Reimagining Childhood Studies

ALSO AVAILABLE FROM BLOOMSBURY

Celebrity, Aspiration and Contemporary Youth, Aisha Ahmad,
Kim Allen, Laura Harvey and Heather Mendick
Disabled Children and Digital Technologies, Sue Cranmer
Using Film to Understand Childhood and Practice, edited by Sue Aitken

Reimagining Childhood Studies

**EDITED BY SPYROS SPYROU,
RACHEL ROSEN, AND
DANIEL THOMAS COOK**

BLOOMSBURY ACADEMIC
LONDON • NEW YORK • OXFORD • NEW DELHI • SYDNEY

BLOOMSBURY ACADEMIC
Bloomsbury Publishing Plc
50 Bedford Square, London, WC1B 3DP, UK
1385 Broadway, New York, NY 10018, USA

BLOOMSBURY, BLOOMSBURY ACADEMIC and the Diana logo are
trademarks of Bloomsbury Publishing Plc

First published in Great Britain 2019

Cover design: Anna Berzovan
Cover image © MirageC / GettyImages

A catalogue record for this book is available from the British Library.

A catalog record for this book is available from the Library of Congress.

ISBN: HB: 978-1-3500-1922-5
       PB: 978-1-3500-1921-8
       ePDF: 978-1-3500-1924-9
       eBook: 978-1-3500-1923-2

Typeset by Integra Software Services Pvt. Ltd.
Printed and bound in Great Britain

To find out more about our authors and books visit www.bloomsbury.com
and sign up for our newsletters.

CONTENTS

LIST OF FIGURES

NOTES ON CONTRIBUTORS

Sarada Balagopalan is Associate Professor of Childhood Studies at Rutgers University—Camden, New Jersey, USA. Her research focuses on postcolonial childhoods, child labor, children's rights, and compulsory schooling. She is the author of *Inhabiting "Childhood": Children, Labour and Schooling in Postcolonial India* (Palgrave, 2014). She is an associate editor for *The SAGE Encyclopedia of Children and Childhood Studies* and serves on the editorial board of *Childhood: A Journal of Global Child Research*.

Clémentine Beauvais is Lecturer in English in Education at the University of York. Her fields of research are at the intersection of children's literature theory, cultural studies of childhood, and the history and philosophy of education. She has published widely on politically committed children's literature, the history of the concept of giftedness, and is currently working on translation and children's literature.

Stephen Bernardini, PhD, is Lecturer in Psychology and Women's and Gender Studies at Rutgers, the State University of New Jersey. His research focuses on race, space, gender, and children and youth cultures. Stephen is currently working on a book based on his doctoral research—an urban ethnography on the lived experiences of Black queer young people.

Jo Boyden, a social anthropologist, is Professor of International Development and Director of Young Lives, a comparative mixed methods, longitudinal study of childhood poverty based at the University of Oxford. Her research has centered on children's education and work and the association with aspirations and social mobility, as well as young people's experiences of and responses to poverty, armed conflict, and forced migration, specifically the developmental and well-being outcomes of risk exposure and the factors that contribute to vulnerability and resilience.

Kristen Cheney is Associate Professor of Children and Youth Studies at the International Institute of Social Studies in The Hague, Netherlands. Her research has focused on children's survival strategies amid difficult circumstances in Eastern and Southern Africa. Her most recent research examines the impact of the global "orphan industrial complex"—including orphan tourism, childcare institutions, and intercountry adoption—on child protection and welfare in developing countries. She is also studying youth sexual/reproductive health and has participated in child-/youth-related research, consultancy, and capacity-building projects in Africa, Europe, and the Middle East. She is on the editorial board of *Childhood* (Sage).

Daniel Thomas Cook is Professor of Childhood Studies at Rutgers University—Camden, New Jersey, USA. His work explores the various ways in which tensions between the "child" and the "market" play themselves out in various sites of children's consumer culture, such as advertising, food, rituals, clothing, and media. Author of *The Commodification of Childhood: The Children's Clothing Industry and the Rise of the Child Consumer* (Duke University Press, 2004) and of numerous articles and book chapters, he has edited several books, and presently serves as an editor of *Childhood, A Journal of Global Child Research* and *The SAGE Encyclopedia of Children and Childhood Studies* (forthcoming).

Matías Cordero Arce is Independent Researcher and Educator at a Young Offenders' Institution in the Basque Country. He holds an LLB (Catholic University of Chile) and an MA and PhD in Sociology of Law (University of the Basque Country) and has presented and published widely on issues related to children's rights. He currently lives in Vitoria-Gasteiz, Basque Country, with his wife Ainara, daughter Maialen, and son Xabier.

Jason Hart is Senior Lecturer in the Department of Social and Policy Sciences at the University of Bath. He is also Visiting Lecturer at the Centre for Children's Rights Studies, University of Geneva. Much of his work has explored the experience of and institutional response to young people on the margins of society and the global economy, embracing themes including protection, rights, notions of "home," militarization, and asylum. Jason has served as an author, researcher, evaluator, and trainer for various UN, governmental, and non-governmental organizations. He has also advised UN bodies on the formulation of studies, guidelines, and policies.

John Horton is a geographer based at the University of Northampton, UK. He is the editor of two international academic journals: *Children's Geographies* and *Social and Cultural Geography*. With Peter Kraftl, he is coauthor of the book *Cultural Geographies* (Routledge, 2013), and series editor of a new major book series on *Spaces of Childhood and Youth*.

Stavroula Kontovourki is Assistant Professor in Literacy and Language Arts Education at the Department of Education, University of Cyprus, where she teaches undergraduate and graduate courses on languages arts teaching methods, language and literacy development, and multiliteracies. Her research interests cover literacy and language arts education, the performance of literate identities in and out of school, multimodality (textual and embodied), the enactment of literacy curricula in schools, literacy teachers' professional identities, and literacy policy and educational change.

Peter Kraftl is Professor of Human Geography at the University of Birmingham, UK. He is also an Honorary Professor at the School of Education, RMIT, Australia. He has published over fifty journal articles and seven books, including *Geographies of Alternative Education* (Policy Press, 2014) and *Children's Emotions in Policy and Practice* (Palgrave, 2015). He is editor of *Area* and was formerly an editor of *Children's Geographies*.

David Oswell is Professor of Sociology and Pro-Warden for Research and Enterprise at Goldsmiths, University of London. His publications include *Television, Childhood and the Home: A History of the Making of the Child Television Audience in Britain* (Oxford, 2002), *Culture and Society* (Sage, 2006), *Cultural Theory: Volumes 1–4* (Sage, 2010), *The Agency of Children: From Family to Global Human Rights* (Cambridge, 2013), and various journal articles and book chapters. His current research interests concern the social life and history of children, childhood and children's rights.

Rachel Rosen is Associate Professor in Childhood at University College London (UCL). Her scholarship is situated at the intersection of materialist feminism and the sociology of childhood, and focuses on unequal childhoods, care and social reproduction, and social relations between women and children. Recently, she has been researching separated child migrants' experiences of care, and caring for others, as they navigate the complexities of the immigration–welfare nexus in the UK. She is coauthor of *Negotiating Adult–Child Relationships in Early Childhood Research* (Routledge, 2014) and coeditor of *Feminism and the Politics of Childhood: Friends or Foes?* (UCL Press, 2018).

Karen Sánchez-Eppler is L. Stanton Williams 1941 Professor of American Studies and English at Amherst College. The author of *Touching Liberty: Abolition, Feminism and the Politics of the Body* (University of California Press, 1993) and *Dependent States: The Child's Part in Nineteenth-Century American Culture* (University of Chicago Press, 2005), she is currently working on two book projects *The Unpublished Republic: Manuscript Cultures of the Mid-Nineteenth Century US* and *In the Archives of Childhood: Playing with the Past*. She is one of the founding coeditors of *The Journal of the History of Childhood and Youth* and past President of C19: The Society of Nineteenth-Century Americanists.

Spyros Spyrou is Professor of Anthropology and Sociology at European University Cyprus. His research interests include children's national identities, borders and border crossing, and children's constructions of immigration. In his current research, he explores the intersections between motherhood and babyhood within a global, neoliberal context. He has coedited *Children and Borders* (Palgrave Macmillan, 2014) and is the author of *Disclosing Childhoods: Research and Knowledge Production for a Critical Childhood Studies* (Palgrave Macmillan, 2018). He is a coeditor of the journal *Childhood* and of the Palgrave book series *Studies in Childhood and Youth*.

Eleni Theodorou is Assistant Professor in Social Foundations of Education at the Department of Education Sciences at the European University Cyprus, where she teaches undergraduate and graduate courses in the social and cultural foundations of education. Her research interests include sociological and anthropological constructions of childhood, (immigrant) children's identities, multicultural education politics and policy, family involvement, and sociological understandings of teacher professional identities, mainly investigated through qualitative research methodologies. Her work has been published in international peer review journals and in edited book volumes.

Mary Wickenden teaches and does research about disability, mainly in the Global South. She uses qualitative and participatory methods to explore the lifeworlds of disabled adults and children. She is particularly interested in the perspectives of disabled children and their families, at home, school, and in the community. She uses innovative approaches to talk to them in the UK, South Asia, and East and Southern Africa. With a background in social and medical anthropology, her current interests are intersections between disability and childhood studies, participatory evaluation methodologies, issues around gender, sexuality and violence for disabled people, and the needs of their carers.

PREFACE

Reimagining Childhood Studies represents a meeting point, a space of convergence, for a set of scholars who have been harboring an unease of sorts—an unease centered around the conceptions animating the very core of their work. The promises of problematizing the child and childhood remain fundamental preoccupations of many who teach, write, publish, and engage in consequential public and institutional practice with and about children. Yet, the long-standing conceptual undergirding of a distinctive childhood studies perspective—i.e., the non-passive, non-derivative, agentic child as a being worthy of study in its own right—while remaining consequential can ring hollow particularly when it begins to enter the imagination and discourse as a given or verity to be known, rather than as a problem to be engaged. An unease sets in for some when the questions posed by instructors, texts, or colleagues no longer demand effort to attempt a new vision or approach but instead seek to elicit a known response.

Perhaps responding to an underlying feeling of professional disquiet, Spyros Spyrou approached Rachel Rosen and Dan Cook in 2015 at the 3rd International Childhood and Youth Research Network conference in Nicosia, Cyprus, to inquire if we, in a sense, suffered a similar restlessness. The answers were swift in coming. Each of us, after all, works in programs and centers that have more or less directly arisen out of the "new" social studies of childhood and which underwrite and promote research and scholarship in that vein—i.e., Spyros with the Center for the Study of Childhood and Adolescence and the ICYRNet in Nicosia, Rachel at the UCL Institute of Education, and Dan in Childhood Studies at Rutgers–Camden. Our respective positions at these different crossroads, we thought, placed us well to be able to curate a volume of this kind. As we set about to see if others would be interested in contributing to a project, our central driving concern focused on gathering together those who actively pursued a "reimagining" of the field, or aspects of the field, in some manner.

As the project unfolded with the participation of the enthusiastic and capable contributors represented herein, all of us, coeditors and authors alike, encountered the presence and resistance of extant ways of knowing and seeing pressing upon each of us. Indeed, it is rather easy to imagine a reimagining than to perform it, especially in brief chapters within the fairly traditional format of an edited collection intended for a readership of relatively like-minded peers. Engaging in a careful and informed critique of contemporary conceptualizations often formed the initial step, the first impetus, toward formulating a statement or demonstration of a reimagination of childhood studies. As we worked with authors to move from their well-thought-out critiques, we came to appreciate the stretch we were asking them to take—i.e., to move beyond a close appraisal of the known and extend themselves into the unstable, and certainly less supportable, realm of conjecture. It is perhaps the same kind of move many of us demand of students every day, but perhaps not so much of ourselves. And it carries its risks, to be sure. Unavoidably, it seems, disciplinary and theoretical toes must be stepped on along the way. Yet, stepping on another's toes reaffirms where paths have converged and so can help indicate how they also diverge.

The result of this process, taken on in earnest by both authors and coeditors, speaks well to the kind of ethos *Reimagining Childhood Studies* aspires to foster. It is an ethos of attempting and making voyages, not simply for the sake of individual adventure, but as an invitation to others to endeavor their own. We commend our contributors for their willingness to step out a bit farther than they might have and for the trust placed in us implicit in that act. In the end, we hope readers will find this effort sufficiently provocative to respond and thereby ensure continued and diverse kinds of dialogue.

Spyros Spyrou
Rachel Rosen
Daniel Thomas Cook

ACKNOWLEDGMENTS

We are indebted to many people who have over the years helped us think about and reflect on childhood studies as a field. *Reimagining Childhood Studies* builds on the significant contributions of many colleagues who have inspired and motivated the course of this book. We take this opportunity to express our appreciation to all these individuals who are too many to mention here but are a continuous source of inspiration to our work!

Two colleagues in particular, Jan Newberry and Sharon Bessell, have provided valuable feedback and helped us sharpen our arguments in the introductory chapter. Thank you Jan and Sharon!

Two anonymous reviewers have also provided valuable feedback to the book manuscript, and we are thankful for their time and constructive insights which we, as editors, and the contributors of the chapters found extremely productive.

We benefited greatly from the support of Matt Prickett and Jessica Schriver, doctoral students in Childhood Studies at Rutgers–Camden. They provided desperately needed assistance in the organization of our efforts and in manuscript preparation. We greatly appreciate your help Matt and Jessica!

And last but not least, we would like to express our gratitude to Maria Giovanna Brauzzi, our editor at Bloomsbury, for her enthusiasm and constant support throughout this project.

CHAPTER ONE

Introduction:

Reimagining Childhood Studies: Connectivities ... Relationalities ... Linkages ...

*Spyros Spyrou, Rachel Rosen,
and Daniel Thomas Cook*

After three decades, a good deal of childhood studies *in practice* finds itself stuck, in many ways, in a mire of its own articulation. The urge to conceptualize children as "active in the construction and determination of their own social lives" (James and Prout 1990: 8) and to grasp childhood as a social fabrication constituted in and informed by history, politics, culture, and geography rings no less relevant and necessary now than it did in the 1980s. Yet, the inventions and interventions forged by one generation of scholars rightly bent on disrupting largely unquestioned and uncontested notions of children and childhood have transfigured, subtly though perceptibly, into the givens, the truisms, and sometimes the platitudes of another. Most insidiously, the generative problematic of the field—i.e., the constructed, agentive, knowing child—regularly enfolds back onto itself, often reappearing as the solution to the problem it poses. No question or inquiry in the arena of childhood studies, it seems, can attract a satisfying response without some recourse to this figure—this skeleton key of sorts—which is increasingly apprehended as sufficiently self-explanatory or, at least, analytically self-contained. It may very well be the case that the "child" of childhood studies—as it has been forged and reforged collectively over the years—stands as a foremost obstacle to ways forward.

Reimagining Childhood Studies arises from a self-conscious recognition that the production of knowledge in a field—particularly in a "new" field still excited about its possibilities—can, like a boomerang, rebound and ensnare the producers and products of that knowledge in ways unintended and counter-intentional. This effort—represented in this Introduction and in the collection of chapters to follow—joins other voices in the field to offer possibilities to revisit some tensions, distinctions, and presumptions of childhood studies scholarship with an ambition to disrupt what we see as a detrimental, self-referential tendency of so much scholarship which calls itself "childhood studies." Admittedly, not every aspect of every chapter achieves this goal. The value, we hope, also lies in the cumulative reflexive attempts to engage in a reimagining along these lines and when, put together, these works encourage dialogic engagement with similar efforts that have come both before and into future scholarship.

Childhood studies, as a field of thought, arose at a particular moment in the social sciences, when modernist and what might roughly be called "post" and "neo" framings (post-modernist/post-colonial/neo-Marxist/etc.) were jostling for dominion in ways of understanding and explaining the social world. As Prout (2005) points out, childhood studies largely oriented itself toward putting forward arguments for children and childhood that spoke to the still dominant modernist frames which sought stability and coherence, often reducing ambiguity and complexity through dualistic categorization. Yet, because childhood studies jumped into the fray at a time when discursive explanations or the "linguistic and cultural turn" were on the rise across the social sciences, from the outset, the field participated in an extended period of rejection of economism, totalities, and "grand theory." A part of this effort entailed asserting a fundamental difference and rupture from political economy modes of inquiry and explanation (e.g., Butler 1997b)—a difference which the bourgeois, Global North "child" subject as the theoretical center of the field made manifest and robust (as Sarada Balagopalan, this volume, discusses).

Entangled in the analytic, moral, and political structures of its founding, a good deal of contemporary childhood studies scholarship also remains reactive to the ghostly presence of developmental psychology (see Burman 2017) and tethered to a cultural heritage derived from the UN Convention on the Rights of the Child (UNCRC) and its ongoing aftermath (see Cheney, this volume; see Balagopalan, this volume; see Wickenden, this volume). The specter of invoking, wittingly or unwittingly, some version of the psychological child in particular haunts the periphery of investigation as pre-emptive constraint. Child development continues to represent the negation—the foundational distinction—against which and upon which childhood studies builds its epistemology at both the level of the subject and the level of structure. Considerable attention and effort expended by authors, instructors, and editors serve to police and reinscribe the boundaries delimiting the child of psychology and that of childhood studies from each other. With near ritualistic formality at times, article after article and talk after talk painstakingly revisit and rehearse, to greater and lesser extents, origin stories of how the child of childhood studies has been rescued from universalism, cultural monotropism, and essentialism by virtue of this "new" perspective.

Hence, it should come as no surprise that, as a field, childhood studies has ventured into an immense historical and collective investment in a particular "problem of the child" which is, in many ways, existentially consequential for the discipline. Childhood scholarship and the production of childhood scholarship have together been complicit in valorizing children's agency to the point of a fetish, making of it a moral and analytic bulwark against the encroachment, or perceived encroachment, of anything that feels like psychological, biological, or indeed structural ways of knowing. Wide swaths of thinking and research accordingly exhibit a decided aversion to centering anything that suggests a decentering of the child subject as the consequential actor or force under consideration—as in, for example, most notions related to child development (in its many forms), or the determinative flows of capital and power or non-human and technological forces as found in other theoretical perspectives. There are certainly notable exceptions (e.g., Lee 1998; Stephens 1995; Prout 2005; Wells 2009, to name but a few). However, the thrust of approach and conception continues to favor singular—if socially, culturally, and historically embedded—subjects who display, or must be allowed to display, creativity and active engagement of the world in the here-and-now (see Cook, this volume; Oswell, this volume). Consequently, we contend, something of the vital relationality of the child remains at arm's length and kept out of reach conceptually, analytically, and politically.

Indeed, one would be hard-pressed, for instance, to traverse the landscape of childhood studies course modules, textbooks, and conference presentations without encountering the sentiment that "children are beings not becomings" (Qvortrup et al. 1994: 2). Clearly, a significant epistemological intervention into presumptions about reading children as *merely* in the process of undergoing change (i.e., especially learning and development), the notion of "being" in this sense has effortlessly taken its place among the new clichés, often deflecting rather than inviting critical reflection. Evidently preferential to "becoming," "being" supposes a desirable state or, at least, a favored perspective on childhood as something to be released from the teleology of adult conceptions and institutions that tend to favor single, linear trajectories of learning, development, and perhaps being (see Uprichard 2008; see also Oswell 2013). "Being" seems a reasonable place to repose from the vantage point of those of us who sit atop Maslow's hierarchy of needs. For others, like some of the queer of color youth Bernardini (this volume) discusses, "being" signifies navigation and struggle *within* multiple structural vulnerabilities, and "becoming"—becoming "sideways" (Stockton 2009) perhaps—might appear as both desirable and undesirably uncertain. The hesitancy to embrace "becoming" speaks to a generalized reluctance to let go of the foundational distinction from developmental psychology and the individualized, monadic child which carries or holds agency unto itself.

The flight from becoming in this way encodes, paradoxically, a kind of denaturalized child which exists in a here-and-now, often for the sake of claiming academic positional distinction. Consequently, the underlying epistemological and moral privileging of agency, usually particular types of agency (see Sanchez-Eppler, this volume; Cordero Arce, this volume; and also James 2007; Spyrou 2011; Oswell 2013), cultivates an analytic blind spot—a space of perpetual unsight—which undoes or disables possibilities of seeing differently. Indeed, presuming "being"—and presuming that a particular sort of being is realized through the exercise of a particular sort of agency—arguably discourages inquiry into how multiple and connective scales, relationalities, and structural entanglements also make the "child" of childhood studies possible and viable. Discussing existentialist readings of politically committed texts for children, Beauvais (this volume) notes: "Doing childhood studies without agency ready at hand" enables "wonder" about "temporal inflections" (this volume). Kontovourki and Theodorou (this volume), as well, lay bare the obstacle of children's agency—of a presumed shape and content—rather than seeking to liberate them from non-agency.

Such fetishization does not only result in an intellectual loop but has serious political consequences. Much like Nancy Fraser's (2009) depiction of feminism's "uncanny double," a version of itself that has not just been co-opted by neoliberalism but has a strong affinity with the very constitution of late capitalism, the "darling figure" of childhood studies (see Cook, this volume) bears marked similarity to the idealized subject of neoliberalism. At once innovative and chameleon-like, this figure demonstrates a remarkable ability to constantly remake itself anew, well-befitting a regime of "flexible accumulation" (Harvey 2007). Because this ontological production is rendered sacred, it can obscure interrogation of its productivity for capitalism, and indeed arguments developed in childhood studies about the agentic child may even be used to bolster neoliberal projects, from the "Girl Effect" (Shain 2013) to early childhood interventions aimed at the human capital development of the active child (Newberry 2017).

The point for consideration here is not simply that scholars have produced and entertained "wrong" or "inappropriate" conceptions of children's agency, or that it has remained entirely unexamined in the field. It is that agency itself—in its centrality, dominance, and hegemonic position in childhood studies—may very well stand in the way of reaching for alternative ways of knowing. Efforts to move beyond individual and individuated agency span from Alanen and colleagues' (2000, 2001) insistence on generation as a relationally inflected time-scale of knowledge and measurement to Oswell's (2013) theorizations of multiple and varied agencies. As well, those in educational studies (see Edwards and D'Arcy 2004), literacy studies (Fisher 2010), and children's geographies (e.g., Ansell 2009; Kraftl 2013b) strive to problematize and, in some ways, decenter the child by attending to the materialities and geo-scales which surround and construe children and their worlds. Agency here arises as a relational dynamic—not so much a property of an entity, but an element of a complex, an assemblage of sorts which, as Oswell states, "is always in-between and interstitial" where "the capacity to do and to make a difference is necessarily dispersed across an arrangement" (2013: 70).

We strive to position *Reimagining Childhood Studies* as an invitation to readers and colleagues to engage in further dialogue about the nature and boundaries of this shared endeavor. Our concern at this historical juncture centers on how childhood studies, as it is being practiced and deployed across a range of institutional domains, might be becoming ossified despite the rather robust efforts of many scholars to the contrary. To breakthrough a long-standing epistemological and conceptual impasse in childhood studies requires a commitment to aspire to dislodge some of the foundational notions of the field without completely dismantling the entire enterprise. In what follows, we attempt to perform this difficult trick, not as an exemplar of some ideal new reimagining of the field but as a contribution to a larger, ongoing conversation regarding our own endeavors to engage with the child, children, and childhood beyond received frames. In so doing, we place ourselves alongside, not above or apart from, the contributors to *Reimagining Childhood Studies*, and other colleagues in the field, who welcome the excitement as well as the risks of stepping past boundaries. Most important, we place our conceptual move in this volume within an emerging current of scholarship in childhood studies, a current which is not always sufficiently forceful and influential but which is however greatly important and valuable in helping disrupt the orthodoxies of the field we described above. Some of this work is mentioned in this Introduction and throughout the various chapters of the volume, although we acknowledge that the purpose of this volume is not to review this emerging literature but to offer a reflective attempt at reimagining childhood studies alongside other efforts that do so.

Our initial effort to assert our own (re)thinking about childhood studies starts with a discussion of ontology. In many ways questions of ontology lie at the heart of childhood studies, with its efforts to reclaim the passive, developing child, and yet the fascination and recapitulation of the field's favored agentic child have meant that more pressing questions about ontology have largely been neglected. In response, we gesture here to the productivity of relational theories of ontology and explore what these can offer to childhood studies, not just as a theoretical enterprise, but as one that is fundamentally bound up with the ethics and politics of knowledge production. Which child, children, and childhood do we bring into being through our scholarship and which do we preclude? Repositioning relationality as the core focus of writing, conception, and research prods scholarship to push past conceptualizing children in essentially monadic terms—i.e., as beings which have (i.e., "own" or "possess") agency—and into realms where children and childhood can only fruitfully be located by way of linkages with other human and non-human aspects of the world. Thinking relationally about the child in this manner thereby invites a relational posture not only toward bodies and persons but also toward objects, technologies, systems, epistemes, and historical eras. Such a focus begets and informs attention to blind spots in the field, areas which we do not see, or are not even aware of, because the ontological and scalar frames which dominate the field do not allow for their existence. Political economy along with its multi-scalar operations, we argue, is one such blind spot. In centering the relational and foregrounding ethical and political commitments, we then proceed to interrogate the political economy of childhood under contemporary, financialized capitalism, suggesting this can open up lines of inquiry and offer critical ways to address new, and more invasive/pervasive, means of capital accumulation and the concomitant heightening of inequities.

In so doing, our point is not to engage in a zero-sum game of replacing one ontology, scale, or "turn" with another. At root, we make the deceptively simple point that the complexity and dynamism of life itself necessitate making a "cut" around the object of study, and demands of us decisions as to the theoretical and conceptual resources we mobilize: *What kind of child do we choose to bring into light? What kinds of inclusions and what kinds of exclusions result from our choices?* We do not suggest that the issues we raise in this Introduction are the only lines of inquiry in childhood studies. In offering an explicit reimagining of ontology and new imaginings of the contemporary political economy of childhood, we set out to make the case that these have a crucial role to play in advancing the intellectual and political project which is childhood studies, including in providing the basis for interventions which have preferable material consequences for children and those human and non-human others with whom they live their lives.

Reimagining childhood studies with relational ontologies

Though not explicitly discussing issues of ontology, a number of the chapters in this volume argue for the need to turn our attention to the relational and interdependent aspects of children's lives as well as the ethics and politics which characterize them. Cordero (this volume) argues for the need to rethink the child legal subject, abandoning the "petrous ontology" of the independent legal subject and moving toward an interdependently autonomous one who is a full-fledged rights holder and duty bearer. Balagopalan (this volume) offers her own critique of the autonomous, independent child-subject of contemporary childhood studies and argues for a non-sovereign kind of relationality based on an ethics of responsibility toward others, while Oswell (this volume) makes the case for an expanded political vision for, and on the basis of, childhood studies, which would also include infancy by accounting for infrastructures and supports, vulnerabilities and solidarities. Together with these contributors, we explore what it might mean for childhood studies to rethink its object of inquiry—the child—with relational ontologies.

Of course, the field's concerns with ontology are not new. The "new paradigm" was in many ways a reaction to the essentialist ontologizing of the child by the developmental and socialization theories which preceded it. In the early 1980s, Chris Jenks expressed his clear dissatisfaction with the ontological assumptions which guided much of the scholarly thinking until then: "It is as if the basic ontological questions, 'What is a child?', 'How is the child possible as such?' were, so to speak, answered in advance of the theorizing and then dismissed" (1982: 10). The "new paradigm" offered a fresh and welcomed answer to the ontological question by positioning the child as socially constructed rather than universal; as a reflexive, social actor rather than a passive presence within overwhelming structural determinations; and as an individual whose very ontological existence needed to be acknowledged as independent and autonomous. The "new paradigm" also offered a set of methodological tools that would help bring forth this new ontological understanding of the child through a commitment to the use of qualitative methodologies, which would highlight children's voices and agency in the local contexts of their everyday lives. But despite these early ontological concerns of the field, its social constructionist orientation and emphasis on epistemology have largely failed to move discussions on ontology beyond the agentic child.

Without downplaying the critical insights of the cultural turn, the call of the "ontological turn" is to embrace a more expansive terrain where human, non-human, and technological forces are recognized as entangled in the constitution of the social world, and producing knowledge about its character. What the ontological turn offers is the theoretical possibility of recognizing the materiality of life while understanding that discourse is entangled with, produced by, and productive of this materiality. A concern with the "real"—the material presences of life—as these acquire their status within discursive fields of meaning and power is what is of interest here. It signals, in this way, a move from a concern with categories and essences to emergence stemming from children's relational encounters with the world. Asking us to rethink our ontological commitments and certainties, this theoretical orientation takes us back to that basic question of the field:

"How is the child possible?" The question invites us to reimagine the child, not by reducing our understanding to essentialist assertions but through a fresh look at matters of ontology, which highlight the complexity of the child. Placing childhood and children within this larger relational field of human, non-human, and technological forces, we are led to explore their becomings as necessarily and inevitably interdependent "on other bodies and matter (Hultman and Lenz Taguchi 2010: 525, 531; see also Balagopalan, this volume; and Cordero, this volume)," as well as social relations which both precede and are transformed through this intra-activity but without resorting to romantic claims about authenticity (Rautio 2014: 471–472). These becomings are not without history as Balagopalan (this volume) shows, nor are they free from social, cultural, economic, and all other kinds of constraints. But, and this is the important point here, they are nevertheless constitutive of change, however small or slow it may, at times, be.

This kind of relational ontologizing signals a shift from a view of children as individual, bounded entities and independent units of analysis to an understanding of children as ontological becomings: what matters is not what they are but how they affect and are affected in the event assemblages they find themselves in (see Lee 2001; Barad 2007; Fox and Alldred 2017). Relational ontologizing also signals a shift from childhood as an identity category to the practices which enact it as a particular kind of phenomenon: from what childhood is to how childhood is done. These shifts, to the extent that they inspire empirical and theoretical work, are in many ways attempts to decenter children and childhood and to contribute to childhood studies' overcoming of its child-centeredness and inward-looking gaze (see Spyrou 2017; see also Beauvais, this volume). To decenter children and childhood through relational ontologizing is precisely to identify and examine those entangled relations which materialize, surround, and exceed children as entities and childhood as a phenomenon diversely across time and space.

Alanen (2017: 149) has recently noted that "to encourage a turn to ontology in this sense means to invite childhood scholars to study and to think 'deeply' of their philosophies of science" and indeed the nature of "reality." A move toward a reflexive and critical consideration of knowledge practices may contribute toward childhood studies' development as a critical field which is not merely aware of its own limits and biases but also capable of making political and ethical choices. Anne Marie Mol (see 1999 and 2002) argues for the need to acknowledge ontological multiplicity insisting that it is our practices which enact particular realities (Mol 1999: 75). Because our knowledge practices are performative we are, as researchers, *partly* responsible for "the world's differential becoming" (Barad 2007: 91) through the material-semiotic configurations we make possible and bring into being through our ontological assumptions and epistemological choices including particular methods for studying the social (Law 2004; Ruppert, Law, and Savage 2013: 33; Fox and Alldred 2017).

A turn to ontological enactments therefore reintroduces the childhood researcher into the research assemblage, not simply as a reflexive figure capable of critically assessing her positionality and biases but as an entangled and co-constitutive presence in the assemblage which produces knowledge—her physical presence, her preferred methods of data collection and analysis, her theoretical and philosophical assumptions, and her own emotions and desires, to name just a few—are all entangled in the knowledge practices at work when investigating any particular event assemblage (Haraway 1992; Barad 2007; Hultman and Lenz Taguchi 2010; Fox and Alldred 2017). Such moves in the context of research are constitutive of the knowledge practices at work as Kontovourki and Theodorou (this volume) illustrate through their reflexive account of an interview encounter with immigrant children: their own presence as researchers co-constituted children's subjectivation and agentive performances in ways that could not be made meaningful outside of the particular research assemblage. Thus, a move to decolonize childhood research, as Cheney (this volume) suggests, through the co-production of knowledge with children constitutes a disruptive intervention which might lead to other, and potentially more ethical, ways of knowing. It reconstitutes the research assemblage in such a way that new affects and effects are possible.

Inevitably, all interventions in research entail a certain kind of ontological politics (see Mol 1999, 2002; Law 2004): if reality is multiple (because entities materialize differently as a result of the multiple event assemblages they become a part of) rather than singular and if it is partially shaped by our knowledge practices (because entities materialize differently, in part, as a result of our theoretical and methodological choices) rather than existing entirely independent of them, then it is also inadvertently political (see Fox and Alldred 2017). To claim that reality may be multiple (because processes of materialization ontologize the world relationally and hence render any claims to essential entities meaningless) is not to resort back to the purely ideational; nor is the claim that our knowledge practices enact certain realities, a claim that as researchers we construct reality based on our own wishes. As researchers we partake in processes of materialization: to claim otherwise is to once again pretend that we can keep the "real" at a distance and simply describe it. As our discussion of political economy further down illustrates, we do take the materiality of life and its outcomes (e.g., multiple forms of exploitation and oppression, including expropriation as we discuss below) as the cornerstones for a critical discussion of knowledge production in childhood studies.

This demands that a critical childhood studies does not simply reflect in a retrospective manner on its ontological enactments but is cognizant and strategic about the way it chooses to exercise its politics in the first place. As Mol (1999: 75) argues, the ontological, when combined with the political, offers options, so that the critical question to ask is which, out of the multiple realities we could enact through our knowledge practices as researchers, do we strive to bring into being (Law 2004: 39). Which ontologies of childhood do we hope to enact? What particular effects, for instance, do our methodological and theoretical choices have on the knowledge we produce? And, more important, what difference do such realities make in children's lives? As Hekman puts it:

> We can compare those material consequences and make arguments about which ones are more useful. We will not convince everyone with these arguments. We cannot appeal to an objective reality to trump the argument. But we have something to argue *about*. (Hekman 2008: 112; emphasis in the original)

If childhood studies is to be ethically committed in relation to its knowledge practices, it will have to grapple with the relativist inclinations of its social constructionist thinking and opt for political interventions with preferred material effects on children's lives. Enacting an ontology of the child as a vulnerable victim versus one where the child is a reflexive agent, as in the ongoing debate on child soldiers, can clearly have diverse material consequences on children's present and future. Rosen (2007), for example, has shown how children who participate in the military as soldiers and engage in violence are often denied by humanitarian organizations and international law their agency and considered to be victims who are coerced into participating despite the historical and anthropological evidence which suggests that children often participate in the military willingly and express a sense of pride for doing so. To claim that these children are capable of making their own decisions rather than being coerced by adults is to enact a particular ontology of childhood— the child-as-actor—which considers the child, like the adult, as a being, while to claim that these children are vulnerable is to enact a very different ontology which considers them as fundamentally different from adults, as incapable of making their own rational choices, in short, an ontology of the child as a developmental becoming. Each position entails both a political and an ethical stance which may, in real life, result in diverse material effects on these children's lives, interfering, for instance, to "save" them in one instance, considering them and treating them as no different from other (adult) soldiers, in another instance. This is an illustration of how childhood studies scholarship may offer more nuanced accounts of children's lives by attending to the multiple ontologies at work, challenging in this way simplistic and uproblematized forms of knowledge which insist on specific and immutable understandings of what a child is (see Spyrou 2018: 214). In a similar vein, bringing into focus the *indebted child* (see our discussion further down) in the context of heightening global inequalities and wealth concentration through a systematic account of the relational processes which materialize her entails a certain kind of ethical and political positioning which informs rather than detracts from the knowledge produced.

Thinking with relational ontologies in childhood studies also signals a willingness to reflexively experiment and rethink the very concepts and tools we use to understand children and their worlds by allowing our empirical materials and the contingencies of daily life to offer us new possibilities about what things are and what they could be. Producing alterity through ontology—whether in the face of the post-colonial child (see Balagopalan, this volume), the queer child (see Bernardini, this volume), or the disabled child (see Wickenden, this volume)—can therefore result in knowledge which is not simply different but also carries political and ethical commitments which can make a difference in children's lives (Hekman 2008; Holbraad and Pedersen 2017).

Scale and scale-making in childhood studies

To rethink childhood studies' object of inquiry—the child—with relational ontologies also invites reflection on a much neglected, mostly taken-for-granted referent and unproblematized dimension of knowledge production in the field, namely, scale-making. Attending to scale-making as a knowledge practice may offer an opportunity to reflect more critically on the processes by which childhood studies scales its empirical field of inquiry and to question the ontological status of the scales it uses to produce knowledge. Far from being the way things are, scales must be created through concerted effort; they must be "proposed, practiced, and evaded, as well as taken for granted," as Tsing (2005: 58) reminds us, and can be used to "contextualize experience, imaginatively placing the phenomena of experience in wider (or narrower) relational fields" (Irvine 2016: 214) to ultimately create hierarchies of importance and centrality through the sorting, grouping, and categorizing of things, people, and qualities (Carr and Lempert 2016: 3).

Scaling-up or scaling-down can provide a different picture of reality, although such moves do not in themselves provide necessarily a more real, complex, or complete picture (see Strathern 2004). In that sense, all scales offer a particular point of view and therefore profess a political and ethical stance toward the world; they are, in other words, ideological, though they are rarely, if ever, explicitly addressed as such by the implicated actors, researchers included. But the fact that there is nothing inherently more real at one scalar level as compared to another does not prevent the kind of ideological work which enlists specific ontological, epistemological, political, and ethical discourses to justify and naturalize particular scale-making projects. Such was indeed the case with the "new paradigm" in childhood studies whose desire to document the competent, agentic child signaled the scale of choice as the local, micro context of children's everyday activity. This meant, however, that other potential scales of interest, such as the macro political-economic scale (see our extended discussion of political economy in the next section; see also Hart and Boyden, this volume; Ansell 2009) would find limited resonance among the committed followers of the "new paradigm" who saw an ethical and political imperative to make visible what was, until then, ignored in research—namely, children's status as beings rather than developmental becomings.

Despite their centrality in elaborating a more critical understanding of knowledge production, questions about scale-making have yet to capture childhood studies' imagination. Ansell's (2009) attempt to rethink scale for childhood studies by exploring the multiple connections children have with a spatially and temporally diverse world made up of events, policies, or discourses which often lie beyond their immediate environments is a notable exception and an invitation for the field to attend to scale-making more seriously. We take this invitation to reflect on scale-making in childhood studies as a call to "play with scale" (see Sánchez-Eppler, this volume), to experiment with new sets of knowledge practices at different scales, and to enact new ontologies which allow for more politically responsible and ethically sensitive understandings of children and childhood. Far from being an exercise in perspectivism, to "play with scale" is to engage in scale-making and to rethink the ontological, epistemological, and ethical assumptions at work (see, for example, Kraftl and Horton, this volume, who argue for a more expansive temporal and spatial scale for the entire field that would help rethink childhood studies' remit in the Anthropocene; and both Sánchez-Eppler and Balagopalan, this volume, for efforts to trans-navigate scale in ways that challenge a cartographic bifurcation of the world into core-periphery or North-South at the same time as remaining vigilant about the ongoing violence of the colonial project and empire).

In the next section, we invite readers to consider with us what "playing with scale" might mean for the field. In recognizing that the scale and ontology being brought into being in childhood studies is easily taken up by, or even bolsters, the project of neoliberalism, we take our cue here from Fraser (2009) and flag up the importance of disrupting our field's "uncanny double" by keeping abreast of the changing social, economic, and political circumstances of global capitalism, which until now has been of limited concern in much contemporary childhood studies. By engaging with recent theorizing on financialized capitalism, we participate in a scale-making that occupies neither the macro-global of traditional political economy nor the preferred micro-local scale of childhood studies, but scale-jumps between and across them. Conscious that the scalar and ontological choices we make have import, we do so to illustrate the dynamic entanglements between generational social relations and contemporary patterns of accumulation, as well as to consider what role we allow, produce, and desire for childhood studies in such contexts. Indeed, to do otherwise risks adding momentum to childhood studies' "uncanny double."

Reimagining through contemporary political economy

We are not alone in making demands on the field to think children and childhood through political economy. In her groundbreaking essay, Sharon Stephens (1995: 20) argued that children's lives and the child figure are impacted by global forces *and* a crucial site for "exploring capitalist society and its historical dynamic." Similarly, Sue Ruddick (2003: 337) argues that "far from being a byproduct of capitalism in its various phases, youth and childhood can be located at its literal and figurative core." She demonstrates, for example, that the experiment with part-time and part-year jobs for young people in the United States in the 1970s, based on assumptions of the malleable and schooled child, was one of the sites where today's flexible labor practices were tested and entrenched.

At the heart of their, and others' (e.g., see also Hart and Boyden, this volume), arguments are not only the conviction that political economic understandings are crucial for understanding childhood but that without attending to children and childhood, understandings of global capitalism are impoverished. As Anna Tsing (2009) demonstrates, the figures we use to think through social processes allow us to do different sorts of conceptual work and are productive of different conclusions. With Stephens and Ruddick, we suggest that thinking through the figure of the child, and the real beings we call children, has much to add to understandings of the variations, expansions, and dynamism of capital. In building on this work, what we are proposing is a sustained engagement with recent developments and debates in the social sciences and cognate disciplines which highlight the specificities of this conjuncture and seek innovative ways to move beyond the false divisions between political economy and the cultural turn of the late twentieth century. More specifically, what is distinctive about our approach is the centering of attention on changing patterns of *capital accumulation* and the relational ontologies this brings into being. Our reimagining involves placing regimes of accumulation at the heart of our studies of the child/children/childhood and by corollary moving the child/children/childhood from the margins of scholarship on financialized capitalism. We add to our ongoing preoccupation with ontological concerns about what makes the child as such possible the question: "How are the child, children, childhood constituted by, and involved in the constitution of, financialized capitalism?" This is not to simply mobilize the child as an object for our own enlightenment. Attending to child figure and the way she is generated by the social relations of financialized capitalism offers insights into child subjectivities and the changing institution of childhood, as well as offering richer conceptualizations of contemporary processes of accumulation.

We situate these arguments within a widening consensus in the wake of the 2008/2009 financial crisis and widening politics of austerity that social theory must re-engage with political economy. The proliferation of interest in the finance sector can be understood as part of the effort to account for the seismic transformations of social life since the post–Bretton Woods period when the gold standard was abandoned. Referred to alternatively as the financialization of daily life (Martin 2002), debt society (Lazzarato 2011), and financialized capitalism (Fraser 2016), this is a periodizing concept which draws attention to the increased portion of global economic activity which is located in the finance sector, as opposed to, *inter alia*, land, industrial production, and the service sector. From student loans for education, to payday or credit card loans to cover the costs of social reproduction in contexts of massive state retrenchment, or repayment obligations incurred through World Bank micro-financing projects, debt is now omnipresent. Individual, municipal, and sovereign debt lies at the heart of financialized capitalism, with securitization, the bundling, and slicing of debts for trade on the market becoming the dominant form of accumulation since the 1970s (Adkins 2017). Financialized capitalism simultaneously refers to "the way financial measurements, ideas, processes, techniques, metaphors, narratives, values and tropes migrate beyond the financial sector and transform other areas of society" (Haiven 2014: 1). Here, the language of the market, technologies and practices of securitization, as well as the shifting of relations of exploitation to those between distant financiers and (often impoverished) debtees, instantiate new types of subjects ensnared by possible futures created through debt (Adkins 2017). We "invest" in our relationships sometimes in the hope of long term "returns" or "owe debts" to people in our social networks, with middle-class childhoods increasingly tied to and enacted in such terms. Schools and early childhood programs are treated as sites for "investing in children," or more precisely their "human capital," with the World Bank even offering an "early childhood calculator" for quantifying profits from investment programs (Penn 2011).

What is notable about much of the recent political economic theorizing is that this is not a return to either a benign market logic inhabited by rationally choosing actors nor a reinvocation of deterministic base-superstructure models. Instead, this work attempts to work with the lessons from the cultural turn with its emphasis on intersectional subjectivities, socio-cultural vernaculars, and struggles for hegemony. As such, this scholarship is productive for childhood studies for both its insistent historicity and the wider conceptual apparatus that it introduces. Notwithstanding the inevitable debates occurring within this vast body of work, here we tease out some key themes and trajectories in a culturally inflected political economy, focusing on those which have particular purchase for reimagining childhood studies.

Efforts have come from several directions to de-naturalize "the economy." Critiques take issue with the depiction of the economy as a simple moniker for market-based activity in more (neo)liberal accounts, or the site of commodity production in more orthodox Marxist accounts.

This new work does not separate "economic" practices from other life-world activities, reduce the economy to a certain set of motivators for social action (e.g., calculability, gain), or pre-determine actors (e.g., wage earners) and mechanisms. In their effort to "rethink the economy," for instance, Narotzky and Besnier (2014: s5) propose a definition that includes "all the processes that are involved, in one fashion or the other, in 'making a living,'" as well as a concern with making lives *worth* living across generations. They draw attention to the effort, value(s), and power differentials involved in such activity. This understanding, and here they acknowledge their "debt" to feminist scholarship on care and reproductive labor, highlights the importance of the reproduction of life itself for people, but also for capital, therefore marking this as a site of conflicting value(s).

Such an opening of "the economy" is also evident in works on the financialization of everyday life. Haiven (2014: 4), for example, draws attention to the way that subjectivities, social relations, creative agency, and social practices are produced, enacted, and "conscripted into an increasingly sophisticated order of capitalist accumulation." In a particularly relevant example, he traces the lucrative Pokemon phenomenon, arguing that its success is—in part—due to its resonance with financialization. It involves a repertoire of "zealous" (113) accumulation and speculative trading, "merg[ed] with a militaristic theme" (115), at the same time valorizing creative expression and individual preferences as long as they don't interfere with the market. Haiven's broader point is that financialized capitalism is not just "out there," imposed on people. Working with notions of economic performativity (e.g., see Callon 2010), where expectations and predictions shape rather than map finance, he argues that financialization is a "bottom up" process made in everyday life. Here a tight web of matter (e.g., Pokemon cards), possible subjectivities (e.g., self-accruing personhood), relations of competition and appropriation embedded in the casino economy, and long-standing efforts to expand markets to the playful and creative consumer child combine to materialize the Pokemon phenomenon and its child subject. At the same time, Haiven insists that we need to account for domination and stratification. This requires simultaneously holding on to understandings that financialization is used by capital as a "fix" for its crises of overproduction, where debt, for example, facilitates continuing consumption by the increasingly impoverished working class despite wage stagnation and serves as a mechanism for generating profit through debt servicing and ever-new financial products.

These insights are important for childhood studies, not least because they indicate that to be attentive to the political economy we do not need to focus on particular groups (e.g., *working* children). Such sectors are surely important, but they need not exhaust our focus. Furthermore, these insights suggest that just because social and legal decrees mean that many children are precluded from wage work, trading on the market, and holding debt or income in their own right, this does not mean that their lives are irrelevant for political economic consideration. No singular site or scale is the site of the political economy; financialized capitalism is just as "real" in the operations of the market as in the play of children. What appears to be a bigger picture (e.g., "global capitalism") is really another depiction of reality which is rendered possible through scalar aggregation. For instance, the impoverishment experienced by children at a local site is aggregated by a statistical service to create a numerical reality which is, however, neither bigger nor more complex than the experiences of impoverishment collected by the ethnographer in her encounters with poor children. Beyond recognition that the multi-scalar levels in which financialized capitalism effects and is produced, we suggest that childhood occupies a central place in political economy. "The economy," in this broad understanding, is animated by temporalities of nostalgia and dreams, often heavily inflected with generational anxieties (Narotzky and Besnier 2014). This reconfiguring of intimate relationships via speculative temporalities, and the existential concerns this produces, borrows from and materializes the trope of child as the embodiment of such futures (as Clementine Beauvais explores, this volume). Still here, we recognize the classed nature of such imaginaries and their productivities. While privileged children are "niche-marketed to secure success in the insecure future," working-class children become the seemingly disposable "waste" or detritus of financialized futures, to mobilize Cindi Katz's (2008: 10) powerful metaphors. Often deeply tied to systemic racism and anti-migrant sentiment, as in the "school to prison" or "school to deportation to export processing zone" pipeline, this is a harsh reminder that debt-spurred dreams cannot evade the structural conditionalities of children's lives.

A second, and connected, emerging conceptualization lies in the insistence on the centrality of the historical and spatial dynamism of capitalism, rather than a reliance on pre-determined models. Local cultures of kinship, varying cultures of production and divisions of labor, colonial histories and the neo-colonial contemporary combine in what has been called "vernacular capitalism" (Birla 2009). Rather than aberrations from a "true" capitalism, such vernaculars highlight emerging and contradictory forms of capital, as well as how these become stitched together, albeit in often fragile forms. For childhood studies, this implies starting our investigations with people's life projects, their efforts to make lives worth living, tracing outward lines of value, economic and moral, as well as accumulation, rather than imposing abstract logics of global scale. Cindi Katz's (2004) seminal study linking children's lives in Howa, Sudan, and New York City is a remarkable example of such efforts to examine the impact of global economic restructuring across spatial–temporal scales. Financialized capital has wrought marked changes on relations between states and increasingly transnational governance structures, markets, and families, in the process creating new conditions of childhood. Reminiscent of Haiven's Pokemon children of financialized capitalism, children in Howa engaged in play emboldened by the introduction of consumerism and monetization, "domesticat[ing] capitalism as they outfitted themselves as new subjects of its terms" (102). In New York, global restructuring shifted the costs of social reproduction away from the state, making impoverished children's futures "moot" and rendering them sources of accumulation through rentierism. Katz depicts diverse childhoods, without losing sight of their interstices, using attention to scale and political economy as a way to make these relations visible.

In an era of financialized capitalism, a focus on debt and reproductive labor is one fruitful avenue for childhood studies to continue such explorations (see Rosen and Newberry 2018), although by no means the only. Mass indebtedness has become increasingly necessary for assuring everyday existence as well as making lives worth living into the future. As Sylvia Federici (2014) points out, this changes the temporality of accumulation linked to reproductive labor. While feeding, clothing, cleaning, caring for, and socializing others are directly tied to accumulation in that, among the working classes, these activities are involved in reproducing workers for capital; in both daily and longer-term temporalities, debt has meant that "many reproductive activities have now become immediate sites of capital accumulation" (Federici 2014: 233). Here Federici is referring to both the provision of social reproduction by private companies (in some cases because of state retrenchment), which is paid for through debt, and accumulation through debt servicing and the explosion of securities trading.

For childhood studies, this prompts questions that we have largely neglected through our scalar and ontological choices, such as: What are the different ways that we can understand debt through the child figure? What childhoods are engendered in the changing relations between matter, discourse, value(s), and process of accumulation in varying contexts? By asking such questions prompted by new scholarship on financialized capitalism we make possible, indeed enact, very different types of children to the always-already active and innovative child-as-agent. For instance, we might explore *the child born of debt*, considering how her life is made and sustained through familial debt as well as how she serves, in the anticipatory imaginaries that make indebtedness possible, as a symbol of hope for brighter futures. We could study the *indebted child*, considering the ways that children in different contexts take up debts in the form of student loans, debts owed and paid to families through migratory remittances (Heidbrink 2014), or as a shared member of an indebted household with the anticipation that debt will be a constant companion into the future (Horton 2015a). As Adkins (2017) points out, a key feature of contemporary debt is that it is no longer premised on a temporality of repayment at a final point in the not too distant future, but ongoing debt servicing into unpredictable futures. We might consider the *child as debt*, exploring the ways that "investing in children," a sustained effort on the part of both children and adults, is premised on borrowing from the future adult the child will become. Here, the temporality of accumulation is perhaps slowed down, until "quality enhanced" labor power of working-class children and adults (Rikowski 2003) enters the wage nexus. Alternatively, this can bring into focus relational questions of gender and generation where the idealized *subject of investment* (the child) is linked to the idealized feminized *subject of debt*. Financial institutions are increasingly seeking to apprehend women's strategies for survival in precarious economic conditions, such as their (real and imagined) steadfastness and reliability in relation to obligations to children and their social networks, as systems for self-management and policing of others, all to ensure debt servicing obligations are met (Federici 2014). Such explorations, prompted by relational ontologizing, have often been downplayed, despite their enormous significance, or even depicted as intrinsic antagonisms between women and children, undercutting the possibility of intergenerational solidarities (Rosen and Newberry 2018).

An insistence on the vernacular also gestures to diversity, and its stratifications, as central to global capitalist projects—not mere happenstance (Tsing 2009). Here we turn to Nancy Fraser's (2016) work on the interstices of racism and capitalism. While concurring with Marx's analysis of exploitation as the private appropriation of the surplus value produced by ostensibly free workers, she makes the case that at least as central to accumulation is "expropriation." Rather than working through wage labor, expropriation involves "confiscation" of land, labor, and human beings including organs and reproductive capacities, and "conscription into capitalist circuits of value" either directly, such as through slavery, or indirectly, such as through debt or unwaged reproductive labor. Other contemporary examples include home and land foreclosures or appropriation, residential and school segregation, and lack or underfunding of public services. Expropriation is key to accumulation for obvious reasons: it provides resources and labor that capitalists do not (fully) pay for. This is not, however, simply an economic distinction but a political one made through concerted effort: between the free worker and the dependent subject, who are often institutionally and legally defined by their relationally produced differences. In contrast to "free" workers, the expropriated are unfree, non-waged, and dependent subjects, including colonized subjects and those who do not have independent legal status, such as children (see also Arce, this volume). Fraser roughly traces the shifting relationship between exploitation and expropriation, arguing that in the current era of financialized capitalism we are increasingly seeing a hybrid figure: "The expropriable-and-exploitable citizen-worker, formally free but acutely vulnerable" (Fraser 2016: 176). Introducing such concepts into childhood studies can help materialize deeply historicized assemblages of social class, the legal and political status of childhood, and new regimes of accumulation.

The complexity of these interconnections is certainly relevant for childhood studies, as the queer youth of color who act as Bernardini's interlocutors (this volume) demonstrate with their refusal to be pinned down as expropriable-victim-subjects while deeply aware of the structural vulnerabilities which shape their lives. They make short work of childhood studies' "go to" concept of agency as self-possession, which offers little by way of understanding the relational fields in which financialized capitalism and contemporary subjects emerge. The political economic processes which make the expropriable-and-exploitable subject are further helpful, we suggest, for interrogating the reproduction and dynamism of adult–child generational distinctions, rather than simply mapping their contours (Mizen 2002). The concept of expropriation allows us to materialize ontologies of childhood which are fundamentally linked to capital accumulation, and therefore engage in knowledge practices which can elaborate their rupture.

Conclusion

In this introductory chapter, we offer our own attempt at reimagining childhood studies alongside the contributors to this volume. In the process of reflecting on and writing this piece we asked ourselves: *How can childhood studies move beyond its current, limited, and limiting preoccupation with the independent, monadic and agentic child on which its own very identity as a project seems to rest? What would childhood studies look like if the "child" was located somewhere other than at the center? How can scholarship and practice take seriously the political presence of living, biographical children while also implementing a wide scalar and temporal view (extending to past and future) of the worlds in which they exist and from which they arise?* Admittedly, such questions may never be answerable in any simple manner, but we felt they must be posed if only to beget initially unsure, hesitant responses.

We have suggested that thinking about childhood through relational ontologies may help the field rethink its very object of inquiry—the child/childhood—in ways that counteract its own inward tendencies and release the hold of its fixation with the agentic child. A move to decenter children and childhood through a relational perspective, we argued, can also offer childhood studies an opportunity to expand its scope of inquiry and to rethink the ethics and politics of its knowledge practices. Our scales of choice, for instance, and the work they do through our knowledge practices illustrate how the field can experiment with new ways of knowing that tackle some of its blind spots. Our discussion of childhood under financialized capitalism (as one instance of such a blind spot) illustrates not only the centrality of childhood in political economy but also the need to disrupt the field's "uncanny double" by turning our attention to the way our field might contribute to, or at least serve to unwittingly justify, wider developments of global capitalism and their impact on children's lives. Without losing sight of the local, a rescaling of the field's empirical project in this sense can bring forth worlds and relations that are both different and consequential. Our interventions in children's worlds through the knowledge we produce, however limited, can, we suggested, be mindful and reflexive about the material consequences they have on children's lives.

As a dynamic scholarly field and practice, childhood studies has much to offer to the human sciences and beyond. Overcoming the desire to "own the child" need not weaken the field's intellectual and political project. On the contrary, we feel that such a move might re-energize it through cross-fertilization. Being open and receptive to dialogue with what lies beyond—to borrow and integrate but to also offer and contribute—is not only a sign of intellectual maturity for a field but also a bold affirmation for its raison d'être. The project of reimagining childhood studies no doubt looms larger than this attempt in *Reimagining Childhood Studies* wherein the contributions, individually and collectively, strive to reach beyond extant boundaries of thought and conception to venture elsewhere. In the end, we feel each of us faces the challenge—in our own ways, our own spheres, our own work—to move past the "child" without recklessly leaving childhood behind. Recognizing the limits of any attempt at reimagining a field, and the sense of humility that comes with attempting to do so, we nevertheless feel that at this particular moment in childhood studies' trajectory, such attempts may provide impetus for new explorations, and not just any explorations, but ones that matter for the historical times in which we live.

PART ONE

Spatial and Temporal Challenges and Interventions

CHAPTER TWO

Childhood, Culture, History: Redeploying "Multiple Childhoods"

Sarada Balagopalan

Introduction

Toward the end of her introduction in *Children and the Politics of Culture* (1995), the anthropologist Sharon Stephens reminds us that the aim of the volume is neither to undermine international human rights discourse nor to frame this as a choice between cultural relativism and universalism. Instead, she seeks to make rights "more powerful and more flexible" (Stephens 1995: 40) in an effort to "disabuse them of their aura of timelessness, absoluteness, universality and naturalness" (1995). Over the past twenty years, the framing of childhoods as "multiple" (James and Prout 1997) has worked to productively reduce the aura and assumed universality (and timelessness) of several key concepts including "biological age" (Huijsmans et al. 2014) and "children's work" (Bourdillon et al. 2010). The rich body of ethnographic research that this framework has produced, on children's lives in the majority world, has significantly attempted to address what Said (1978) characterized as "the dreadful secondariness of some peoples and cultures." Yet, a closer inspection of how these accounts get included in childhood studies research (and teaching) would more than likely disclose that, in a majority of instances, these ethnographies continue to serve as empirical examples. They serve as case studies of difference that supplement or oppose conceptual categories that are drawn from children's lives in Euro-American contexts without ever fully disabusing their universality. Effectively then, these dense and rich narratives of children's everyday lives in majority world context have seldom been mobilized for broader theorization within the field of childhood studies. This implicit but foundational divide, between the empirical "south" and the theoretical "north," that continues to frame research on children's lives, more than twenty-five years after this multi-disciplinary field materialized, begs the question around whether the recognition of childhoods as "multiple" has necessarily reduced the *conceptual weight* exercised by the normative ideal? Adrian James (2010) has explored this tension in terms of its more pragmatic effects around whether a recognition of children's lives as multiple might end up condoning the "exploitation" of children within a cultural register. While this is a critical point, it is also one which fails to adequately interrogate our current allochronic[1] orientation toward subaltern children in the majority world, and the ways in which our temporal and hierarchical distancing of these lives continually reinforce, albeit in multiple ways, the higher truth of an universal, linear, and singular narrative of childhood. Working instead with Stephens' plea to disabuse certain universal certitudes of their naturalness and timeless aura, this chapter utilizes a postcolonial lens to offer two separate, although inter-related, moves which would allow childhood studies to assume a more critical and conceptually precise stance in relation to childhoods in the majority world. The first is to demonstrate how a sustained focus on the present circulation of universal certitudes, like children's rights for example, can gain by factoring the traces of the colonial past in the present. Reading contemporary cultural practices as historically mediated isn't limited to knowing the "history" of these communities as a set of facts. It is more about foregrounding the continued effects that this past exercises on the present lives of subaltern children in order to disrupt the field's current privileging of a linear, historicist account of childhood. It is this linear reading that allows Euro-American childhoods to emerge out of a complex "history" while the lives of the rest of the world's children remain mechanically slotted within "culture." The second is to take a self-evident explanatory term that has been singularly employed to read subaltern childhoods in the majority world, namely, "responsibility," and to critically reframe this in terms of its potential challenge to the field (Bissel 2003; Bourdillon et al. 2010; Dyson 2014). I do this by drawing upon assumptions of "non-sovereign relationality" that underlie "responsibility" and the challenge that this poses to the autonomous, liberal subject that frames existing understandings of "agency" within childhood studies (James and Prout 1997). In what ways does the privileging of purposive actions by rational actors exclude the ethical actions of a majority of the world's children?

Let me begin, however, by briefly recapping my critique of "multiple childhoods" as it is my frustration with and the need to move beyond this "yet another example" inclusion of children's lives in the Global South that propels my efforts in this chapter. As stated at the beginning of this chapter, multiple childhoods did enable a re-assembling of the earlier prescriptive, universal, and historicist lens that underlay a normative childhood. However, these detailed ethnographies are often epistemologically arranged and leveraged within older notions that equate cartographic "place" with a discrete "culture." The resulting slippage not only frames these children's "agential" actions and behaviors within deterministic, structural-functionalist logics, but the failure of these ethnographies to more critically engage a normative childhood further bolsters the parochializing of these children's lives (Hurtig 2008; Swanson 2010; Dyson 2014). Elsewhere, I have argued that "multiple childhoods" in effect works out as a project of "liberal tolerance,"[2] with its "separate but equal" reading of children's lives in the majority world often aiding in consolidating, rather than denaturalizing, the "cultural" difference between the normative "us" and the othered "them" (Balagopalan 2014).

To a certain extent this parochialization has been both directly and indirectly addressed by research that foregrounds a political economic reading of the discrete lives of children throughout the world by locating, for example, their everyday experiences of work, consumption, and schooling, within larger global economic transformations (Katz 2004; Wells 2009; Honwana 2012; Williams 2016b). Not only does this embedding of the culturally discrete lives of children within global economic processes offer us a more political handle with which to engage these lives, but this framing also constitutively rejects a relativist reading. Instead, it brings into focus visible shifts in the "local" brought on by the universalizing logics of global capitalism, including neoliberal modes of governance, new modes of consumption, the commodification of bodies, and the role that the increased mediatization exercise on youth sociality and aspirations. While this research appears to have successfully transcended the material–ideational divide, its privileging of the working of a distinct "global" on a discrete "national" ignores the global and the national as co-constituted within an earlier and more fraught colonial past. It is thus the historical and cultural particularities of global connections, the "symbolic domination" they reassert, and the ways in which they challenge and maintain asymmetries in social relations set in place by the colonial past (and reinforced in projects of national development) that play out in the contemporary.

Postcolonial scholars have, for several decades now, worked to map, interrogate, and disaggregate this colonial past and have produced a critical lens that is alive to colonialism as a significant rupture with enduring effects (Chatterjee 1993; Bhaba 1994; Chakrabarti 2000; Dirks 2001). Edward Said (1978) has discussed colonialism as a "fate with lasting, indeed grotesquely unfair results," while Gayatri Spivak (1993) has delineated the "altered normality" that colonialism set in place by tracing its continued effects on forms of knowledge and everyday cultural, social, and material practices in the colony and the metropole. This inclusion of the metropole has produced postcolonial theory as a critical node for scholars researching Aboriginal childhoods in Australia as well as Black and minority childhoods in the United States. Through deploying frameworks that remain cognizant of the continued effects that a violent and exclusionary colonial past exercises on the present workings of the liberal state,[3] the productivity of a postcolonial optic lies in its critical scrutiny of universal categories like "rights," "freedom," "development," etc., categories whose emancipatory potential is usually taken for granted. This wide and expansive terrain of scholarship has generated several different lines of inquiry and this chapter draws on the work of theorists who have interrogated the assumed "subject" of these universal projects of emancipation. Spivak's (1992, 2004) tracing of the strong effects that past and present exclusions exercise on the formation of subjectivities and her astute theorization on inability of the subaltern to become proper subjects of reason have been variously mobilized by postcolonial theorists. They've utilized this inability to both critically foreground the limits of these universal imperatives and highlight the crucial need to redraw the universal in relation to the particular (Mbembe 2003; Mahmood 2011). Their critique of underlying assumptions—like reason within liberal subject formation—is not necessarily a rejection of these universal projects but more an effort to continually be alive to the exclusionary logics that frame these universals in an attempt to move toward a more substantive realization of social justice for all. Thus, they force us to continually keep open the ethical imperative within these universal projects of emancipation and thereby also recalibrate our imagination of the political (Spivak 2004; Chatterjee 2004). By alerting us to the workings of the past in the present, postcolonial theorists force us to recognize that the categories we employ in our research—whether it be universals like "labor" and "rights" or particular categories like "manush" and "khatni", that emerged from my research with street children and child laborers in Calcutta (Balagopalan 2014)—require to be read as historically specific constructions to more meaningfully address the substantive exclusions that mark "progress."

Historicity and "children's rights"

Although the colonial "civilizing mission" took various forms, depending on the colonial power,[4] its workings engendered a violent insertion into modernity for the majority of the world's peoples. Postcolonial scholars have highlighted this formative violence to interrupt the hegemonic narrative of "transition" within which modernity gets often read as a singular, linear, and predetermined trajectory. In this reading not only does the modern West represent the end of this evolutionary process but countries in the majority world are always already found to be lacking/lagging (Chakrabarty 2000; Chatterjee 2004). This singular reading of modernity is what childhood studies constitutively contended with in its recognition of childhoods as socially constructed. Despite the richness of archival research on children's lives in these ex-colonies—which discusses native subaltern childhoods as dominantly constructed through a "difference" that needed to be defined and maintained and was therefore seldom stable (Grier 2006; Pomfret 2009; Vallargada 2011)—our ethnographies unintentionally privilege an ahistorical reading of "culture" that naturalizes and reifies these childhoods instead of continually alerting us to their constructedness. The colony was where the adult natives appeared "child-like" noble savages and where the very meaning of efficient colonial administration meant adapting to the supposed heterogeneity of the natives through technologies of enumeration of religious, caste, tribal, and regional differences (Nandy 1992; Chatterjee 1993). Within this "ethnographic state" (Dirks 2001), the "child-figure" did not materialize within a shared liberal understanding of "protection" as its underlying humanism would have destabilized the rule of colonial difference. Instead native children and childhoods circulated as that which had to be locally qualified, broken down, and made to fit specific sites in the colonial governmental apparatus including crime prevention, public health, and education. The state's accommodation of this diversity was a central feature in the introduction of modern apparatus of discipline and protection around the "child" in the colony. Although this apparatus reflected bourgeois constructions around the "child" that underlay emergent ideas of "protection" in the metropole, in the colony these ideas were indexed within a more extractive logic. The economic expediency that often underlined these "civilizational" imperatives not only produced indigenous natives as plantation, factory, and other types of laborers but also worked upon their children to naturalize their learning of labor through the manipulation of laws, policies, and pedagogic instruction (Sen 2005; Greir 2006; Balagopalan 2018).

Even when we include this colonial past, we read this more as a historical event and less in terms of its historicity or namely the continued effects that this colonial past exercises on the present (Stephens 1995; Balagopalan 2002, 2011, 2014). While recent discussion around reparations to former colonies highlights the more material and economic dimensions of colonialism's continued effects, my dwelling on historicity focuses on the circulation of abstract assurances, like children's rights in the majority world, in light of this colonial past. At a time when states in the Global South show a previously unseen willingness to implement the provisions of the UNCRC into national laws, what is our critical purchase on the idea of children's rights? Is it only to reprimand postcolonial states for poor implementation and governance? Or, might we need to combine ethnographic and historical research to better theorize this moment's promise as well as its disempowering moves?

While the ethnocentrism that underlines the UNCRC has been skillfully exposed (Burman 1996; Boyden 1997; Neiwenhuys 1998; Pupavac 2001), there has been less writing on the translation of these rights in different national-cultural contexts (Balagopalan 2012; Hanson and Neiwenhuys 2012). This translation is not only about the effects of social stratification on the uneven realization of children's rights but also a recognition of the fundamental difference in the ways in which elite and subaltern communities in postcolonial societies understand and engage this discourse. The newness of "children's rights" is an insufficient explanation for the varied engagement between elites, who easily adopt this language of children's rights, and subaltern communities, who appear more "baffled" (Spivak 1992). Instead, if we factored in the postcolonial predicament in which children's rights sits upon, and co-exists with, the colonial and the "developmental" apparatus, then we would need to work with an understanding of modernity as an uneven, violent, and coercive process in these lives, with past exclusions continuing to exercise a significant role on the formation of subaltern subjectivities. Subaltern communities don't necessarily resist these liberal discourses, neither are they uninformed nor averse to mobilizing claims to resources. However, through all of these moves they appear less conversant with liberal certitudes and often have to be motivated and encouraged to take on children's rights initiatives as a lawful exercise to their claims to citizenship. Several campaigns around children's rights, including efforts to eliminate corporal punishment and make schooling compulsory, have often misinterpreted these communities lack of ease as a clash between a modern and progressive rights discourse and static, archaic "cultural" traditions. However, what this reading elides are the ways in which these populations have been marginalized by political, social, cultural, and economic policies, processes, and practices of the colonial and postcolonial state. As a sphere of rational action, these policies and processes do not just preclude and order these "cultural" practices but are also grounded in particular interests, contingencies, and exclusions that have affected and shaped these "cultures." Historicizing these communities relationship with the state and capital,[5] including its exclusions which result in their continued lack of access to "lines of social mobility" (Spivak 2004), would allow us to delve deeper into how certain hierarchies of knowledge that underpin children's rights discourses also produce an anti-political front for schemes of poverty reduction that disguise governmental practices of resource extraction, dispossession, and the casualization of labor. Becoming aware of the continuing effects of this apparatus on the present abilities of subaltern populations to act upon their entitlements as citizens would allow our research on disparate aspects of children's lives—ranging from livelihoods, schooling, consumption, media access, marriage, sexuality, mobility, and migration—to be construed less as interpretations of isolatable domains of child-specific "cultural" practices and to instead be viewed as, fundamentally, political.

This broad framing of the political is also that which helps realign the inability of subaltern communities to fully participate in contractual obligations, a central tenet of liberal, individuated subject-formation. In India, for example, although the country's liberal Constitution contains a surfeit of progressive legislation that guarantees and works affirmatively to engender equality, this does not produce individuated understandings of citizenship and equality which circulate as the norm within modern Western liberal democracies. Why this difference persists, despite provisions in the Indian Constitution and the passage of various laws which guarantee and uphold equal and individuated citizenship, is best understood through a comparative historical explanation. Postcolonial scholarship has foregrounded this differentiated engagement with citizenship and rights that marks ex-colonial countries (Mbembe 1992, 2003; Chatterjee 2004).[6] According to Partha Chatterjee (2004), citizenship develops chronologically in the modern West from the institution of civic rights in civil society to political rights in the nation-state. In the modern West, the idea of citizenship as an ethical, normative category that implies participation in the sovereignty of the state historically precedes the state securing its legitimacy through ensuring the well-being of populations. Only in the nineteenth and twentieth centuries, with the emergence of an apparatus of welfare provision around the vectors of schooling, health, and employment, did the social come to be organized in the modern West. However, in former colonies, the creation of nation-states was preceded by colonial rule that produced its own technologies of governmentality, which administered colonial subjects while not recognizing them as citizens. Instead, the colonial state worked upon native populations through an elaborate apparatus that classified, categorized, and enumerated them as population groups for a range of purposes linked to concerns of colonial governmentality, including crime prevention, education, and public health (2004). After decolonization and with independence, India and several other ex-colonial countries adopted a democratic form of government with universal adult franchise which meant that these national populations received the right to vote without necessarily embodying the particular citizen subjectivity that Western liberalism assumes.

While the discourse of "children's rights" may be a more recent introduction in the majority world, the liberal language of rights that it upholds is not necessarily new. In several ex-colonial countries, constitutional provisions and the legal apparatus are based on an enlightened citizen-subject who desires the tradition of rights, reason, and freedom. But this does not necessarily translate into the assumed hegemony of liberal practices in these societies. This absence is what Ranajit Guha (1998) has famously called "dominance without bourgeois hegemony"; it does not mean that these countries are non-modern, but rather that modernity took a different form in former colonies. Ranajit Guha (1998) has discussed the ways in which the formation of modernity and citizenship in former colonial countries constructed the domain of the political as split into two distinct sensibilities that get woven together continuously. While the first is the formal-legal and secular networks of governance, the second is that of relationships of direct domination and subordination that derive their legitimacy from a different set of practices. Everyday understandings of equality, entitlement, rights, and the state are thus not necessarily framed within a liberal understanding of the same, although the Indian Constitution upholds this liberal text.

In former colonies, the creation of nation-states was preceded by colonial rule that produced its own governmental apparatus to administer, classify, and enumerate colonial subjects for a range of purposes, including education, hygiene, law and order, etc. With this colonial governmental apparatus continuing to endure when these nations became independent, the majority of the population interacted with the legal-bureaucratic apparatus of the postcolonial state as targets of various programs (like improving nutrition of mothers and babies), processes (gradual increase in school enrollments), and campaigns (improving awareness of hygiene) rather than through discourses of individuated citizenship. The latter was limited to a small section of the nation's elite who were a part of civil-social sphere. Although NGO workers who are employed in children's rights organizations may in their professional capacities employ this individuated discourse of rights, their everyday lives are embedded within a recognition of the split in the political, between secular networks of formal-legal governance and forces of direct domination and subordination (Pells 2012; Balagopalan 2014).

Given this dense and complex postcolonial predicament, critical research on children's rights would need to extend its current focus beyond this transnational terrain's investments in neoliberal logics of practical and moral improvement, and also be alive to the ways in which this discourse risks reproducing, albeit in new forms, the fraught relationship that subaltern communities have had with the national and local state and its social welfare apparatus. Foregrounding the enduring effects of these communities lack of access to "lines of social mobility" (Spivak 2004) as the starting point of our research, that is adopting a more historicist perspective, would allow us to realign these communities engagement with citizenship and the discourse of rights; not as a historical "lag" that children's rights will rectify but as that which risks setting in place new exclusionary logics while effectively leveraging the speculative futures of subaltern children.

These speculative futures often rely on a binary reading of these lives; a simplification of dense realities into a "before," which is often vexed by family circumstances and community traditions, and an "after," or a potentially improved future made possible through children exercising their rights. What this binary framing often jettisons is these children's sense of "responsibility" as this is viewed as having emerged from an earlier, more fraught arrangement of these lives. The next section of the paper opens up this deterministic framing of "responsibility" in an effort to realign responsibility as a conceptual category that contains the potential to destabilize, and thereby expand, existing understandings of children's agency within childhood studies.

Reframing "responsibility" as an universally desirable mode of being

Learning to become responsible is an important aspect of children's socialization. We understand this as contributing to self-discipline, tolerance, the public use of reason, and the development of self-restraint. Studies on adolescent morality in the United States often include adolescent awareness and exercise of responsibility as a critical indicator of their moral development (Hart et al. 1998; Ochs et al. 2009). However, when responsibility is used to read marginal children's lives in the Global South, it usually serves as a shorthand for the overwhelming control and determination of lives. Interpreted as expectations that bind children to families and communities, responsibility is often viewed as the zone of the non-modern, of a gendered tradition that inhibits these children's self-interested and free movement. Whether deployed as a constraint or as an explanation, "responsibility" is often interpreted as a natural, ahistorical character trait that subaltern children are socialized into.

Elsewhere, I have discussed how historicizing "responsibility," in terms of the enduring effects of colonial and postcolonial policies, can aid in denaturalizing this as a character trait (Balagopalan 2014). In this chapter, I draw on Spivak's (2004) discussion on responsibility to foreground the epistemic contributions that "responsibility" can make to childhood studies. Spivak's writing on responsibility grows out of her critical reading of what she characterizes as the social Darwinism of human rights and its binary division of the world. This bifurcation of the globe between "rights-based" and "responsibility-based" cultures maps onto Euro-American and the Global South, or ex-colonial, contexts, respectively. Spivak argues that the self-evidence of this division is tied to the universal privileging of human rights which allows persons in Euro-American contexts to view as their "manifest destiny" the key role they play in improving the lives of others. When juxtaposed against the universal referent of human rights, "responsibility" takes on a more provincial register, with the naturalness of understanding this as a set of cultural practices serving to routinely circumscribe its potential as a generative and more conceptual category. In contrast to this, Spivak's (2004) analysis propels responsibility into a more universal orbit through recognizing this as the "lost imperative within postcapitalist societies." She interrogates the juridical-citizenship inflected idea of responsibility as "duty" and juxtaposes this formal contractual relationality against the ability to be defined by a less formalized and less contractual mode of reciprocity. This "call of the other," a term she borrows from Emmanuel Levinas, is not about formally learned rational set of behaviors but rather a sensibility that appears to be thinned out or lost within postcapitalist societies. In these societies "duty," as invoked by Churchill in his aphorism, "the price of greatness is responsibility," is the widely prevalent episteme of a rationally induced sense of liberal benevolence that human rights discourses contain. In contrast to this, Spivak foregrounds that in marginalized communities the question of responsibility or "being called by the other before will" is that which is prior to a rationally learned intent. Thus, by bringing non-rational actions into the sphere of ethics, Spivak effectively expands this domain to go beyond its current investments in individuated, autonomous agents who calculate, with rational certitude, the right actions that require to be taken in a particular situation.

Although Spivak relies on philosophy to make her point, research on reciprocity and reciprocal social relations has been a very significant line of inquiry in cultural anthropology. These ethnographic investigations and broader theorizing have often provided insights into the cross-cultural workings of this mode of intersubjectivity, self-making, and sociality. Such interconnections repeatedly find expression in the root metaphors of a culture and forms the habits and idioms of exchange which are never separate from these communities sense of cultural, bodily, and interpersonal meaning-making. The anthropologist Michael Jackson (1998) eloquently explains this when he states,

> Language articulates social relationships more than it expresses information and ideas. And agency is not so much self-expression as self-restraint tied to an ability to foster mutually beneficial alignments within a wide field of social and extrasocial relations. In such a world, civility, etiquette and emotions are less a matter of inward disposition than of interactive performance, and "we" replaces the discursive "I." (Jackson 1998: 12)

Becoming responsible is then always already part of the dense cultural fabric of these everyday worlds and therefore "half archived" within the consensual working of kinship relations and often generates an intrapsychic response to the "call of the other."

While this sociality, intersubjectivity, and non-sovereign relationality take different cultural forms across the majority world, they continue to structure relations even in urban, upper-class, and socially mobile ethnic communities. It is not its absence, its missing, but more its diminishing and attenuation ("the lost episteme") within post-capitalist Euro-American contexts that Spivak alerts us to. The relational nature of human existence has been foregrounded in Western thought including phenomenology, hermeneutics, and post-structuralism, while psychological anthropology has focused on the ways in which the psychic self is constructed through language and social relations. In postcapitalist societies, however, this has been reduced to formally learned behaviors with the ascendancy of reason normalizing individuated, purposeful actions that we undertake to create and maintain familial, personal, professional, and civic socialities. Positive freedom or the capacity to realize your autonomous true and individuated self is foundational to liberalism and produces "duty" as a set of rational ethical acts of benevolence. Critics of liberal citizenship and politics in Euro-American contexts have often highlighted the limits of this rational benevolence and disclosed the racist, gendered, and classist exclusions, including the violence that liberal projects rely upon and cultivate (Brown 2005; Duane 2013; Berlant 2016). This chapter does not have the space to go into these critiques at length, but these foreground the limits of this contractual understanding of a citizen's duty which underlay the promise and the inevitability of a "good life" in Euro-American societies. This promise has in the past few decades entered an immense crisis as rising inequality, shrinking wages, "footloose capital," and crumbling infrastructure have become the everyday conditions of late capitalism.

Given these degradations of capitalism, scholars have begun to discuss the significance of non-sovereign relationality as a desirable mode of being. Scholarship has mobilized the productivity of this mode of being to foreground existing relations of "everyday communism" that already operate between individuals in postcapitalist societies (Graeber 2011), while others have used non-sovereign relationality to rethink current conceptualizations of subject-formation in US democracy by denaturalizing existing notions of sovereignty, autonomy, and individuality and making a compelling argument for "belonging" instead (Berlant 2016).[7] Rosine Kelz (2016) explores the writings of Arendt, Butler, and Cavell on the formation of the self to foreground the appeal of a non-sovereign notion of the self. She argues that this notion can aid in expanding our understandings of political connectivity and agency by linking these to an ethics of responsibility toward those "others" who are marginalized within our current political-national contexts. These writings not only frame this mode of relationality as desirable and required within Euro-American contexts, but Graeber and Kelz also make the point (as did Spivak with responsibility) that this mode of being already exists, although in a diminished form, in these societies.

Perhaps there was no need for me to highlight the valence of this mode of being in Euro-American contexts, as the first thing that comes to mind when we think about the non-sovereign relationality that "responsibility" embeds is the "child." Our relationships with children as parents, siblings, immediate and extended kin and children's relationship with their peers and with adults are largely governed by a "call to the other before will" or non-sovereign relationality. Our irrational worrying about the children in our lives and our efforts to "protect" them coexist with the rational decisions we make for and with them. Although this chapter does not have the space to undertake this discussion, the dialectic between given-ness and choice that frames our relationship with children makes the "child" figure a productive node through which to further explore the broader potential of non-sovereign relationality (and thereby also amplify the import of childhood studies).[8] However, I do want to flag one aspect of this concept that directly relates to the ways in which we currently conceptualize children's "agency," and the following section focuses on this discussion.

Realigning agency in light of responsibility

Recognizing children as competent social actors is a constitutive component of childhood studies. In the past few decades, scholars in the field have greatly expanded and complicated our notions of children's "agency": from its earlier circulation as active, autonomous, and individuated participation (Esser et al. 2016) to a more nuanced recognition of power dynamics and silences (Spyrou 2016), and assemblages and arrangements (Oswell 2013). These multiple iterations of agency are anchored, however, in the hegemony of reason. This hegemony is also reflected in our framing of children's subjectivities in the majority world through the idiom of "responsibility." Ranging from street children's survival tactics (Hecht 1998; Aitkin 2001; Scheper-Hughes 2008; Balagopalan 2014) to rural children's intimate understanding of nature and respect for the rhythms of local forestland (Katz 2004; Froerer 2011; Dyson 2014) and working children's subjectivities (Bissel 2003; Leibel 2004; Bourdillon et al. 2010), all of this research foregrounds children's "agency" as a set of rational and contextually mediated, purposeful actions. This includes, for example, the recognition of children's competence across varied contexts, their astute decision-making, their creative interpretation of existing practices, and their knowledgeable engagement with multiple hierarchies.

What at times get left out, or are often less attended to in these descriptions of the "agential," are the non-sovereign aspects of these relationships, or namely the multiple, daily, interactions that affirm children, while not necessarily foregrounding aspects of their autonomous selfhood nor emphasizing processes related to choice-centered, rational actions tied to individuated self-making. It is the child's dependency that prompts these non-sovereign interactions, and in our efforts to adequately distinguish and detach the "agential" from the "dependent" child we've naturalized and affirmed autonomy as a developmental and generational matter. Haunted by Locke's assertions around the incapacity of children to participate in contractual obligations, our reification of autonomy has foreclosed an exploration of the non-sovereign relationalities that sustain children's agential actions. The largely unconscious psychodynamic processes that allow them to relate to others "before will," or as a sensibility (as opposed to rational actions), when they are "dependent," might diminish, but is seldom erased, as they grow older. Instead, these processes continue to both shape and be shaped by children, through socially charged everyday interactions in which the countervailing needs of self and other are balanced (Chapin 2014). Several cultural anthropologists have highlighted the given-ness of social relations, with their work on kinship foregrounding this sensibility by describing how individuals act both alone and with others. The given-ness of these relationships combine dependence with autonomous actions. This is reflected, for example, in everyday rituals that require conformity while also allowing for inversions, fulfillment, role reversals, and delinquency, that is, processes through which persons challenge and reconstitute this given-ness and thus also exercise control over it (Jackson 1998).

In a similar manner, the overdetermined terrain of "responsibility," as Spivak's theorization makes clear, consists of agential practices even though these practices are not necessarily rational. Although an intentionality of action undergirds responsibility, the given-ness of these actions might be motivated by less than rational attachments, obligations, and sentiments. Thus, far from being limited to the contractual, responsibility exists as a sensibility that both precedes and exceeds rational actions. In our privileging of rational, agential actions of the child, we quell the possibilities opened up by children's sensibility to continue to be moved to action by non-rational sensibilities produced by their being alive to the "call of the other." This half-archived sensibility is dominant in the non-sovereign relationships that form an integral part of everyday relations in the majority world. Opening up children's "agency" to incorporate the ethics of non-sovereign relationality would centrally challenge autonomy as an ontological feature of the subject (Mahmood 2011) and would enhance current efforts that interrogate developmental psychology's universal grammar around the "child." Moreover, our current understandings of children's self-restraint as passivity as well as our friction with children's non-verbal communication might be realigned through our renewed efforts to expand "agency" to include irrational and non-sovereign attachments that have always marked children's actions.

However, working with "responsibility" as a critical concept is to also be alive to its perversions. The deep inscription of this mode of being has direct and deleterious effects when used by communities to further legitimize and strengthen existing hierarchies of caste, gender, religion, and ethnicity as witnessed in the myriad rationalizations across the majority world, preventing and curtailing girls' schooling. In addition, there is also the risk of subaltern practices of non-sovereign relationality being leveraged by the state to naturalize the enduring poverty of these communities within a depoliticized reading of culture. The latter is well demonstrated in the Indian government's recent amendment to the child labor law which I explain in some detail to reinforce the central role that historicity exercises in our efforts to mobilize responsibility as a conceptual category.

Despite India's phenomenal economic growth and all children being guaranteed their "right to education" in 2009, the state's 2016 amendment of the country's child labor law appears to rely upon the affective relationality indexed in responsibility to legalize the bulk of child labor. Although on the surface the amendment appears to ban all children under 14 years from engaging in labor, a more careful reading discloses that they can continue to work in "family or family enterprises." This is further augmented by the absence of any regulation around how many hours these children should work. Instead, the amendment leaves this decision to parents and simply states that children may work "after school hours or during vacations." Given that roughly 80 percent of child laborers in India work with family members in various occupations ranging from agriculture, home-based assembly, and street vending, this move by the Indian state masterfully deflects the more enduring historical exclusions based on caste, religion, ethnicity, and gender into the personal decision of parents, with their "responsibility" toward their children serving as a mark of their correct actions. While it might be argued that this amendment is only formalizing what in effect already exists in practice, that is, the family does determine the child's involvement in labor, what is different is that the Indian state has effectively privatized and depoliticized what was earlier a key national developmental concern. Ironically, this privatization of child labor has been skillfully camouflaged in large part through the state's amplified rhetoric around the right to education. With all children now being able to exercise this right, the state is, in effect, leveraging schooling as the antidote to child labor, an antidote that puts the onus on parents to capitalize on school access while inversely blaming them when they are unable to do so.

What this framing elides is the long history of colonial and postcolonial policies that deliberately, as well as through a politics of neglect, and continually worked to affirm child labor as auxiliary to the country's development. The highly class-specific terrain of compulsory schooling in India with its low-quality schools for the country's impoverished populations further reinforces this earlier politics of neglect but with an added twist that the new right to education enables. This is namely the state's ability to manipulate this right to free schooling to signal its commitment to children and thereby construct subaltern communities as irrational, as mired in cultural traditions and practices that continue to prevent them from taking advantage of this new entitlement. To better attend to the complex inequalities which constrain the meaningful realization of right to education in India, it is not enough for us to only focus on the present assurances of the state and their ineffective implementation as this reading would legitimate the logics of the state and its framing of subaltern populations. Instead we would need to interweave two lines of analysis—the first that opens up subaltern childhoods to a more historically grounded understanding of the ways in which the colonial and the postcolonial state constructed and worked upon subaltern communities and their children, and the second that employs an ethnographic lens to dwell on the everyday working of non-sovereign relationality and how it meaningfully sustains lives lived within this longer history of enduring poverty and structural neglect (Balagopalan 2014; Phiri and Abebe 2016). Only focusing on the latter risks "culturalizing" these communities inability to rationally act upon liberal certitudes, like the right to education. While a singular focus on the former risks reinforcing a universal childhood norm within which these communities attunement to the "call of the other" cannot be included in terms of its conceptual potential. Redeploying multiple childhoods, from its current circulation as an empirical referent to have it serve instead as a more conceptually productive frame, requires us to foreground the uneven histories of the state and capital in our current context-based reading of childhoods in the majority world, as well as be more open (given the steady crumbling of liberal assurances in post-capitalist societies) to learning from societies that idealize non-sovereign relationality as a desirable mode of being.

Conclusion

According to the anthropologist Michel-Rolph Trouillot (1995), there are four crucial moments during which silences enter the process of historical production. These include "the moment of fact creation (the making of sources), the moment of fact assembly (the making of archives), the moment of fact retrieval (the making of narratives), and the moment of retrospective significance (the making of history in the final instance)" (26). I share Trouillot's analysis because it foregrounds *silences* that mark the *production of historical knowledge* while noting that each of these moments are conceptual tools that feed on each other and help us understand that not all silences are equal. It would be complicated to attempt a similar mapping of silences in the production of knowledge on children in the majority world within childhood studies but what Trouillot draws our attention to is the ways in which the norm (the making of history in the final instance) is as much a product of silences as it is of the exercise of hegemony. Recognizing the inseparability of the two on the ways in which the "child" was constructed is what prompted the new sociology of childhood to emerge more than twenty years ago. While we've made great strides in theorizing children's lives, the recognition that the particular optic through which we view childhoods in the majority world produces conceptual silences remains one of our greatest challenges. This chapter's attempt has been to realign the gaze through drawing attention to the continued effects of the colonial past on the present lives of children as well as to rethink the critical contribution that "responsibility" can make as a conceptual category of normative significance. Mobilizing this particularistic reading of "responsibility" and positing it as universally desirable is not intended to merely challenge, or flip, the false universalisms that underlie a normative childhood through reifying a mode of being that decisively challenges childhood "innocence." Instead, by signaling the, surprisingly overlooked, parallel between the normativity of non-sovereign relationships in the everyday lives of a majority of the world's children (and adults for that matter) and the historical construction of the modern Western "innocent" child as a figure who constitutively embodies and engenders non-sovereign relationships of love and affection, I wish to suggest that future research in childhood studies might productively align "responsibility" and "innocence." Not only as concepts whose interrelatedness starkly foregrounds the continued colonial and racial logics that affect the lives of children across the globe and the binary representations in which these are mired, but as that which forces us to work with the complexities of non-rational relationality that undergirds them both. An analytical exploration of these relational complexities contains the potential to propel the study of children and childhoods as central to, and not as a by-product of, current efforts to re-imagine the contemporary political terrain.

Notes

1 I borrow this term from Johannes Fabian's (1983) classic discussion of the constitutive role of time in Anglo-American and French anthropology in *Time and the Other*. His comprehensive analysis is focused on the contradictory ways in which time functions in fieldwork and in ethnographic writing with well-known term the "denial of coevalness" serving to signify the hierarchical and temporal relationship within which the "other" is produced. While this term is not explicitly discussed in this chapter, its strong trace can be found in the chapter's arguments against a relativist, parochial reading of children's lives in the majority world.

2 My critique draws on Wendy Brown's (2005) theorization of tolerance as that which skillfully masks the universalism that is at the heart of liberalism. According to her, the liberal subject's tolerance of the "other," or those who violate the norm, is based upon a self-recognition of themselves as conforming and upholding the norm. A double autonomy underlies this masking of the normative powers of liberalism—the first of the individual subject who extends this tolerance and rejects and retains aspects of a cultural framing, and second, the autonomy of law and politics from culture.

3 Research on African-American and indigenous lives in North America and Aboriginal lives in Australia has contributed to postcolonial theorization on the continued traces of unfreedom and analysis into settler modernity and colonial efforts to civilize populations through the use of brutal force. This includes research on the "stolen generation" or the 10 to 30 percent of Aboriginal children who were forcibly removed from their parents between 1910 and 1970 as part of the state's mission of cultural assimilation (Povinelli 1999). In addition, research on African-American childhoods has used critical race theory and postcolonial theory to discuss the persistent brutality of state and institutional violence as well as the structural exclusions that continue to mark the lives of these children in the United States (Bernstein 2011).

4 While the vast and varied scholarship on colonialism broadly asserts that it clearly lacked a transhistorical essence (Comaroff and Comaroff 1992; Appadurai 1996), they also reinforce the ways in which disparate indigenous practices were indubitably affected by these multiple circuits of ideas, institutions, and persons that made up these colonial processes of modernity, capital expansion, racial exclusions, disciplinary practices, and bureaucratic governmental functioning.

5 This reading also embeds an awareness of the contemporary loss of state power in development and children's rights projects and its dispersal among NGOs, donors, private sector providers, and social entrepreneurs.

6 While I am most familiar with the workings of the postcolonial state in India and the writing of postcolonial scholars who work on theorizing the Indian state, Mbembe offers a different analysis of the state. He addresses postcolonial state power as a distinctive symbolic system and regime of violence based on a fraught relationship between postcolonial states and their subjects. Domination in the postcolony works through the performance of the obscene and grotesque, which undermines action and resistance. In addition, he also traces the origins of the current "state of exception" and racialized forms of subjugations to the slave plantation and colony, and argues that Foucault's notion of biopower is not enough to account for contemporary forms of power that subject many to conditions of life akin to the status of "living dead." Instead, we need to understand power as "necropower." For more read Mbembe (1992, 2003).

7 David Graeber (2011) in his majestic treatise on debt discusses the reciprocal relations that we already share with each other in Euro-American contexts. Arguing that communism is the foundation for all human sociability, Graeber distinguishes between mythic communism, or the political organization of all aspects of society in terms of communist principles, and "everyday" communism. In the latter, communism is less a political ideology but more an operative principle that often frames our interactions with each other in which we are often inclined to instinctively help the "other." Whether it be a stranger asking for directions or a person on a ladder who drops their hammer while working, in both instances our spontaneous (and not yet rationally worked out) reaction is to help. It is this spontaneity, the ways in which we comply with small requests without even thinking about it or even perform spectacular acts like jumping into water to save someone from drowning, that Graeber mobilizes to highlight the ways in which "the call of the other before will" already manifests in postcapitalist societies. On the other hand, literary theorist Lauren Berlant (2016) develops the idea of "belonging" in relation to the "commons" and through this theorizes the possibility of replacing existing understandings that frame democratic subjects as those who are sovereign, autonomous, and free from constraints. She suggests that we construct "individuality as a genre carved from within dynamics of relation rather than a state prior or distinct to it" (395); thereby, signaling a sensibility that is open to the kind of attachment, both intense and fraught, that kinship societies with their sense of responsibility contain.

8 One of the several issues that I have in mind is feminist critique of this relationality and their work to disclose the various patriarchal forces that compel women to conform to this norm. In addition, several theorists have critiqued the privatization of the child's "dependence" and the ways in which it reifies multiple inequalities of race, class, and other differences. However, more recent feminist conceptualizations of "care" have increasingly adopted ideas of non-sovereign relationality in their theorization on nurturance by retaining within the notion of non-sovereignty, a critical stance for individual actions directed at questioning and interrogating our social environments (Kelz 2016). By effectively weaving together singularity and relationality to critically reformulate "community," Kelz realigns this combination to serve as a precondition for emancipatory political action and moral relationships.

CHAPTER THREE

Geographies of Play:

Scales of Imagination in the Study of Child-made Things

Karen Sánchez-Eppler

Reimagining Childhood Studies demands a respect for imagination. This chapter affirms imagination as a conceptual resource for thinking the world differently, and in doing so it demonstrates the value of attending to the experiences and activities of children—and in particular to the stuff they leave behind. Child-made things and the material traces of children's play remain a largely under-utilized resource for childhood studies. Adopting imaginative play as both an object of study and a generative methodology, this chapter models what is at stake in looking at the things children make and shows how children's play is shaped by and expresses its social context.

I have spent much of the last twenty years locating cultural artifacts produced by nineteenth-century American children and devising strategies for interpreting these invariably enigmatic items.[1] The obstacles to such work are by now deeply familiar. Child-focused research is hindered by bibliographic and classificatory conventions that have rarely considered age a salient category: the archives of childhood call for new collection agendas, age-sensitive classifications, and more robust descriptors. We hardly even have names for the genres of childhood production, nor any sense of the prevalence of different sorts of child-made things, nor even clear guidelines for how to identify whether or not something actually was made by a child. The available archives of child-produced materials from the past tend to be preserved only through the mediating actions of adults. Adult systems of valuation structure not only the keeping and categorizing of childhood production but also the efforts to analyze and interpret the items preserved. The curation of all histories traces lines of power, but this is most particularly true for childhood studies where—even if all once were children—not a single scholar may presently be a member of the group studied. "Reconstructing the history or histories of childhood through children's materials seems deeply entangled with more personal retrieval or recovery projects," Kenneth Kidd (2011: 2–3) acknowledges. Thus, the allure of accessing childhood experience comes steeped in adult nostalgia and desire. It is important to recognize all these practical and psychic particulars of what Jacqueline Rose (1984) identifies as the "impossible" aspects of studying childhood. Impossibilities, however, invite imagination.

Valuing things made by children pushes against most historical, cultural, and sociological assumptions about what matters.[2] The "childish" is defined as dependent, foolish, and so trivial. These liabilities of immaturity are in fact bound up with how and why the study of childhood impacts a broad range of historical questions. The treatment and experiences of children entail economic, institutional, governmental, and social dependencies, while their care and education establish norms. Childhood thus connects, as Steven Mintz (2012: 17) summarizes, "the personal and the public, the psychological and the sociological, the domestic and the state." In these pairs the child provides the pivot between shifts in scale, encapsulating the ways that an individual life engages with societal structures. To think across scales is to recognize similitude despite difference in magnitude. Changes in scale frequently characterize imaginative play. They also prove a constitutive feature of the kind of microhistory attention inherent in studying child-made objects. In short, the study of childhood requires shifts of scale. My contribution to this book, *Reimagining Childhood Studies*, affirms the value of children's imaginative play to this endeavor, but as an exercise in scale. Rather than offering a celebration of the separateness of play or of childhood, as classic play theory would have it, I intend to chart connections. I trace how adult expectations and the pressures of the real inform children's play and are transformed by it.[3]

The division between childhood and adulthood has often been depicted as the difference between playing and reality. Gillian Brown (1999) recognizes this mirroring as characteristic of childhood experience and as one of the obstacles to adult apprehension of that experience:

> These two realms within childhood, the provinces of actuality and imagination, restage within the child the poles of adulthood and childhood. The child's imagination stands apart from the actuality in which the child lives, an actuality identified with and ratified by adults. In this geography of childhood experience, children appear simultaneously accessible and inaccessible to adults. (79)

In Brown's account children are constantly negotiating this borderland between imagination and reality, experiencing these realms as simultaneous and permeable, while adults appear stuck on one side of a rigid binary. What might a "geography of childhood" look like if we trespass across that border and recognize play as consequential? This is not in itself a new question; there is a widespread understanding of play as the significant "work" of childhood and a key mechanism for children's incorporation into social norms. Yet historians of children's play largely base their arguments on adult evidence: supervisory records and nostalgic memoirs.[4]

This chapter exemplifies its geography of childhood through the examination of a nineteenth-century American geography textbook and the playful way one young girl used it. I have selected this object because in its doubleness—as lesson and as play—it literalizes the inter-relations of reality and imagination, adulthood and childhood. My analysis of this hybrid object demonstrates the importance of paying attention both to what is taught to children and to what they do with those lessons, and hence the need for historians of childhood to attend both to facts and to imagination. Schoolbooks rank among the most efficient tools of socialization, explicitly produced to instruct the next generation in those skills and values that their elders consider important to pass on. That their pages can sometimes simultaneously prove sites for play makes them powerful emblems of childhood's duality: the blank slate primed for inscription with social norms and the free spirit gleefully determined to roam. The doubling of docility and delight I discover in this schoolbook and discuss in this chapter strikes me as different from the pairings of hegemony and subversion that have long underlaid literary and historical patterns of critical analysis. The marks of play I find in this schoolbook do not simply indicate resistance. Children play *with* their schoolbooks, their marks of play occurring alongside the processes and tasks of socialization. Imagination, in other words, remains circumscribed by a host of social realities, but it is not reducible to them. In the terms of debate laid out by Brian Sutton-Smith, I seek to pair "progress theories" of child development through socialization with "power theories" that acknowledge children's capacity "to make themselves into their own social beings" with their own "play culture" (Sutton-Smith 1997: loc 2318–2424).

William Swinton's *Elementary Course in Geography* claims to be "a compromise between two extreme methods of treatment": this 1875 school textbook combines "the hard, curt, matter of fact style of question and answer which characterizes most primary geographies" with the "flowing description and animated narratives" that "though charming as mere reading lessons, fail in leaving that precise and definite knowledge which in our public schools must be obtained" (Swinton 1875). Thus, in the pedagogical design of his geography textbook Swinton seeks to bridge the "provinces of actuality and imagination" that Brown considers the "geography of childhood experience." Swinton's *Elementary Course in*

Geography is itself deeply invested—as pedagogical structure and marketing ploy—in the recognition of the doubling relation between didacticism and pleasure.[5] As Swinton's headnote explains, the first lesson "is designed merely to be read aloud in the class," a story rather than a list of questions. Although Swinton's *Elementary Course in Geography* is explicitly marketed as a school text, decorated with directions to teachers, these opening pages suggest a dual location since the lessons begin at home around a breakfast table: "Geography in a Cup of Coffee" (Figure 3.1). Here Uncle John,

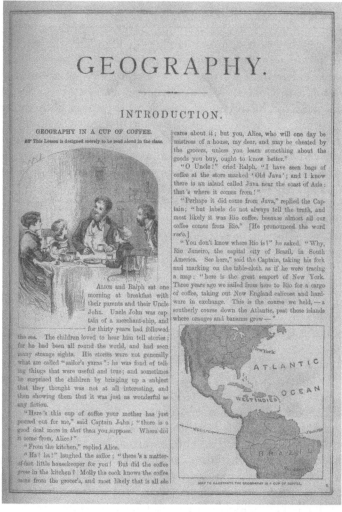

FIGURE 3.1 *"Geography in a Cup of Coffee" in William Swinton,* Elementary Course in Geography *(1875). Courtesy of the Winterthur Library: Joseph Downs Collection of Manuscripts and Printed Ephemera.*

captain of a merchant ship, regales young Alice and Ralph with "useful and true" tales about the origins of his breakfast brew—although not without a fair bit of embedded quizzing about the sources of his coffee, sugar, silver spoon, and china cup. The two illustrations on this opening page may appear to be opposites: the charming drawing of the charmed family circle set against the "precise and definite knowledge" offered by maps. Yet the narrative merges them in the imagination's conditional realm of "as if": the first illustration depicts Uncle John sketching with his fork on the tablecloth "as if he were tracing a map." Thus, the drawings in the book present Uncle John imaginatively transforming the breakfast table into the very map this schoolbook prints to demonstrate the networks of extraction, production, and trade that stock this well-laid table (1). Uncle John's geography lesson insists that all the items of domestic life come from and link a wider world, but as both consumers and as learners these children remain seated at the family table, venturing nowhere in body even as they are urged to circle the globe in their minds.

The historical record of what adults think about children and what adults want children to think about the world overwhelms in its enormous prescriptive bulk the available evidence of children's own experiences and perspectives. The fictive children of this introductory story are instructed about their raced, classed, and gendered roles as affluent white Americans in a global web of production and trade.[6] Children's literature and especially its didactic texts are such useful tools of social history because in their function of passing on information and values to the next generation they provide an explicit record of cultural norms. Swinton in his depictions, Uncle John in his address, and no doubt too the teacher in implementing these lesson plans all embrace the social replication import of the information they teach. The commodity chains of this geographical pedagogy double as ideological chains. As Hopkins and Wallerstein (1986: 159) convincingly showed, the "network of labor and productive processes whose end result is a finished commodity" was significantly international since at least the sixteenth century. The study of such chains has become a standard feature both of contemporary American business schools, where it aids in maximizing profit, and of a critical pedagogy, at the university and even the high school and elementary level, that generally seeks to expose the labor and environmental costs of a globalized consumer culture. Still it is striking to see the explicitness with which such insights structure this nineteenth-century schoolbook, and Swinton's complacent assurance that an understanding of commodity chains will invariably affirm white, bourgeois America's increasing world dominance. "The idea of childhood pervades the rhetoric of nation and citizenship," Christopher Kelen and Björn Sundmark (2012: loc 190–2) remind, "etymologically, 'nation' refers us to the idea of being born." The ties between the national prestige of the United States and geographical study prove particularly strong since comparative historical maps of North America document the United States's consistent territorial enlargement in a way that is not the case for the more stable or more erratic borders of European nations (Schulten 2012: loc 314–7). Thus, it is not surprising that from the period of the early republic through the nineteenth century, American schoolbooks turned to geography to teach the nation's origins and to confirm its territorial expansion and growing prestige.

The national, class, and gender lessons to be found in Uncle John's coffee cup are legion. When Uncle John quizzes the children about the source of his coffee, Alice helpfully announces that it comes "from the kitchen," and Uncle John contrasts such routine responses suitable to "Molly the cook" with the global knowledge needed by a girl "who will one day be mistress of a house" (1). This understanding of domestic space—and the domestic responsibilities of women and girls, servants and mistresses—recognizes the home as inextricable from the marketplace, not cordoned off and privatized but rather the very core of a vast network. Enacting his gender difference the more publicly observant and geographically informed male child, Ralph, proclaims that he has "seen bags of coffee at the store marked 'Old Java'; and I know there is an island called Java near the coast of Asia: that's where it comes from!" The story makes clear, however, that while there may be differences in how Alice and Ralph relate to the global economy, true geographical knowledge is equally crucial for girls and boys. To Ralph, Uncle John advises skepticism: "'labels do not always tell the truth,' he warns and notes that most coffee sold in the United States 'probably comes from Rio.' [He pronounced the word *ree'o*]" (1). While Uncle John cautions against a market economy where deceptions abound, Swinton's explanatory brackets generously recognize and guard against the limited foreign knowledge not only of the students but of the classroom teacher as well—teaching distrust and trust at once.

In three tightly printed and illustrated pages this story depicts the "negroes" laboring to gather coffee beans on Brazil "plantations" or grow sugarcane in Louisiana or Cuba. In this story, published a decade after the close of the Civil War, neither characters nor author mentions slavery. A later section of the book describes Africa as "the least important of the Grand Divisions because it is the seat of no great civilized nations ... the commerce of Africa is limited," its exports blandly listed as "gold, ivory, ostrich-feathers, dates, gums, drugs, and negro slaves"(121). In "Geography in a Cup of Coffee," Uncle John does describe the ports that ship and receive plantation products and the merchants who distribute them, the Nevada silver mines that produced the metal for Uncle John's spoon, and the Chinese origins of the cups he himself had brought from Asia, although patriotic Uncle John avers that there is no need "of our going to that far-off land for our crockery, when such excellent ware is made in our own country" (3). The commodity chains Uncle John traces present the American family as the beneficiaries of the world's labor without threatening American ingenuity or productivity. The lesson urges Alice and Ralph and the book's child auditors to imagine this "panorama" of labor, the "great multitude" whose "hands" and "work" are "getting this cup of coffee ready for us." Thus, this story models the imaginative act of seeing in the daily rites of domestic life both the vast interconnections of a global market and the white, middle-class, American child's own gendered but privileged place within it.

The copy of Swinton's *Elementary Course in Geography* in the collection of the Winterthur library is battered with a broken spine and some missing pages. Inside the front cover of this schoolbook published in 1875, May Durgin has written her name in pencil, and below it inscribed in sharp black ink "Vineland N.J. 1887." There is a pencil squiggle, perhaps the letter M for "May," along the edge of the picture of Uncle John enjoying his geographical cup of coffee. The lines curve above the figures of Alice and her mother: could this pencil line be a slight sign of readerly identification with these domestic, female figures? While frequent among all book owners, such marks of possession, the random traces of bookish activity, are particularly prominent features of child readership. They demonstrate, as Patricia Crain puts it, the ways in which children's literacy "enacted and enabled practices of ownership, and once claimed as their own, the ways in which their books became repositories, registers, and mediums for social and emotional attachment" (Crain 2016: 109). If the book's content celebrates the white, American child's position in a global marketplace, and perhaps especially the feminine role of domestic consumer, the book itself has become a thing to own. I do not know what sequence of exchanges brought this 1875 schoolbook into May Durgin's hands more than a decade after its publication—how it traveled from schoolroom to home. But by inaugurating its lessons at young Alice's breakfast table, Swinton's *Elementary Course in Geography* had already predicted and plotted just such a circuit.

I do know that May Ruth Durgin, the only child of Flora and Harrison Durgin, was born in Vineland, New Jersey, on May 8, 1878. The 1880 census sheet that lists the Durgin family shows six other children, 5 years old or younger living in houses neighboring 2-year-old May ("New Jersey, Births and Christenings Index"). Vineland itself was fairly young; May's father had settled there within the city's first decade. Harrison Durgin is identified in his obituary as a "Vineland Pioneer" ("Death Notice"). In 1861 Charles Kline Landis purchased 30,000 acres of woodland along the newly completed West Jersey railroad line thirty-five miles southeast of Philadelphia, with the goal of developing a model planned community: the imagined becoming real. "I conceived the idea," Landis reported in an 1875 essay, "of starting a settlement upon virgin land, near the great seaboard markets of America." Landis (1875) understood that his profits depended on the contentment and prosperity of the settlers:

> I therefore had to deliberate carefully upon all possible things which would benefit the settler directly or indirectly, develop industry, protect it—make the improvements of one man, in usefulness and beauty, redound to the benefit of each neighboring man, make families contented by giving them religious and educational privileges ... In short, selling land to them was

but the beginning of the business; without their prosperity the sale of land would soon stop, before a fifth of my immense purchase could be taken up ... The broad design of the Settlement was that it should be agricultural, manufacturing, commercial, and educational—one object could not well prosper without the others.[7]

Landis's development project, his speculation, explicitly envisions the relation between spiritual and material welfare, between social and economic networks, between contented families and prosperous manufactories. He recognizes domestic life at the heart of profit. Landis's advertisements succeeded.[8] Harrison Durgin, a New Hampshire native, was among the many residents of other states attracted to this venture, and in 1871 Durgin purchased a lot on the corner of Landis Avenue and Fourth Street. In laying out his model city Charles Landis had named its central avenue after himself. A grand 100-foot-wide boulevard, by the time Durgin acquired this lot, Landis Avenue was already lined with young shade trees. A Vineland directory for 1875 lists Harrison Durgin as a glove manufacturer, with a business at this address just one block from the railway station and a few blocks from the center of the city grid. In January, 1877, Harrison married his significantly younger, second wife, Floretta Maria Taylor of Rumney, New Hampshire, and she joined him in Vineland. A Vineland directory from 1887, the year their daughter May signed her name in this geography book, records "Durgin, Harrison, gloves" still on the Landis Avenue corner of Fourth Street.[9] Through these years Vineland remained a swiftly growing city—the Vineland directories repeatedly call it "flourishing"—its prosperity built as Landis had hoped on good railroad lines and flat fertile land.[10] An 1885 map of Vineland emphasizes this tidy grid plan and celebrates the city's fine public buildings and multiple factories (Figure 3.2). The 1887 directory gives Vineland's population as 4,000; the 1895 directory lauds it as "an exceptional point for manufactories" and notes that the city "has been most remarkable for increase in population, having attained a population of 12,000." Thus, when May Durgin, by then 9 years old, took possession of this geography book she was living in a city self-consciously built to produce and profit from the very networks of manufactory, commerce, and distribution Swinton's geography lessons sought to teach and normalize. Indeed, Vineland was founded upon the "Geography of a Coffee Cup" presumption that such networks require and support contented families.

Besides inscribing her name, and occasional small pencil markings in the margins, the volume at first appears to offer little indication of May Durgin's relation to this book and its lessons. Then unexpectedly, completely covering the text of pages thirty-eight and thirty-nine—and inverting the pattern of the book's opening story where the world comes to the breakfast table—this geography textbook becomes a room, furnished with a table set with china cups, silver spoons, and sugar urn, and occupied by a little girl holding a coffee pot (Figure 3.3).[11] If the elusive aspiration of archival work in childhood

FIGURE 3.2 Map of Vineland, New Jersey, *1885. O.H. Bailey & Co. (Boston, 1885). Courtesy of the Library of Congress Geography and Map Division.*

FIGURE 3.3 *May R. Durgin, Scrapbook House—Collage Album (1887). Courtesy of the Winterthur Library: Joseph Downs Collection of Manuscripts and Printed Ephemera.*

studies is to glimpse at childhood through its detritus, May Durgin's book emblematizes this effect, pasting a paper figure of a girl over the text. Creating a room to house a paper-self on the pages of a book about the world is an imaginative act: a bit of play that demonstrates how deeply these lessons in domesticity and commerce have been learned. If, as Robin Bernstein (2011) has argued, books are remarkably "scriptive things," inviting particular behaviors and beliefs—especially true of nineteenth-century schoolbooks with their imperative tone, catechizing form, and didactic aims—the use of this book clearly resists the script: not just reading in it or even writing in it, but pasting over its pages with sheets of wallpaper and images cut from other kinds of print sources. Yet, at the same time, in her creative play with this book, May Durgin enacts its lessons, conjuring the domestic scene, preparing the very cup of coffee that the text describes. As Allison and Adrian James (2008) observe, it proves "surprisingly difficult to provide a child-focused definition of play" because the liberated and purposeless understandings of play articulated by theorists of adult play fail to register the "immense purposeful load" that play carries for children, the ways in which play often figures as a "more obligatory activity" for children. In using her book as a plaything, a room in a paper doll's house, Durgin participates in an act of imaginative world-making that is both liberated from and continuous with the gender, class, racial, and national obligations of her education.

The transformation begins with pasting two sheets of wallpaper over the text. The strong brown pattern was likely intended to hang with its small stripes running vertically; here it is used to form the carpet of the room, the stripes placed as grounding horizontals. The paler pinkish second paper is displayed as wallpaper, the more natural flowers of its pattern twining up the walls. The placement of these two papers—dark and light, horizontal and vertical, stylized and natural—demonstrates a strong aesthetic sensibility and intentionality, and the orderly grid logic that Landis used in laying out his model city. The world-making trivialized as play has multiple and deep connections with the world-making valued as development. Standing open, the book ceases to be a book and becomes a physical representation of the furnished corner of a room. Expressing the play dimensions of this transformation, this paper room is capped with a theatrical pendant border carefully assembled out of many short pieces. Furnished with a paper cabinet, table, and chair, the interior decorations were probably culled from magazines or advertising sheets. The mix of very different sorts of paper—colorful heavy paper made to decorate real houses (wallpaper used as wallpaper, the thing as a representation of itself), and black-and-white printed pictures of domestic objects that originally circulated as illustration or advertisement in the commercial press (images standing-in for objects)—plays with and destabilizes the distinction between representation and reality, decoration and information.

May Durgin did not invent this art form; period magazines and newspapers touted the transformation of unwanted books into paper doll's houses as "a simple yet effective way of amusing children." Jessie E. Ringwalt (1880) provides detailed directions for making such multi-room houses in her "Fun for the Fireside: A Help to Mother's" column in *Godey's Lady's Book*.[12] Ringwalt's account presents the child as "owner" and "little architect" of such dwellings, but also presumes some level of adult involvement. In a preliminary 1896 survey of children's doll play, G. Stanley Hall (1907: loc 3211) includes an account of a girl who marked having grown too old for dolls "by putting her paper dolls in a scrapbook as a house." This type of paper play is promoted as a mature, helpful alternative to the more physically active forms of play, potentially destructive to household decor and decorum, that children might undertake if confined inside a real house. In his register of the kinds of play activities adults recorded in their autobiographies, Bernard Mergen (1992: 165) finds that many adults who were children during the nineteenth century recall using parlor furniture to create horses, carriages, houses, and forts. May Durgin's paper doll's house obliterates two pages of this old schoolbook, but it leaves the rest of the volume intact and does no harm to the Durgins' actual china cabinet.

Paper doll's houses were generally constructed by cutting furnishings out of magazines and catalogs and then gluing the items into a book, the clippings arranged so as to create a separate room on each page or spread. In her instructions on making paper doll's houses, Ringwalt registers how much this play entails a collage of disparate systems of valuation:

> The many unconsidered trifles that constitute the treasured wealth of children—scraps of paper, lace, silk, with fragments of torn picture books, and the multitudinous illustrations now presented as business advertisements, will all find a fitting place in the construction of such a book; while the work furnishes a wide scope for the exercise of that inventiveness which is so great a delight to many children. (162)

While the "scraps," "fragments," and "unconsidered trifles" of adult assessment may "constitute the treasured wealth of children," images drawn from "business advertisements" demonstrate how deeply this play is embedded within commercial networks. Ringwalt suggests "advertising sheets" as a particularly good source for "cuts of chairs, tables, sewing-machines, stoves, pianos, and other furniture" (162). The use of such commercial images to populate and furnish Durgin's paper room demonstrates an intimate appropriative relation to the plethora of ephemeral print forms that facilitated nineteenth-century commerce. The increasing reliance in the postbellum period on attractive illustration to promote sales for all sorts of domestic goods actively enlisted children—if not as child consumers at least as child advocates for consumption—in the web of commerce, an early step in the process that Daniel Cook characterizes as the commodification of childhood, and one aimed with particular intensity at girls.[13] The effort in Swinton's geography book to assure that students become knowledgeable consumers may register the deceptive risks of the marketplace—"labels do not always tell the truth"—as it presumes and prepares for children's engagement with "the multitudinous illustrations now presented as business advertisements" that make such good sources for furnishing paper houses. The play of constructing scrapbook houses surely serves to induct children, and specifically girls, into domestic economy and consumer culture. Yet as Ringwalt seems to recognize, even viewed in economic terms, the "treasured wealth" that builds such a house does so as imaginative scavenging at the edges of adult systems of exchange. This capacity to appropriate is, as Miguel Sicart (2014) notes, a crucial characteristic of the playful. Beverly Gordon (2006: 49 and 55) argues, in one of the few critical studies of this odd genre of child-made things, that the children who made scrapbook houses "were in effect making an entire world" and "even subverted the consumer model" since in this activity advertisements prompted not purchases but creative play. If, as Arjun Appadurai (1986) argues, commodities are not particular kinds of things, but rather a situation of exchangeability in the social life of any "thing," imaginative play may be one of those special modes of transfer that can yank an object out of its commodity state.[14] Approached in these terms children's imaginative play appears not as frivolous, but rather as a tactic that appropriates fragments of the structured and the real in a manner that makes them available for other purposes. The transformations play effects instance the alongside conception of play and socialization I trace in this chapter. Play enables children to construct their own place, exercise their own power and vision, but it does so out of materials scavenged from adult culture, and the process of such play seems equally likely to enmesh children in the web of national, commercial, and gendered hierarchies as to snap their threads.

G. Stanley Hall's (1907: loc 2777) extensive list of "doll substitutes"— "pumpkins (dressed in own clothes), towels (knotted in the middle), rubber balls, brooms"—instances the core transformative activity of doll play in particular: not only do children bring dolls into animate life, but with similar transformative ease they set about "dollifying" a host of objects most adults would consider intractable.[15] The transformations worked on the pages of May Durgin's book produce a scene that Swinton has depicted as the culmination of a network of labor and exchange and turns it into something else. There are obvious structural echoes in the transformations achieved through commodity exchange and those wrought by the imagination; I am arguing that such closeness with a difference, like Brown's adjoining "provinces of actuality and imagination," should be a key methodological and attitudinal aspiration for childhood studies—recognizing children's experiences and perspectives as both distinctive and relevant.

The play of making a paper doll's house requires, however, more than imagination; it calls for a fairly high level of production skill. The cut-out work in this room is meticulous. There are only a few small places (the rails atop the china cabinet, the spaces between chair legs, the tiny spots of white amid the ornate carvings of the table) that show the background of the page from which the picture was cut. May must have been a very precise and capable 9-year-old, or perhaps she created this room some years after she signed her name in this book, or perhaps her mother or her glove-maker father or some other older hand assisted with this project and wielded these delicate scissors. It is impossible to determine whether this room was made in collaboration with May Durgin, or made for her rather than by her. In truth children's play can never be fully separated from the world of adult expectations and interactions. Indeed, recognizing such contiguity and overlap maybe a crucial aspect of the task of understanding children's play.

The furnishings selected for this room do docilely seem to illustrate the opening story of this geography book, and as Rodris Roth notes of scrapbook houses as a whole, the scene proves "surprisingly ordinary" replicating "the prevailing taste in home interiors." Yet the scene, despite its realism, deploys a fairy-tale aura, largely due to incongruity of scale. Roth (1998: 302, 311, and 303) describes such differentials of scale as a frequent characteristic of scrapbook houses, since furniture pictures from varied sources would rarely come in compatible scale, and the makers of these houses seem to have differed in how important they considered proportion in choosing the furniture for their rooms. In Durgin's room the table and cabinet are reasonably consistent in size, as are the lamp and cups. The chair is too small for the table, and the landscape paintings hung a bit too high on the wall are smaller still: tiny worlds framed within this miniaturized world and in their odd placement perhaps the strongest evidence of a child's hand. But most strikingly, the little paper girl with the coffee pot pasted near the center of the spread appears decidedly too small for her paper doll's room, adrift in the large pattern of the wallpaper floor, as if she could be drowned in its swirls, or as if she were a fairy child in a garden of stylized blooms. In a book that generally makes no presumptions about what its students know—including explicit instruction on how to point!—Swinton's chapter "How Maps Are Made" gives remarkably little attention to teaching scale. The only mention comes within a bracketed insertion of instructions to teachers:

> Pupils may be required to draw a plan of their school-room. They should be shown that it is necessary to draw it to some definite scale. Thus, suppose that the room is shown to be 40 X 30 feet: pupils will readily understand that it would be impracticable to draw lines 30 or 40 feet in length. Let the scale be 1 inch to 5 feet; then the line representing the longest side of the school-room will be 8 inches in length, and that representing its width 6 inches. (7–8)

Scale seems to be one of the few bits of cartographic convention or geographical knowledge that "pupils will readily understand." Yet as Wai

Chee Dimock (2006: loc 791 and 74) explains, "asymmetry of scale makes human knowledge infinitely problematic"; she proposes literature as "the home of nonstandard space and time." In the literary imagination, erratic shifts of scale that forge links across continents and eras are indeed "readily understood." Scale incongruity proves a similarly obvious and potent feature of children's play and of the study of childhood: "On every hand we see that a large part of the charm of doll play is the small scale of the doll world," Hall (1907: loc. 3306 and 3315) observes with uncharacteristic absoluteness, "to make small will always be of itself alone a most pedagogic method and will always exact a potent fascination." The relations between adult and child, world and breakfast table, reality and play entail changes of scale. Shifts in scale alter the perceptual field and the processes of valuation. Child-made things prove such resistant—but also such fruitful—objects of study because they disrupt the usual scales of historical significance, enacting and inviting imaginative play.

Notes

1   For examples of my work with child-made materials see *Dependent States: The Child's Part in Nineteenth-Century American Culture* (Chicago: University of Chicago Press, 2005); Karen Sánchez-Eppler, "Practicing for Print: The Hale Children's Manuscript Libraries," *Journal of the History of Childhood & Youth* 1, no. 2 (March 2008): 188–209; "Marks of Possession: Methods for an Impossible Subject," *PMLA: Publications of the Modern Language Association of America* 126, no. 1 (January 2011): 151–59; and for a more theoretical account of the stakes of such work see "In the Archives of Childhood," in *The Children's Table Childhood Studies and the Humanities*, ed. Anna Mae Duane (Athens: University of Georgia Press, 2013), 213–37.

2   A testament to this marginalization, one of the few modes of scholarly analysis attentive to marks made by children, is the growing field of marginalia studies. See H. J. Jackson, *Marginalia: Readers Writing in Books* (Yale University Press, 2002) for a general account; and for studies particularly attentive to children see M. O. Grenby, *The Child Reader, 1700–1840* (Cambridge University Press, 2011).

3   I join Miguel Sicart in recognizing that "play is not detached from the world; it lives and thrives in the world," *Play Matters* (Cambridge: MIT Press, 2014), loc. 252, yet it is interesting to note that Sicart himself tends to treat children's relationships to their toys as the ideal, ur, and "purest" form of play, loc. 605. For the classic articulation of play's separate world see Johan Huizinga, *Homo Ludens: A Study of the Play-Element in Culture* (Martino Fine Books, 2014).

4   Howard P. Chudacoff, *Children at Play: An American History* (New York: New York University Press, 2007), provides an extremely valuable wide-ranging history of play that acknowledges the imbalance in its sources: "My major resources consist of several dozens of children's diaries and several hundred autobiographical recollections of childhood," loc. 97.

5   John Newbery (1744/1770) printed the phrase "instruction and delight" below the frontispiece of *A Pretty Little Pocket-Book: Intended for the Instruction and Amusement of Little Master Tommy, and Pretty Miss Polly*; a text generally considered the first true children's book in English. The phrase references Horace's dicta a commonplace of Renaissance definitions of poetry; see Hardison and Golden 1995 (946).

6   "Geography in a Cup of Coffee" thus provides an early instance of the sorts of lessons in American imperialism that Clif Stratton identifies in early twentieth-century Geography textbooks in *Education for Empire: American Schools, Race, and the Paths of Good Citizenship* (Berkeley: University of California Press, 2016).

7   After touring British social experiments, Landis published this account of his planned community for an English audience. For photographs of Vineland during this period and a brief history of the city's origins see Vineland Historical and Antiquarian Society, *Vineland* (Arcadia Publishing, 2011).

8   Vineland prospered, but Landis's personal history was more mixed including a scandalous trial for the murder of a local newspaper editor. See "Building Vineland, New Jersey from a Vast Wilderness."

9   Multiple Vineland directories and census sheets containing listings for Harrison and/or Flora Durgin can be accessed through Ancestry Library: Ancestry. com. Their marriage is included among the Durgin family information in Ezra S. Stearns, William Frederick Whitcher, and Edward Everett Parker, *Genealogical and Family History of the State of New Hampshire* (New York: Lewis Publishing Company, 1908), 759. Although never one of Vineland's most prominent or wealthy residents, Harrison Durgin seems to have prospered. He purchased additional real estate on neighboring streets, and by the 1890s had become Deacon of the Baptist Church; see "No Christian Unity Here," *New York Herald*, October 10, 1894. A 1901 Vineland Directory lists Harrison Durgin, no longer a glove maker, manufacturing "fruit juice" at 401 Landis Avenue. Thomas Welch invented his unfermented grape juice in Vineland, and Durgin seems to have been one of many Vineland residents to open grape juice manufactories in the early 1900s; see *Vineland*, loc. 361–67. Later directories show May (Durgin) Comins living as an adult in the same 339 Landis Avenue house on the corner with Fourth Street where she had lived as a child. The 1910 and 1920 census list her married to George Comins ("owner of a grape juice factory"), with a son they had named Harrison after her father. Widowed in 1909, Flora Durgin lived with them.

10   Indeed, in 1872 Landis had lobbied for and invested in the construction of a second central New Jersey rail line: the short-lived Vineland Railway. Soon after, burdened by debts, it was consolidated with New Jersey Southern Railroad; but although the line itself did not prove profitable, it did significantly expand the city's distribution network. *Vineland*, loc. 276–79.

11   My thanks to Christina Michelon for drawing my attention to this fascinating genre. May R. Durgin, "Scrapbook House/Collage Album 1887" (Vineland N.J., 1887), Winterthur Museum and Library. The Winterthur collection contains quite a few scrapbook houses, many far more elaborate than this one.

12   "This Will Amuse the Children," *Times Picayune*, October 30, 1901; Rodris Roth, "Scrapbook Houses: A Late Nineteenth-Century Children's View of

the American Home," in *The American Home: Material Culture, Domestic Space, and Family Life*, ed. Eleanor Thompson (Winterthur, DE: Winterthur Museum, 1998), 301–23, describes the kind of mixed medium artistry Durgin demonstrates in this room, and provides a useful classification of the varied types of scrapbook houses. Durgin's room can be categorized as belonging to the "wallpapered" and "permanent people" types.

13 For a discussion of the use of trade cards to attract children to an enormous range of domestic items with little acute childhood connection, see Ellen Gruber Garvey, "Readers Read Advertising into Their Lives: The Trade Card Scrapbook," in *Adman in the Parlor: Magazines and the Gendering of Consumer Culture, 1880s to 1910s* (New York: Oxford University Press, 1996), 16–50; Daniel Cook's study of the modes of marketing children's clothing from the late nineteenth through the twentieth centuries provides a rich theoretical account of what such commodification entails. Daniel Thomas Cook, *The Commodification of Childhood: The Children's Clothing Industry and the Rise of the Child Consumer* (Durham: Duke University Press, 2004).

14 Such a re-definition works to dissolve the conventional opposition between commodity exchange and the exchange wrought through barter or gift giving.

15 Hall coins the term "dollifying," loc. 2815.

CHAPTER FOUR

Thinking the Adult–Child Relationship with Existentialism

Clémentine Beauvais

In this chapter I propose an existentialist reading of the adult–child relationship. By a "reading," I do not mean a totalizing explanation, but rather, in the sense generally attributed to the word in literary studies, an adjusted theoretical lens, allowing us to pay attention to chosen structural, aesthetic, narrative, or discursive patterns when observing the representations of that relationship. The reading I advocate here is especially attuned to the temporal tensions within the adult–child relationship; in particular, it probes the implications of the notion that children, symbolically if not in reality, have a greater *time left* than adults.

That notion, well explored in childhood studies, has sometimes been contextualized as distinctly modern. In James and Prout's list of clichés surrounding contemporary childhood, children are "'the next generation,' 'the guardians of the future' on whose shoulders time itself sits" (1997: 239). Child time has been analyzed, in its contemporary iterations, as both intensely hopeful in symbol and intensely controlled in reality. We know about the processes through which the speeds, rhythms, and durations of childhood have been historically fixed and modulated by adults (e.g., Foucault 1975; Ball et al. 1984; Adam 1995; Symes 2012; Duncheon and Tierney 2013); but we also read about "the child" as being in waiting, and about childhood as a moniker for potential, its symbolic temporality stretching into a future full of promise (James and Prout 1997; Qvortrup 2004; Reynolds 2007).

That ambiguous child time, both hyper-regulated in the present and charged with symbolic potential for the future, has been connected historically and ideologically to neoliberalism; seen as a construct of adult discourse and practices, peopled with adult dreams and fantasies; and therefore treated with a healthy dose of hermeneutics of suspicion. Yet the vexing question of time in relation to childhood has also elicited some of the most sophisticated thinking about childhood in contemporary theory (Arendt 1960; Agamben 1993) and childhood studies (Uprichard 2008; Wallace 2008; James and James 2010).

I want to add to the discussion on the temporal dynamics within the adult–child relationship by focusing on one prominent aspect of those dynamics: namely, that the child will (or should) continue to live after the adult dies. This is, of course, a context-dependent assumption, recent and privileged, and one that surrounds the child of the minority world in particular. But in that context, the inherent presence of adult death within the adult–child relationship, I contend here, is of interest not only for the exploration of constructions of childhood, but also because it has existential implications, complicating the social and political dynamics of the adult–child relationship, and nuancing the power (im)balance between adult and child parties.

Existentialist approaches within the philosophy of education

I take "existential implications" here not in the psychological sense sometimes weakly attributed to the word "existential," but in reference to existentialist philosophy. There is no such thing, however, as a unified existentialist tradition; there are, rather, a number of central concerns and lines of questioning common to so-called existentialist philosophers. Those are, centrally, a phenomenological epistemology, the positing (variously articulated) of existence as preceding essence, and in most approaches, the awareness of death not so much as a source of psychological dread than as undergirding the individual's existential project, in its endeavors, frustrations, and choices.

Existentialism has long enjoyed a fruitful relationship with the philosophy of education, yielding a varied spectrum of perspectives and applying theoretical pressure onto many different aspects of the adult–child relationship and of pedagogy. Within that tradition, we may distinguish, for instance, between the following strands:

- Early Sartrian approaches: popular from the 1950s to the 1970s, when it chimed with progressive education, this type of existentialist educational philosophy foregrounded concepts from the "early Sartre" of *Being and Nothingness* (1943), such as, prominently, freedom and authenticity (Niblett 1954; O'Neil 1964; Morris 1966; Denton 1968). Following critiques (e.g., Lindsey 1972), later work put greater emphasis on concepts such as individuality or humanism (e.g., Lieberman 1985; Kakkori and Huttunen 2012).

- Neo-Heideggerian approaches, more in vogue today, have yielded many insights, informing, for instance, the influential work of Michael Bonnett on educational practices sensitive to human beings' phenomenological entanglement with space and the environment (e.g., 1999, 2002), or the no less prominent contributions of Gert Biesta on the educator's vulnerability, the existential violence of the pedagogical relation, and the unpredictability of educational processes (e.g., 2006).

- Kierkegaardian approaches to the philosophy of education appear to be on the rise (Saeverot 2011; Jaarsma et al. 2016).

- Some existentialists wrote themselves about education and childhood; Simone de Beauvoir's works on the matter (e.g., 1948) have recently attracted more critical attention (Scholz 2010; Beauvais 2015a).

What those works have in common are, first, a phenomenological understanding of being; second, a belief at least to a degree in human existence as defined through action and responsibility; third, they generally subscribe to the notion that human relationships are always situated, irremediably unstable, and potentially violent.

Existentialism and childhood studies

(Neo)existentialist approaches, although important in the philosophy of education, have little influenced childhood studies, at least in its sociological declensions. There were, from the beginning, insuperable clashes. The constructivist paradigm of the New Sociology of childhood, while superficially aligned with existentialism in its anti-essentialism, was always radically at odds with two of the central tenets of existentialist thinking: namely, that human beings are fundamentally free and responsible for their actions. Admittedly, the "freedom and authenticity" line of early Sartrian existentialism was nuanced by Sartre himself and worked by Beauvoir (1952) into sociological, psychological, and anthropological reflection, more accommodating for constructivism. Still, we find only the slightest traces of the existentialist canon in the New Sociology of childhood.

Today, childhood studies continues to find existentialism decidedly uninspiring. The so-called material turn is as uneasily reconciled with such approaches as its constructivist predecessor, foregrounding, as it does, ways of thinking about things and beings directly opposed to existentialism's. At least for Heidegger (1927) and Sartre (1943), there is an incontrovertible ontological difference between inanimate objects or animals (beings-in-itselves in Sartrian jargon, characterized by complete self-adherence) and human beings (for-itselves, characterized by a mixture of freedom and facticity). As such, the Latourian framework, for instance, where actants—be they bacilli, microchip, or human—all interact and effect change upon each other in a decentralized network, is virtually illegible from even the most generous existentialist perspective. Furthermore, what may seem phenomenological about new materialism— the notion, for instance, that choices and actions are situated, and that relations, rather than essences, are the locus of meaning—is very far from the anthropocentrism of most existentialist perspectives, where the focus of interest is above all the human being: certainly, individuals exist within networks, but networks are illuminated by consciousness. Finally, the ethical landscapes of constructivism and new materialism are profoundly different to existentialism's; the former locates "what is wrong," so to speak, within systems and structures; the latter tends to suspend ethical judgment. Existentialist approaches, to various degrees, foreground individual responsibility.

There is much, however, that existentialism can offer to childhood studies today. This chapter details only one of many approaches, but by focusing on the temporal dynamics of the adult–child relationship it proposes perhaps an especially childhood studies–friendly possibility. In order to clarify that possibility, I first explain my own research background as a children's literature scholar. I then suggest how an existentialist reading of selected children's texts may inform our understanding of the temporal power imbalance between adult and child. Lastly, I explore the applications of existentialist readings of the adult–child relationship to research closer to the heart of childhood studies.

Reading the adult–child relationship

While most existentialist approaches to childhood are rooted in educational philosophy, my own interest for them began in a different room of the ivory tower. A doctoral student in children's literature, I was attempting to understand and, hopefully, theorize a corpus of texts that had always gathered academic scorn, yet had been rising again since the early 2000s: politically committed children's literature. Such literature may be defined as texts targeted at children that actively and purposefully defend (or oppose) ideological positions with wide-scale political ramifications and consequences for social organization. In their "transformative" iterations, typical of left-leaning committed children's literature, such texts advocate sociopolitical change in the future, often through the action of child characters.

Politically committed children's literature, de facto, is a modern, principally Western phenomenon, often bourgeois in aesthetic and modes of production. It is important to note, however, that there has been a rise for the past two decades in the production of politically committed children's literature in majority world countries, too, with the emergence of radical independent publishers with clearly committed editorial lines (Zubaan, a feminist publisher in India, is a good example). South America is also dynamically involved in the production of committed fiction and non-fiction for young readers, often under the impulse of independent presses, such as Cinco Puntos Press or Ekaré. Thus, the theorization of politically committed children's literature is not solely relevant to a middle-class, White, Western adult–child relationship, even though there are huge contextual and geopolitical variations in its applicability.

Studying those texts, I became frustrated with existing theorizations, which seemed to me, whether Foucauldian, Althusserian, Bourdieusian, or Bakhtinian, overwhelmingly negative, concluding to the authoritarian streak of such literature. The only neutral studies were historical (Mickenberg 2006; Abate 2010), and only a handful of studies were celebratory (Mickenberg and Nel 2008; Reynolds 2007). A recurring, though rarely defined, word in the debate was *didacticism*, generally implying that those texts told children what to do and think, hearkening back to a time when children's literature was written solely for the purpose of moral edification and preparation for future life.

Yet it became clear to me that such texts have great theoretical interest, not just for the children's literature scholar, but also for philosophical and sociological approaches to childhood, because they condense with unique intensity a fascinating paradox of the adult–child relationship. Those texts explicitly present stories that advocate change, often showing ways to effect that change; they are thus rather "closed" texts for the implied reader. Yet, simultaneously, they identify children as privileged targets for transformative messages. Those texts thus betray both a strong adult authority *and* a strong belief in a special power of childhood. Importantly, they cannot be reduced to either. They cannot be celebrated as simply "giving a voice to the child"— written, as they are, by adults, for children, with the purpose to persuade children to act upon the word. Equally, it is intellectually unfair to dismiss them as fantasies of dictatorial adults: fundamentally future-bound and revolutionary in spirit, they cannot be accused of seeking to perpetuate existing social orders.

Children's literature theory, I found, could not quite accommodate that paradox, in part because works in the field were highly suspicious of the adult presence within children's literature. That elusive entity, "the hidden adult," as called by Perry Nodelman (2008), had been most influentially theorized in 1984 by Jacqueline Rose's landmark work, *The Case of Peter Pan, or, The Impossibility of Children's Fiction*. In that text, Rose analyzed "the adult" within children's literature as an immobilizing entity: a fantasy-ridden, frustrated agency eager to immobilize "the child" and project onto it adult fears, traumas, and desires. There is no child, Rose concluded, behind the category *child* in children's literature; it is an empty signifier, peopled with adult definitions. The effect on real child readers of children's literature is egregious, she said: children are condemned to perform the expectations set by a phantom concept. Rose's book, seismically unsettling for the very category of children's literature, had a long-lasting influence on children's literature scholars. Perhaps its most important effect for the question that concerns me here is that, for a while, it rendered *impossible* not so much children's fiction as the thought that the adult within children's literature could be anything else than an oppressive entity.

I pause here to clarify that everything in that debate is at the level of text. By "the adult" there, as in this whole chapter, I mean a synthetic adult intentionality, which cannot be reduced to one individual in particular; it is a symphonic persona, composed of the intentionalities of authors, editors, mediators, teachers, parents, and others which directly and indirectly format every children's text. That adult presence within texts is extractable using the tools of literary criticism and analysis, specifically those developed by scholars like Umberto Eco, Stanley Fish, Wolfgang Iser, or Roland Barthes, who sought ways to decode the implied authorities and layers of authorship within literary texts. The "hidden adult" in children's literature is not a "he" nor a "she" but an "it": a textual feature.

However, this feature is of course connected from the social, cultural, and political context of its time. Children's literature theory, taking its cue from the cultural sociology of childhood, posits the impossible neutrality of adult attitudes toward children: to quote D. T. Cook, "Each word to a child seems like a directive; each decision made on its behalf or in response to a request favors some aspects of the world over others" (2002: 7)—the historical, social, cultural, etc. situatedness of "the child" inflects and inhabits every adult utterance. In children's literature, which both reflects and sets current parameters of symbolic childhood, the adult presence also sets and reflects current parameters of the adult–child relationship.

This is why I have entitled this subpart "*Reading* the adult–child relationship": when we look at the adult authority within children's literature, we are looking at a point of suture between text and world; more precisely, we are forced to oscillate between thinking of that adult authority as an intentionality for the text, and as an intentionality for the world. It is difficult, if not futile, to determine where that adult intentionality stops being a construct and starts emitting requests and/or carrying them through, namely, starts being a construct*or*. Reading the adult–child relationship with the tools of literary analysis (and with due caution) means extracting from text *and world* the structuring narratives and aesthetics of that relationship, in both its constructedness and its constructiveness.

Adult authority, child might, and a common project

The adult presence in politically committed children's literature, to be theorized without being caricatured, called for an approach that would be sensitive to the authoritativeness of that adult voice, and yet take seriously its chosen locus for future transformations of the world, namely the child. In order to theorize texts that are intrinsically future-bound and intent on change, yet *also* didactic and authoritative, I needed philosophical tools receptive to that tension.

Sartre's foray into literary theory, *What Is Literature?* (1950), tuned mid-twentieth-century understandings of a type of text now widely disregarded in literary studies: the politically committed novel. Sartre's manifesto on (good) literature requests that it be "a demand and a gift," namely spell out transformative exigencies for the world while offering itself to its readers' free will. The committed text, Sartre theorized, engages the double responsibility of author and reader; it is a joint project, begun with the speaker and continued by the addressee, to modify the world. This is why, says Sartre, the novel can by definition never address a powerless reader: there would be no point in addressing someone who could not potentially change the world.

In that reading, a politically committed text directed toward children that would not fundamentally consider them to be actors of change is unthinkable. For a Sartrian, politically committed children's literature by definition cannot "immobilize" or "impossibilize" the child: it must posit an active recipient. More, it must posit a recipient able to act *in the future*. And here politically committed children's literature is particularly interesting compared with equivalent literature for adults. Because the current child will continue to live beyond the current adult, the child's share of the project stretches into a time not encompassed by the adult's timescale.

This would not be an assumption, it is important to note, in a time or place where child mortality is a very present concern. The idea of a potent child, who as a matter of course lives longer than the adult, is a modern Western child (I have discussed its emergence in contrast with the *puer aeternus* figure of earlier children's literature, in Beauvais 2015b). When talking about a child–adult relationship modulated by awareness of the death of the latter before the former, I am locating my analysis within contexts where children's outliving of their elders is a near certainty.

To make sense of politically committed texts for children, we must consider that they constitutionally posit the continuation of their own projects within a timeframe at least partly unavailable to the speaker. Yet, still from a Sartrian perspective, we cannot dismiss that speaker's voice altogether. It is the author, in Sartre's theorization, and the "hidden adult," in ours, who orchestrates the text, endorses responsibility for it, and carefully organizes its mission. For Sartre, that mission is to give an accurate representation of the world both as it is and as it needs to be changed. There is a moral imperative to the mimetic effort: the author, preferably gifted with considerable acumen, must show society's flaws and propose pathways to improve it. In the case of politically committed children's literature, we must consider the adult authority as the orchestrator of that knowledge and the bearer of an accumulated experience that allows that knowledge to exist. The past, and its representative—the adult authority—is a necessary focalizer for any existentialist lens onto a politically committed children's text.

From this theorization, we can sketch an existentialist reading grid for literary discourses charged with transformative projects, such as politically committed children's literature. Like all reading grids, that one is not meant to capture every aspect of a text; rather, it allows for specific characteristics to be captured:

- The politically committed text for children has a future-bound temporal inflection: it seeks to transform the future through the young reader's action. An existentialist reading must pay particular attention to how the text seeks to generate that action.

- The politically committed text for children also by definition depends on a knowledge provider regarding possibilities for change. That provider, the adult authority, is characterized by its *time past*, an accumulated baggage of experience and layers of commitment (in Sartrian lingo, facticity). An existentialist reading must pay attention to how that experience is presented.

- The politically committed text for children, finally, posits an adult–child relationship marked by a temporal imbalance between a future-bound entity, the child, and a past-laden entity, the adult. It is marked by a symbolic distribution of powers for action between the authoritative adult presence and the child who should pick up the text's project. I called this property of the child "might" in my own work (Beauvais 2015b). An existentialist reading will pay attention to the temporal modalities of that relationship and the resulting power (im)balance between adult and child.

The above reading grid allows for the subtleties of politically committed children's literature to be evaluated in ways not previously afforded by other theorizations, because it forces us to look at moments of transition, of transaction, of conversion, of negotiation, rather than thinking about adult authorities and child addressees as opposite entities, the former intent on controlling the latter. It also forces us to contemplate the intrinsic conflict within politically committed children's literature: namely, that it leans on and, to a degree, celebrates the tension between past and future, between current organizers of the world and potential changers of that world. That reading grid allows for analysis of the pains and stretch marks that might result from that tension.

And that, at least, is the theory.

Politically committed children's literature in practice

There is no space here to delve into in-depth close reading of children's texts, but I will describe some of the interesting frictions that occur when looking at politically committed children's literature from an existentialist perspective.

First, my exploration of the texts revealed a number of identifiable literary, aesthetic, and narrative strategies, meant to act as, so to speak, textual converters of adult authority (characterized by a baggage of "time past") into child might (characterized by future-bound action). At their most basic, those "converters" were typically paradoxical utterances: for instance, sentences such as "Break all the rules," "It is forbidden to forbid," or similar. Those self-canceling imperatives reflect at the level of text the wider paradox, which I highlighted earlier, of an adult authority dictating to a child not to follow the rules dictated by an adult authority.

Such "liar paradoxes" constitute obstacles in the path from order to obedience. Paradoxical utterances are not just sentences: many committed children's books are in concept, plot, or structure paradoxical, themselves a command that collapses as it is being emitted (e.g., Seven and Christy 2013). They may even be generic: I analyzed the aspirational biography for children as a *genre* of collapsed injunction, in that it presents to children laudatory accounts of the existences of real—often already dead—people (i.e., of existences that have entirely slid into facticity), yet asks child readers to do something in the future with those already-lived lives. This is a typical example of paradoxical utterance at the level of genre.

I was thus interested in moments where straightforward didactic injunctions fail, and the project of the book for the child becomes unclear, muddled, or unrealizable. Those moments call for extratextual space for future action: the domain of the child reader. Many politically committed stories for children thus rely on tensions created by clear demands followed by unclear, nonexistent, or unsatisfactory descriptions of the implications. For example, *La carie (The Tooth)*, a Canadian picturebook (Slodovnick and Gauthier 2008), features a little girl who has had a tooth extracted and is looking forward to her tooth-fairy money. Leaving the dentist, however, she spots a homeless man and hands him her tooth, thinking the tooth fairy will give *him* money. The picturebook concludes, "Now all he needed was a pillow." That final sentence, equally interpretable as sarcastic or hopeful, leaves the reader—and, indeed, society—hanging: there is no intratextual resolution. Worse, the reader, unlike the protagonist, knows that the homeless man's predicament has not been solved. That surfeit of knowledge entails a surfeit of responsibility; it renders future action imperative, and that action must be located outside the book, in the child reader's hands and informed, but not dictated, by the story she or he has just read.

Politically committed children's literature oscillates between clearly presenting political projects and unclearly instructing as to how they should emerge. It is in textual gaps and interstices, notably in the gaps between text and image—a concept well explored in picturebook theory—that those books address readers as potent, opening up spaces for action. Incentives, nudges, paradoxical utterances, unsatisfactory resolutions, gaps, etc. are intratextual insofar as they are created and contained by texts, underscored by adult intentionality; yet they are also extratextual in that they reach beyond the text, in a future overlapping with, and eventually outlasting, the adult intentionality.

A differentiated reading of the texts in that corpus shows variations in whether they envisage transformative action as occurring within the moment of temporal overlap between adult and child or much beyond it. Texts about environmental change, predictably, tend to posit long timescales for action, with portrayals of child power reaching far past the temporality of adults; even, in one case, beyond the death of all humanity (Serres and Bonnani 2009). Books about revolution tend to lay stronger emphasis on the conjoined efforts of child and adult parties. But, crucially, even those books that envisage transformation as a remote possibility only available to the child—those books that, in other words, see children as pure futurity—remain framed, in the present, by the relationship between adult and child. Children's literature by definition has a double address of child and adult (Wall 1991). Children's books are produced, distributed, mediated, and often bought by adults. In addition, many books, especially picturebooks, set up their own reading event as shared; in that sense, much of their meaning is conceived as co-constructible by adult and child. Some of the books may portray projects whose realization in the story only occurs within a timeframe beyond the adult's life; yet those projects are rooted in an intimate reading event, with both adult and child "powers" temporarily overlapping. In other words, there can be no future beyond the adult without the adult's presence by the child at some point in time. There is something inherently transformative, therefore, in the temporal overlap between adult and child when it is characterized by commitment: it sets the conditions—in existentialist terms, the situation—for future action.

Looking at those texts with an existentialist lens allows for those tensions and contradictions to remain unsolved; or rather, to remain meaningful *as* tensions and contradictions. To a Sartrian, there is nothing nonsensical about calls to freedom (or to action) contained in, and indeed constrained by, situations created by others. Similarly, the theory accommodates, without rendering it either pathetic or gloriously spiritual, the presence of death as the horizon of human endeavors—and therefore the necessity of handing down one's project to other human beings. In the case of politically committed children's literature, the adult presence and its demands within the text can be analyzed serenely, because existentialism allows for that presence and those demands to be marked by both facticity *and* freedom, by both awareness of death *and* consideration of futurity. Such an analysis reveals the complexity of a relationship between two parties whose respective symbolic powers are temporal, and thus deployed within overlapping but different timeframes.

What such an analysis reveals in practice, too, is the variation in representations of the adult–child relationship in politically committed children's literature, which is a wide spectrum of targeted age groups, genres, formats, media, pedagogical approaches, intensity of political opinion, publishing and distribution processes, and, arguably, aesthetic quality and literary merit. There are clear national differences in the prominence and publication of such literature, and interestingly they do not necessarily mean that Western children are always privileged in their access to those books. The case of the UK is particularly intriguing. After a politicized phase in the 1970s, the children's publishing landscape in the UK is now at odds with Western European countries and the United States. The lack of independent publishers and foreign imports means that the UK today produces fewer children's books that could reasonably be qualified as politically committed. These differences alert us to the varying place and role of political commitment not just in one type of discourse—children's literature *in general*—but in its geographical and time-specific iterations. That corpus in itself reflects and models variations in political commitment of adult–child *relationships*, plural.

An existentialist analysis is suited to such a fragmented corpus because it by definition posits the situatedness of any work of art and therefore of the representations within it. The large corpus of aspirational biographies for children in the United States, for instance, may be contrasted with the large corpus of picturebooks depicting collective action in a country like France. This should not (or not just) be analyzed simplistically as a contrast between individualistic-minded America and Commune-nostalgic France, but also as contrasting iterations of the adult–child relationship. An aspirational biography like *Barack Obama: Son of Promise, Child of Hope* (Grimes and Collier 2012) works on several levels of intimate, face-to-face relationships between adult and child: in the story, a young African-American boy is told by his mother about Barack Obama's life; in the story-within-the-story, little Barack's relation to his parents is equally central. By contrast, books extolling collective action, for instance through revolution, tend to set up several relationships as entry-points into the story, some intergenerational, some intragenerational, some within groups, others intimate. Generally, as in books on the French revolution or on the May 1968 protests, a handful of child characters are used for identification, but politically significant relationships are developed within a larger crowd of adults, younger and older, who are the ones effectively orchestrating change (Beauvais 2013).

In both cases, societal and political upheaval occurs; but the biographies lay significantly more emphasis on the already latent power of the child, addressed as an individual by an attentive adult; in the French books, children are addressed as agents further down the temporal line, by an adult presence less invested in the idiosyncrasies of individual children. While no conclusions should be drawn from this very specific corpus regarding the relative cultural and national expectations set on children by adults, or the modulations of their relationships, such differences may mirror divergences in educational systems, or conceptions of children's place in society and of child agency. They might also mirror divergences in what constitutes *the political* in those various countries. Some of that literature emphasizes the political power of inspirational figures who, through merit and virtue, come to incarnate unity and to symbolize, to contain, what might be meant by the *polis*, the organized community of a nation or a state. The political, in that view, is what links together and fuses. Other books lay emphasis on the conflict, plurality, and internal negotiation inherent to the *polis*, its fragilities and internal cacophony. The political, in such texts, is what lays bare the fractured matter of that apparent whole.

Because an existentialist approach captures, without, so to speak, *breaking* them, the multiple aspects of adult–child relationships, the plurality of situations into which they flourish, and the conflicting visions of the political that they allude to, it resists falling into premature judgment of whether a book is "bad or good for children"; whether it dispenses the "right" ideology; or whether it signals an "oppressive" or a "liberating" adult presence. Such analyses reveal that there is no politically committed children's book that fully succeeds at imparting knowledge; it can only transmit a project, which stretches out into an unknown future, and thus cannot succeed without the—necessarily unpredictable—role of the child. An existentialist analysis locates meaning in the failures of the adult–child relationship, in the failures of the didactic injunction, and lets us extract and explore those failures.

What's in it for childhood studies?

I conclude this chapter with what I believe might be retrieved for childhood studies from that admittedly very literary approach to an admittedly specific type of text. As I see it, there are three main applications of existentialist readings of the adult–child relationship for childhood studies.

First, and most obviously, the existentialist reading sketched here is transferable to the study of non-literary texts addressed to children by adults, that is, educational texts, oral and written addresses to children in non- or para-educational contexts, advertising, and all artistic expression targeted toward children, including films, video games, etc. There is evident overlap between analyzing a picturebook about the French Revolution and analyzing a civic education textbook for the same age range. As such, existentialist readings of non-literary texts simply require tuning the type of analysis already being performed by scholars in childhood studies who explore non-literary material targeted at children. This is with the caveat, of course, that such analyses should always remain situated and contextual, and that for now very little work has been done on texts (whether fictional or non-fictional) outside a mostly Western corpus.

Second, existentialist readings of the adult–child relationship can contribute to the ongoing reflection in childhood studies about young people's "voices" or agency, especially political, within an adult-orchestrated world (Bordonaro 2012; Tisdall and Punch 2012). Existentialist readings of the adult–child relationship chime with contemporary attempts to reclaim the ambiguity and the disorderly nature of children's agency. They do so primordially, and quite radically, because agency simply does not exist in their framework; with no equivalent in either French or German, the word is literally foreign to the existentialist canon. Working from existentialist premises, agency and its fraught relation to structure are not available conceptual tools; its neighbors, authenticity, and freedom are not equivalents. Doing childhood studies without agency ready at hand might seem a radical thought experiment, but it entails an interesting shift of perspective. Instead of focusing on the child's agential or non-agential status in the present, we wonder about the temporal inflections of both child and adult projects, with "project" understood as transformative effort stretching through time. How does the young person's project relate to a time past— possibly, but not necessarily, the property of adult influencers? How does it extend into the future—possibly, but not necessarily, with the concourse of even younger agents? We see here how the question of children's "agency" becomes inevitably complicated by considerations of its entanglements with time, and thus with other people's actions and desires, including people not born yet and others already dead.

We might eventually decide to reincorporate the concept of agency, under some guise, within existentialist reflection on childhood; but we can do so only, from an existentialist perspective, by focusing on its temporal iterations. Rachel Rosen (2017: 378) points out the extent to which contrasting conceptualizations of time imply significant differences in theory, method, and knowledge-production among childhood studies scholars. In an existentialist (re)reading of agency, premised on close attention to the temporal dynamics between adult and child, we are sensitive to the necessary messiness and temporal statuses of children's and adults' actions. Children, like adults, are temporal, indeed even *temporary*, agents of a project to which they have been committed in the past and to which they might also commit others in the future. Doubtless, there is a degree of fatalism—or facticity—in that vision of agency as always originally committed, anchored in the past; but it resists solidification through its future developments, by definition unknowable.

Third, and more metacritically, an existentialist reading of the adult–child relationship can contribute to wider disciplinary thinking around the ethical valence of the focal points chosen for analysis by scholars in childhood studies, especially in relation to the "power" of adult and child parties. Childhood studies scholars are very aware of the performative nature, and ideological and moral implications, of method, disciplinary positioning, and epistemology (Komulainen 2007; Spyrou 2011). Locating oneself within childhood studies signals a special interest in "the child," thus entailing responsibility for the "hypermoral arena" (Cook 2002: 7) of childhood as an object of study, and childhood studies is tectonically travailed by the power relations between its conceptual categories.

The ethical positioning of existentialist readings, stemming from their conceptualization of temporality, is that the child cannot be the sole focus of inquiry nor of intellectual curiosity when dealing with adult–child relationships. An existentialist reading of the adult–child relationship cannot be child-centered. It must take into account the questions, desires, and anxieties experienced by adults as a result of the presence of children in the world. Such a reading requires a curious and compassionate stance toward the adult side of the relationship, based on the understanding that it is not existentially neutral for human beings to cohabit with people who will outlive them. Instead of condemning adults for "oppressing" or objectifying children, such readings highlight the fundamental ambiguity not just of children themselves but of adults, too, in the relationship between adults and children. Those beings operate together, possibly conjointly, in a moment of temporal "overlap," yet belong to different symbolic categories to which different powers are assigned. An existentialist reading of their relationship recognizes the full symbolic violence of existing alongside beings who are loaded with greater symbolic potency.

However, this does not mean that such readings are unconcerned with the experiences of real children. By taking seriously adult anxieties, frustrations, and desires in their relations with children, existentialist readings of the adult–child relationship also take seriously their consequences for the daily lives of children. Clearly, children are the most at-risk party in the relationship, both in reality and symbolically; clearly, the frustrations of adults directed toward children are a prominent cause of child suffering. By considering the ambiguity of the relationship from the adult's viewpoint, we do not minimize that suffering, but seek to gain a richer understanding of the problems. An existentialist reading, therefore, implies the moral responsibility to represent, understand, and describe adulthood as a symbolic category and adults as a group of agents.

In that respect, the existentialist reading I sketch here shares some of its purposes and values with the blossoming field of age studies, which attempts to theorize the life course from sociological, philosophical, literary, psychological, medical, etc. perspectives. Age studies overlaps with childhood studies in many places, not least of which in its interest for intergenerational relationships, or for ageism, which might be against children (sometimes called childism) or against adults, especially older adults. Related polemical concepts, such as generational envy—the impression by one generation that another, either younger or older, "has it easier" (Joosen 2017) or the fear of generational usurpation may be handled subtly with an existentialist reading, which allows for those phenomena to be explored without falling into straightforward condemnation.

At their most sophisticated, existentialist readings recognize the possibility for human relationships to be meaningful and enduring, full of projects, energy and desires, yet irreducibly difficult too, hindered by interpersonal obstacles ill-captured by psychology, and rooted in disconnect between what one is and one yearns to be. In the iteration I proposed here, existentialism offers us a peek at that possibility in the adult–child relationship, whose central characteristic is that it is traversed by awareness that the speaker will die before the recipient. As I hope to have shown, at least in the circumscribed field of children's literature, the consequences of that characteristic, perhaps against common misconceptions about existentialism, are not depressing. They show, mostly, and in spite of all the difficulties, projects for the world seeking to endure through time.

PART TWO

Rethinking Materiality and Political Economy

CHAPTER FIVE

Childhood (Re)materialized:

Bringing Political Economy into the Field

Jason Hart and Jo Boyden

Introduction

The decades between the 1870s and the 1930s witnessed profound transformation in the lives of children in North America and Western Europe. According to Viviana Zelizer, during this period there emerged an ultimately hegemonic view of the young as "economically 'worthless' but emotionally 'priceless'" (1985: 3). This transformation did not, however, result simply from a shift in popular sentiment toward the young. For example, it was due to an array of factors—only one of which was growing public distaste—that working-class children ceased to be employed in factory work and domestic service. Similarly, the economic dependence of middle-class children upon their parents was prolonged as a consequence of factors that included, but were not limited to, affect. As Wanda Minge-Kalman noted, "The nascent concern with education by all classes eventually rescued children from the factories and put them into schools" (1978: 460). However, full-time education became the norm across society not only because it was widely felt to be more appropriate for the newly sacralized child, but for reasons that were rooted in political and economic consideration. A skilled and disciplined labor force became the priority for industrialists; while for the poor, education came to be seen as a means of avoiding exploitation and achieving economic advancement.

The shift that resulted in children in high-income countries becoming economically "useless" but emotionally "priceless" can only be comprehended through an analytical approach that integrates the socio-cultural with the political-economic. This chapter is motivated by the conviction that childhood studies has, for the most part, focused strongly on the former while paying insufficient attention to the latter. This is not only unfortunate for scholarship; it has also constrained the contribution of childhood studies to efforts aimed at enhancing the lives of children.

We begin by explaining the manner in which we deploy the notions of "political economy" and "neoliberal": terms that are central to our analysis. We then offer an account of childhood studies, paying particular attention to the history of its emergence and the reasons for its primary interest in the socio-cultural domain. We end by outlining some of the theoretical and methodological work that we believe is needed for the integration of political economy within childhood studies.

Laying out our terms

Political Economy

Our employment of the notion of political economy refers to two distinct but interrelated phenomena. First, we are interested in political economy *as a field of study concerned with the relationship between the exercise of power and the distribution of resources*. Of particular interest is the analysis of how power, applied to and operating through institutions of governance at local, national, and supra-national levels, informs the material conditions and life chances of children. Such power should be understood as differentially distributed across humanity as a whole, taking into account the mediating effect of gender, "race"/ethnicity, (dis)ability, class, and so on. In recent years considerable attention has been given to inequities in distribution along lines of gender, race/ethnicity, and (dis)ability. For us class is a further vital factor that both marks and mediates disparities in distribution between sections of the population. It is a necessary element within an intersectional approach that we consider essential for analysis of childhoods embracing socio-cultural and political-economic perspectives.

We are also mindful of the usage of "political economy" to refer to *a methodological approach foundational to a distinct field of study*. Thus, our suggestion that childhood studies, as a field, embraces political economy relates both to the subject matter requiring attention and to the necessary mode of investigation. Political economy analysis is inherently interdisciplinary and multi-scalar, bringing together, most particularly, economics, sociology, and political science to consider the two-way relationship between action by capitalist elites and material outcomes.

The challenge posed by political economy to childhood studies is to contextualize the domains of children's everyday lives—family, school, work, leisure, etc.—within a larger system in which power is exercised in a highly asymmetric manner. Bronfenbrenner's familiar "ecological model" (1979) can be utilized as a framing device for such a purpose. This model conceives of "the child" (problematically rendered in individualistic terms) at the center of a series of nested and interdependent "systems," some proximal to and some more distal from the young. Within the "microsystem" are institutions closest to children that include immediate family, peer groups, the neighborhood, religious organizations, and school, all of which directly impact them in multiple ways through routine exchanges and participation in close relationships and recurring activities. These institutions also affect children's lives through their interaction and influence on each other, such as when a child's school performance is affected by the involvement of volunteer teaching assistants from the local community. This interaction occurs at the level of the "mesosystem." "Exosystem" refers to settings that children may not engage in directly but which nevertheless exert a strong influence on the microsystem—such as welfare services, the parental workplace, etc. Clearly, the content and working of the "exosystem" may vary according to cultural context and particular circumstances. The "macrosystem" is most distal from the young. Many elaborations of Bronfenbrenner's model place culture, media, and wider society here. A few of the numerous iterations explicitly mention economic conditions and political bodies.

Bronfenbrenner intended this model to indicate that children's lives unfold and are profoundly shaped by interacting systems and processes. However, the model has been subsequently invoked to reinforce normative assumptions around the primacy of the immediate and intimate in children's lives and the attenuated relationship between institutions of governance—through which elites exercise power—and the young. This ignores the evidence that macrosystems function consistently to affect all other systems. The more proximal systems are profoundly influenced by the actions of political-economic elites: from the food that the young consume to the curriculum that they study and the conditions in which they do so; from their access to health services and leisure facilities to the capacity of caregivers to provide effective nurturance.

Neoliberalism

The argument for embracing a clear focus upon political economy within childhood studies is only strengthened by the changes wrought around the globe over the last forty or so years: changes that may be associated with the rise of neoliberalism. The "neoliberal era" has witnessed the rapid and inexorable concentration of wealth and power in the hands of elites (Dumenil and Levy 2005: 9). In mid-2017, the wealthiest 1 percent of the world's adult population owned 50.1 percent of global household wealth (Credit Suisse 2017). Key causes *and* consequences of this concentration of economic and political capital include constraints placed upon organized labor and depressed wage growth for all but those at the top, massive cuts to public spending, tax breaks for the wealthy, the loosening of regulations governing the activities of large multinational corporations, and the flourishing of the tax avoidance industry.

We follow Wendy Brown by attending to neoliberalism as a rationality—"a peculiar form of reason"—that is reshaping state, society, and the human subject (2015: 17). Brown has described the overarching nature of this change as the "'economization' of political life and of other heretofore noneconomic spheres and activities" (2015: 17).

She explains the process as follows:

Neoliberal rationality disseminates the *model of the market* to all domains and activities—even where money is not at issue—and configures human beings exhaustively as market actors, always, only, and everywhere as *homo oeconomicus*. (p.31, emphasis in original)

Childhood should be considered as one of the domains potentially reshaped by the "model of the market." This can be understood as a process of privatization—in various meanings of the term. In one sense it entails reconfiguring children from a section of the population for which the nation or society bears a collective responsibility to mere individuals who are the concern of their families. This goes hand-in-hand with the withdrawal of the state as provider of welfare and the transfer of services from the public to the private sector to be run according to market principles. Facilities particularly used by children such as libraries, youth clubs, and leisure centers have been severely affected by this move. Writing prophetically in the mid-1980s Zelizer noted: "The sacred child is ... a private luxury; children in need of public support are treated unsentimentally, assisted only if the investment is justified in economic terms" (1985: 216).

The reshaping of "human beings exhaustively as market actors" (Zelizer 1985: 216) renders community, exchange, and mutuality as impediments to success and thus has a further significant implication for childhood. This stage in the life course becomes principally the period for human capital formation wherein the central aim is to develop toward maximum competitiveness. In neoliberal understanding citizenship is of little concern. What matters is for children to strive to become winners in the market place of work and other domains, including personal relationships (Brown 2015). Parents, teachers, and youth workers are made responsible for undertaking such investments and, as children grow toward adulthood, they bear increasing responsibility for self-investment.

Serious inquiry into childhood in contemporary society must, in our view, entail focus on the penetration of neoliberal rationality and the market into all aspects of life. In respect of children, this is needed, at the very least, to contextualize their educational, work, familial, and social lives. Yet, with some notable exceptions, scholars in childhood studies have shown little interest in bringing political economy and consideration of class into their analysis. For this to change we need to understand the reasons for such reluctance.

Childhood studies: A socio-cultural project

Countering the hegemony of developmental science

The field of childhood studies emerged in Western Europe and North America during the ascendency of neoliberal rationality in the latter decades of the twentieth century and evolved in direct challenge to child development research. Seeking to identify the factors affecting children's progress toward adulthood, this latter field of inquiry experienced a huge surge in the twentieth century across medicine, psychology, and the developmental and human sciences, with neuroscience a more recent contributor. Its influence on the social sciences has been most evident in economics, which has harnessed the theory and research tools of developmental science toward identification of the determinants, pathways, and outcomes of human capital formation. In the process, the field has become complicit in perpetuating neoliberal rationality, insofar as "successful" development in children is defined in normative terms through cognitive and other outcomes that have been found to promote labor-market readiness, competitiveness, and productivity.

Childhood studies scholars were galvanized by concern about the positivism inherent in dominant approaches to child development. They were also disquieted by the fact that the empirical base of developmental research was largely confined to high-income countries in which only a minority of the world's population live, thus rendering claims of global applicability profoundly misleading (Bornstein et al. 2012). They asserted that childhood is fundamentally a construction shaped by specific socio-cultural conditions in particular settings, with the consequence that the representations, experiences, and competencies of children are highly variable across time and space. Through such a perspective, the diversity of childhoods around the globe became a valid field of inquiry in its own right, with emphasis on the contexts in which boys and girls live, their everyday experiences and actions, and their emic perspectives.

Moreover, childhood studies sought to diverge from the bulk of scholarship around child development by giving weight to the part children play in shaping not only their own lives but also the environments that they inhabit. Research has revealed the many ways in which the young are "active in the construction and determination of their own social lives, the lives of those around them and of the societies in which they live" (Prout and James 1990b: 8; also Corsaro 1986; Solberg 1996). In the process and in alignment with the UN Convention on the Rights of the Child (1989), a new ethic emerged that emphasized the authenticity of children's voices as well as their right to participate to the greatest extent possible in all aspects of academic and policy-related inquiry.

Rejecting "human capital"

Child development research has been integral to work concerned with the formation of human capital, which seeks to provide insight into the ways that the young can be best prepared for their role in capitalist society and is thus oriented toward the future rather than the present. Rejection of this endeavor is paradigmatic for childhood studies. Jens Qvortrup's insistence that the young be viewed as "human beings" and not as "human becomings" (1985: 132) is perhaps the most frequently cited articulation of this position. The argument against seeing the young in terms of what they will become is strongly moral in nature and is at the core of childhood studies scholars' advocacy for children to be viewed as agentive social actors. However, critique of the future orientation of the human capital approach has served to foreclose attention to the potential impact upon children's lives of the larger project in which the conceptualization of childhood as a period for the formation of human capital was embedded. The aim of neoliberalism that children should become competitive in the market place profoundly shapes the domains of children's lives. This includes, for example, organized youth activity. Tania St. Croix in her account of the impacts of changes in UK government policy makes the following observation:

> Success for a young person is not about enjoyment, ethics or living their lives for the "here and now"; instead they should focus almost entirely on their individual future, with every decision a calculated move towards their "outcomes." (2012: 3)

In an era of neoliberal governance, children, as the rest of society, are expected to act as "self-investing capital that constantly attempts to enhance its market value" (Rottenberg 2017). Capitalism's concern with future viability and success is thus a vital force in the everyday lives of children. Yet childhood studies, in its rejection of the human capital approach, has largely forestalled critical engagement with this force.

The politics of culture

Childhood studies emerged as a field during the period that witnessed the collapse of the Soviet Union and, in consequence, the discrediting of Marxist political-economic formulations. For social scientists Marxist critique was over-deterministic, even anti-humanist, in its focus upon macro-level structural analysis. Attention was given, instead, to individual agency, participation, and the politics of identity. Childhood studies reflected this mood, advocating for attention to and participation of children in a manner that echoed similar moves by liberal feminists. As with women, gay people, and the previously colonized, children were seen as a "muted group" that required recognition by society and polity (cf. Ardener 1975; Hardman 1973, Mayall 1994).

In the 1990s, childhood studies scholars largely side-stepped the materiality of childhood that might lead to consideration of political economy. Reflecting on his work a decade and a half earlier in promoting a new paradigm for the sociology of childhood Alan Prout acknowledged that

> [social constructionism] grants discourse (narrative, representation, symbolization ...) a monopoly as the medium through which social life, and therefore childhood is constructed. Accounts of the socially constructed child always privilege discourse. Some versions are distinctly idealist about childhood while others are simply silent or vague about the material components of social life. At best there is an equivocal and uneasy evasiveness about materiality. (2005: 63)

The unease that Prout expresses here resonates with concerns that began to be expressed from the late 1990s about the dominant attention to the politics of identity and recognition. For Carl Boggs, for example, the focus on individual subjectivities was being bought at the cost of blinding ourselves to commonalities in the experience of disempowerment and impoverishment due to the workings of global capitalism. He noted:

> There are two problems: privileging the "discursive field" over structural factors and preoccupation with localized micro concerns in such a way that the macro realm of state governance, corporate power, and global economy is diminished. (2000: 217)

Incipient efforts to attend to political economy

In recent years a small number of scholars have, in different ways, brought together the study of children and childhood with an explicitly materialist perspective.[1] To the best of our knowledge, however, none of these has advocated explicitly for childhood studies to address its lack of attention to political economy. Take, for example, Alison Watson's book on *The Child in International Political Economy* (2009). This volume is concerned largely with encouraging scholars in the sub-discipline of International Political Economy (IPE) to treat children as "worthy of recognition" (p.91). The author draws directly upon key texts within childhood studies to advance her argument in favor of a "'kindered' IPE" through which "the equality of rights between adult and child" (2009) is promoted and "new vistas in traditional debates" within IPE might be opened up (p.90). We do not take issue with the aims or argument in this book. However, it leaves unexamined the converse benefits to childhood studies of embracing the focus and methodology of political economy. The examination by historians, including Hugh Cunningham (1995), Harry Hendrick (1997), and Viviana Zelizer (1985), of the interplay between the institution of childhood and social, political and economic forces over time could serve as a guide to the ways that the socio-cultural may be integrated with the political-economic. However, this aspect of their work has generally been marginal to scholars bringing a sociological perspective to issues around children and childhood.

(Re)Materializing childhood studies

Focus

To be clear, we are not suggesting that emphasis upon the socio-cultural domain within childhood studies should be supplanted by attention to political economy. Rather, we seek engagement with both. The importance of this integrated approach may be illustrated by the effort to understand patterns of non-participation in formal schooling. On one hand, there is a need to attend to the attitudes and behavior of parents, teachers, community leaders, and others who may encourage or obstruct children's participation. In the effort to comprehend access to and experience of schooling such inquiry is vital: potentially revealing, for example, patterns of discrimination that inhibit access, or perceptions of quality that inform the willingness to attend. This focus, however, is insufficient in itself. Also required is examination of such matters as the budgetary allocation to education and its impact upon quality, provision of transport and other vital infrastructure, employment opportunities for those who complete schooling, etc. These are issues determined by the "system," itself shaped disproportionately by the agenda of elites. Education budgets may be redirected to other areas where well-placed individuals can gain profit, such as through military equipment (Feinstein 2013). Or, it could be that state support is skewed in favor of particular geographical areas or specific populations of children with which the relatively powerful are aligned (Williams 2016a).

Challenging discriminatory attitudes and behaviors, while arguing for appreciation of children's agency and for the value of concentrating on their "voices," constitutes engagement in the "politics of recognition" (Fraser and Honneth 2003). In the view of Berry Mayall, "Recognition of (children's) responsibilities may help raise their social status" (2002: 2). However, as Nancy Fraser has observed, "struggles for recognition occur in a world of exacerbated material inequality" (1997: 11). A principal means toward the realization of social and economic justice has to be redistribution (Fraser and Honneth 2003).

Richard Wilkinson and Kate Pickett's 2009 book *The Spirit Level: Why Equality Is Better for Everyone* indicates the impact of mal-distribution upon the young. These authors considered the relationship—at national level and, in the United States, at state level—between income inequality and an index of health and social problems. These problems include several that directly affect the young: infant mortality, school dropout, bullying, teenage pregnancy, social immobility, and obesity. There is not the space here to discuss in detail the explanation that Wilkinson and Pickett offer for the relationship between income inequality and the incidence of these and other problems. At the core of their argument, however, is the issue of societal hierarchy and the breakdown in social trust resulting from a high level of inequality. This loss of trust may have direct impacts upon children's lives—for example, in constraining their movement and activities beyond the home out of fear of harm from strangers.

A focus upon the politics of redistribution is not simply a complement to the politics of recognition, however. It may also serve to rescue scholars of childhood from being co-opted. As Nancy Fraser has argued in relation to the experience of feminism:

The turn to recognition dovetailed all too neatly with a rising neoliberalism that wanted nothing more than to repress all memory of social egalitarianism. Thus, feminists absolutized the critique of culture at precisely the moment when circumstances required redoubled attention to the critique of political economy. (2009: 109)

As well as attending to redistribution (alongside recognition), we also need a consistent focus upon intersectionality. This entails consideration of children's lives as shaped by factors that include gender, ethnicity, disability, and class. The last of these has been masked by the treatment of children as an undifferentiated group in socio-economic terms—even as a class in themselves (Oldman 1994).

There may be several reasons why childhood studies scholars have paid relatively scant attention to the issue of class. Certainly, consideration of class may prompt uncomfortable questions about the unequal distribution of power amongst children. Moreover, children from relatively privileged families may exercise power over adults, for example, domestic servants. Attention to classed difference thus potentially blurs the association of children, as a section of the population, with social marginalization and lack of empowerment. This association has animated the field of childhood studies since its inception. Yet, in an era shaped by neoliberal rationality where the young are obliged to compete in a marketized economy and society of winners and losers, attention to classed difference among children is vitally needed.

Methodology

The concerted effort in childhood studies to promote a view of the young as agentive and as capable commentators on their own lives has coexisted with the contention that the young inhabit a "world," "culture," or "community" separable from that of adults. For example, Prout and James state, "Children's social relationships and cultures are worthy of study in their own right, independent of the perspective and concerns of adults" (1990: 8). Lawrence Hirschfeld takes it further in arguing that

> children ... constitute themselves into semi-autonomous subcultures and as such can be as usefully explored by anthropologists as Senegalese street merchants in Marseille, Vietnamese rice farmers in Louisiana, or high-energy physicists at Lawrence Livermore. (2002: 613)

This contention about children's (semi-)autonomous subcultures, taken together with the view of the young as agentive and as commentators on their own lives, has marginalized perspectives other than those of children. These two contentions have also had important implications for the methodology conventionally employed by researchers within the field of childhood studies. A particular hallmark has been the use of qualitative methodology relying on small samples and the documentation of emic perspectives and the everyday. Such research has typically entailed concentration on intimate relations, such as with peers, family, teachers, and spheres of activity, including, the school, household, and workplace. Ethnographic fieldwork with significant participant-observation has been commonplace, while focus groups and, to a lesser extent, semi-structured interviews have been undertaken as a principal method by researchers more pressed for time.

The young may offer profound and invaluable insights into the experience of children in their community and wider society. They may also articulate insights into local dynamics of power and wealth and how these affect their lives. However, they are unlikely to have access to the vantage point from which to locate such experience in relation to the exercise of elite power through institutions of governance beyond the micro and meso levels. Focusing on the experiences of children in isolation from attention to the larger structural forces therefore imposes particular limits on understanding of their lives. To illustrate we refer to a pilot study we undertook together in Sri Lanka in 2002 (Hart et al. 2007). This research was focused on the impacts of civil war upon Tamil children roughly in the age range 8–15 living in a rebel-controlled area. One source of great concern that emerged from our interactions with children was snakes. Children spoke at length about their fear of snakes entering homes at night and showed acute awareness of the high incidence of child mortality as a result of snakebite. However, they were not able to explain how this fear related to the specific conditions of their locale as produced by political-economic forces.

Through engagement with local NGO workers, parents, and local officials, we were able to comprehend the impact of actions by the warring parties (Government of Sri Lanka and the Liberation Tigers of Tamil Eelam [LTTE]). Programs to contain the snake population and the creation of local clinics equipped with the necessary medicines had been curtailed or denied. Freedom of movement was also restricted. In large measure children were dying as a result of bites due to the unchecked number of snakes compounded by interminable delays at checkpoints and a ban on travel during curfews that often made it impossible to get to a clinic where an antidote might be administered in time. Understanding how and why fear of snakes was an important issue in children's lives it was necessary to attend not only to their experiences but also to the larger structural constraints and the calculations of warring elites that perpetuated such constraints.

An approach to research that serves to identify the linkages between phenomena at the micro, meso, exo, and macro levels is, in our view, essential to the effort to embed a far stronger political economy dimension within the field of childhood studies. In particular, the effort to understand the precise causal channels through which macro-level political-economic forces affect children's lives requires an approach that likely involves mixed methods, that draws upon multiple data sources, and that might entail longitudinal, multi-scalar, and multi-sited study. We illustrate the particular benefits of these different elements through reference to three very different studies.

In their investigation of the impact of maternal migration on the physical growth and cognition of children in Peru, Javier Escobal and Eva Flores (2009) compared the children of non-migrant mothers with those whose mothers had migrated from areas affected by civil war and a third group whose mothers had migrated from communities not affected by conflict. The authors attended systematically to factors that the literature anticipates might influence children's outcomes—such as service access and parental income—that, in turn, may be linked to political-economic forces. These factors were considered in relation to mothers prior to, during, and/or following migration in the context of armed conflict. The authors controlled for the characteristics of the mother preceding her first migration episode and the characteristics of the birthplace by introducing a series of variables, such as the mother's age, years of education, and maternal language; they also included mother's height to proxy for genetic circumstances. In doing this, the authors attempted to parse out other factors that may have influenced child outcomes, in order to isolate the effect of the migration decision.

As may be expected, there were important differences between children from areas of high-intensity conflict and those from areas free from conflict, the latter having higher cognitive scores than the former. However, the study found that, overall, children of mothers who migrated fared better than those whose mothers had not, showing a significantly lower level of stunting and significantly higher levels of cognitive achievement.

By distinguishing the effects of maternal exposure to various environmental conditions, including armed conflict, the study reveals how macro-level political-economic processes play out directly in the lives of children. What remains unanswered and what can perhaps be best addressed through qualitative research is how more specifically the mothers' very different experiences may have moderated their beliefs, practice, relationships, and decision-making in ways that shape children's outcomes.

In making the case for interdisciplinary and multi-scalar research, we thus advocate for the integration of micro qualitative data, which necessarily include children's perspectives, with other data types and sources. Matching micro data with nationally representative cross-sectional data, such as Demographic and Health Surveys, the Living Standards Measurement Study, administrative data or civil registration systems, can provide context for inquiry into children's experiences, perspectives, and outcomes. Some nationally representative data make it possible to disaggregate between groups of children on the basis of place of residence, household economic status, gender, ethnicity, religion, caste, or other factors of social status, and thereby reveal disparities in access to resources, infrastructure, and services, together with associated outcomes in children. Qualitative evidence from a sub-sample of children can be used to interrogate these wider distinctions and explain the many implications for children's lives.

Long-term qualitative research with children and other respondents in the locality can help draw out wider processes that bear down on the young through repeated triangulation. For example, Cindi Katz (2001) documented the effects of government efforts to compel farmers to switch from subsistence farming to the production of cotton for the global market in Howa, a village in rural Sudan, over the course of fifteen years. Among numerous other effects, including the production of unprecedented local-level socio-economic disparities, Katz notes the disembedding of children's economic activity from their social relationships. In place of shepherding livestock in the company of peers—an activity that exhibited elements of both play and environmental learning—boys in Howa became increasingly involved in cash cropping with adults: "activities that produced an income or saved household expenditures for newly commodified goods" (2001: 148). This had important consequences for their lives more broadly:

> If work and play are separated and children's peer groups become settings for play alone, they are gradually isolated from the larger society caught up with work ... If these conditions isolate the peer group, so, too, do they trivialize play as a "childish" activity in the eyes of adults. The conceptualization of play as a trivial and inessential activity consigned

to inferior symbolic status because of its separation from work is surely part of the deracination of everyday life that capitalist "modernization" brings. (2001: 148–149)

In this case, the changes prompted by a state-led endeavor to capitalize Sudan's rural economy were, it seems, intensified by neoliberal rationality which drove the economization of sociality. Diverse aspects of everyday life became commodified to the point that "money came to define a growing number of relationships and exchanges, including those within families" (p.138).

Longitudinal, locally based research of the kind conducted by Katz can give us a valuable picture on the direction of change and how such change is experienced, drawing into question the relationship between macro-level processes associated with the penetration of the global market and children's everyday lives, including play. However, on its own such study may be limited in helping us understand the precise dynamics of causal pathways.

Multi-site research with diverse actors in interconnecting institutional structures with shared discourses and procedures can be very effective at tracing specific routes through which particular political-economic influences touch children's lives. For example, Neil Howard's study (2012) of the policies and experience of "child trafficking" in Benin involved interviews with numerous respondents from diverse governmental, inter-governmental, and non-governmental policy and practitioner organizations internationally, nationally, and sub-nationally, as well as with a purposive sample of former and current migrant working children (mainly boys). Interviews with the child respondents were conducted in both sending communities in rural Benin and in the artisanal quarries in Abeokutu, Nigeria, where they had migrated for work. In addition, the research tracked child protection policies and discourses as explicated globally, regionally, and nationally in a multitude of conventions and protocols, as well as in agency documentation. Focusing on major organizational players, such as the ILO and UNICEF— both at global HQ and on the ground—and revealing how their vision and objectives were echoed by smaller local organizations, Howard exposes the relations of power operating within and between institutions from global to local level.

According to this author the dominant position in policy circles is to label children migrating for work as victims of trafficking. Yet these young people and their communities did not see or experience the situation in such terms. Rather, the movement of children for the purposes of work represented the continuation of a well-established economic and learning strategy in the context of rural poverty. Importantly, Howard does not treat such poverty merely as context—as a "causeless reality" (Howard 2012: 470). Instead his study reveals how economic conditions in rural Benin are bound up with the workings of global capitalism: US subsidies for its own cotton industry in the context of global free trade had depressed the earnings of cotton farmers in Benin over many years. This, in turn, had increased the pressure on families to send their children away to work. Potentially illustrating the impact of elite interests upon, within, and between institutions working to support children in Benin, most of Howard's interviewees among the staff of NGOs, UN agencies, and government side-stepped the link between "the political economy of subsidies and reduced household income" (2012: 470). A small minority pointed to the political constraints that hindered attention of their organizations to "structural issues" (2012: 470).

Howard also describes the very real damage caused by abolitionist child-trafficking policies in contexts where child work is both a form of learning for the young and a valuable contribution to the domestic economies of the rural poor. The making and implementation of such policy illustrate the tendency to frame the situation of children primarily in terms of socio-cultural factors (typically as "harmful traditional practices"). The development of a sharper, multi-scalar focus on the impact of political-economic forces might assist those seeking to challenge the tendency of development actors to divert the attribution of responsibility away from centers of power and wealth toward the poor themselves.

Conclusion

We began our chapter with allusion to the changes for children in high-income countries during the last decades of the nineteenth and early decades of the twentieth centuries. One major element of such change was the ending of children's large-scale involvement in paid labor. That the young became economically "worthless" but emotionally "priceless" was due to the interplay of factors that were technological, cultural, political, and economic in nature. By contrast many millions of children in low-income countries remain economically active, in some cases under highly exploitative conditions that put them at considerable risk of harm.

As a field, childhood studies has aspired to improve the lives of the world's young and with that goal in view has done much to document the perspectives of children exposed to diverse forms of marginalization and exploitation. But if we are to help challenge such harm it is not sufficient to attend solely to experience and to local attitudes and behaviors. We must also address the larger forces that perpetuate poverty, inequality, and lack of access to the services and resources that children themselves value. As scholars we need to develop the capability to situate our analyses of children's lives and of childhood in relation to such phenomena as austerity economics, involvement in the globalized capitalist economy, war-making, and the capture of governance processes by powerful interests. Conversely, the innumerable accounts of diverse childhoods amassed over recent decades may provide a powerful basis to counter neoliberal rationality and the attempted naturalization of children as self-investing entrepreneurs whose early years are primarily a preparation for competition in the marketplace. The requisite blending of ethnographic inquiry with political-economic analysis of the conditions in which those lives unfold has the potential to challenge the status quo at many levels but will require us to rethink the dominant methodological and disciplinary bent of childhood studies. Failure to do so would be an act of negligence.

We write this chapter in 2018 while witnessing the ascendancy of political leaders claiming to serve the interests of citizens, while they work harder even than their predecessors to shore up the wealth and power of elites. At such a moment, reimagining childhood studies as a field focused upon both the politics of recognition and the politics of redistribution has never been more necessary, nor perhaps more daunting.

Note

1 Contributions include Kent (1995), Stephens (1997), Levine (1999), Pupavac (2001), and Ansell (2005).

CHAPTER SIX

Decolonizing Childhood Studies:

Overcoming Patriarchy and Prejudice in Child-related Research and Practice

Kristen Cheney

There is a growing dissatisfaction that childhood studies is not making the desired academic or international development policy impacts that would improve children's lives. This chapter argues that there are two reasons for this. The first has to do with patriarchal tendencies within the academy: childhood studies is often viewed within academia not only as an infantilized subject by virtue of its young objects of inquiry but as a feminized subject by virtue of the fact that the field is dominated by female scholars. Such assumptions undergird a related perpetuation of "childism" in academic research (Young-Breuhl 2012). Second is the colonization of childhood in international development policy by a pervasive universalized children's rights discourse that tends toward protectionism rather than empowerment (Cheney 2014b).

In order to overcome these challenges, I argue for a decolonization of both academia and international development practice. Going beyond recent calls for a postcolonial re-examination of childhood studies (Nieuwenhuys 2013; Balagopalan 2014), I argue for a *decolonization* of childhood research and practice (Tuhiwai Smith 1999; Mutua and Swadener 2004)—both in the conventional sense of confronting Western civilizing constructions of childhood and as a means to challenge the patriarchal underpinnings of the politics of knowledge production about children. This will enable childhood studies as an (inter)discipline to not only critically and reflexively question the politics of knowledge production in the academy but to effectively question established norms, approaches and practices in international development work targeting children. Through examples from my own and others' experiences, I provide an impression of the current state of childhood studies and academia more broadly. I then consider what a decolonized approach to childhood research might look like. Although this line of thinking is still speculative, it can help us imagine how achieving epistemic justice (Fricker 2009) in childhood research could change both the field of childhood studies and child-relevant policy.

Patriarchy in the academy

Despite (or perhaps because of) having gained enough legitimacy to establish separate academic departments, one could argue that the ghettoization of childhood studies persists in the academy. It is an area of inquiry that is consistently infantilized and feminized by other academics, and thus consistently devalued within a patriarchal system. While childhood studies is not the only discipline to suffer this problem, I claim that it has significantly affected the development of the discipline. As Andrea Cornwall has written, making patriarchy visible is "a first step in raising awareness of its costs as well as the ways in which the short-term benefits it offers men … the 'patriarchal dividend', wreak longer-term consequences" (Cornwall 2016: 76).

Here, a comparison with the evolution of women's studies is instructive—not to reinforce presumed affinities between women and children that tend to naturalize childhood studies as a "women's subject" (Twamley et al. 2017: 2), but rather to challenge that view by comparing the experiences of establishing these disciplines as legitimate areas of intellectual inquiry within the patriarchal academy.

Women's studies grew out of the women's movements of the 1970s, gaining an academic foothold within a decade or so because of its close alliance with the women's movement—often referred to as its "academic arm" (Jaschik 2009). Being highly interdisciplinary prompted "a long-standing debate as to whether women's studies should remain its own department and/or discipline, or whether it should be integrated into the entire academic curriculum" that is still contested today (Jaschik 2009). At issue is whether social studies of women's lives deserve their own attention as a counterweight to historical bias in favor of men's experiences and interpretations, or whether each discipline should be taking more gendered approaches to understanding their areas of inquiry. While the latter might be desirable as an end goal, many thought it first required separate departments to teach others why it was even necessary to study women in their own right and how to incorporate gendered analyses into other disciplines. According to Alice Ginsberg, "While this is certainly not a bad thing, women's studies teachers [who were based in other departments] were worried that they would be looked at suspiciously in their home disciplines, and may even be denied tenure because of it" (Jaschik 2009). However, many other social science departments saw the introduction of women's studies as disruptive to their own intellectual pursuits. Stuart Hall even accused feminism of "crapping on the table of cultural studies"[1] (Skeggs 2008: 670).

Nevertheless, decades of women's studies, as well as the infiltration of feminist thought in various disciplines, has not managed to disrupt some of the central tenets and established histories of the social sciences (Skeggs 2008)—nor has it fundamentally altered the functioning of the academy as a patriarchal space. Recent studies have shown that female lecturers are consistently rated lower in student evaluations than their male counterparts— particularly women of color (Lazos 2012)—even when controlling for other variables (Wagner et al. 2016).[2] Male students in particular tend to rate female professors lower (Mengel et al. 2016), and online instructors who assumed female names (whether actually female or not) received lower student evaluations for teaching the exact same online content (MacNell et al. 2015). In other words, just the *impression* that the teacher was female lowered evaluation scores, whether the teacher was *actually* female or not. In addition, female academics are more likely to be penalized in the academy for having children—at the same time as having children generally helps male academics' careers (Mason 2013). Moreover, it is often assumed that women's choices of academic inquiry are closely linked with either their own biographies (in women's studies) or reproductive choices (childhood studies), while this is rarely the case for men (Baxter 2015).

It is therefore ironic that while it is often assumed that women are better suited to study children and childhood, and childhood studies departments are indeed comprised mainly of female students and faculty, the few male scholars in such departments are often of higher rank. These proportions are not necessarily particular to childhood studies but are rather indicative of broader trends in the academy; in fact, they are reflective of the academy as a whole, across the world. In the Netherlands, for example, while women make up a majority of academic staff, they still comprise only 17 percent of full professors nationally.[3] At some Dutch universities, the figure is as low as 7.6 percent.[4]

The continued predominance of men in child and youth-related academic fields—especially among senior faculty—likely has less to do with denaturalizing the woman/child dyad and more to do with the implicit need to lend legitimacy to feminized research topics by including men. Otherwise, such "women's" topics are easily relegated to marginal positions in academia (Baxter 2015). Moreover, in order to gain legitimacy in their own right, female researchers are often compelled to comply with scholarly norms around publishing, research, and funding, yet the rewards are few and far between because they continue to be devalued by a patriarchal academy. Thus, just as women's studies scholars did, childhood studies scholars frequently find themselves having to establish the legitimacy of their research in ways those researching other topics are not. Jane Baxter (2015) writes, "Read nearly any work on the archaeology of childhood and you will find a preamble explaining why studying children in the past is important, necessary, and viable ... This need to justify the study of children is notable because of its persistent ubiquity in the literature—it has never stopped." Likewise, I have also consistently been asked throughout my twenty-year career to justify the relevance of studying children virtually anytime I have stepped outside childhood studies, including in African studies, anthropology, and development studies, and colleagues have complained that their proposals are frequently rejected from conferences and publications in these disciplines.[5]

Childhood studies has some instructive parallels and departures with women's studies (Oakley 1994). Esser and colleagues claim that childhood studies as a political project arose out of feminist concerns for the social justice of marginalized groups: "From a scholarly perspective, the aim was to adequately represent the agency of children, while from a political perspective, this more accurate representation was expected to help improve children's situation." There was thus a "close connection between criticism of the gender order and criticism of the generational order" that had in fact begun in feminist studies (Esser et al. 2016: 5). Childhood studies grew in parallel with—and sometimes out of critiques of—the promotion of the Convention on the Rights of the Child (CRC) in the 1990s. However, children's rights were not a broad social movement like the women's movement; it was mainly a top-down international policy movement. As such, it was widely criticized from the start by non-Western governments and populations.

Also multidisciplinary in nature, childhood studies is still struggling to gain recognition through the formation of distinct academic departments, especially in the United States (the one country *not* to sign the CRC). This may be a symptom of the academy's reluctance to take a certain orientation toward the study of children seriously as an object of intellectual inquiry. Childhood studies has thus had debates similar to women's studies about whether to create and maintain distinct childhood studies departments or to integrate childhood studies into other departments (James 2010). Moreover, childhood studies still struggles with the same issue that also continues to plague women's studies: inclusiveness of non-Western societies, whether in faculty composition or conceptual frameworks. For this reason, I would concur with those who say there is still a need for both distinct women's and childhood studies departments in the academy—especially as we see a backlash against feminism in global politics and a neoliberal agenda that threatens to deepen child poverty and jeopardize children's wellbeing. On the other hand, this further confounds questions of how, despite its interdisciplinary beginnings, to break childhood studies out of its siloed academic spaces and integrate it with other disciplines.

As Cornwall suggests, "To get to grips with masculinity we need to begin to denaturalise the associations that are often made between men, masculinity and power, and bring into clearer view what is going on in terms of power" (Cornwall 2016: 77). But we also need to denaturalize the essentialized association of women with children that is part of patriarchal oppression—and the ways in which women and children are commonly pitted against each other (Twamley et al. 2017). We have to constantly shine a light on deeply embedded institutional structures that re-inscribe these assumptions through daily practices, even in our own socially critical academic departments. A number of scholars have pointed out how academics do not take children seriously, except perhaps as future adults (Hirschfeld 2002), even while using them as window dressing (Friedl 2002). Elisabeth Young-Breuhl (2012) has referred to this as "childism," a persistent prejudice against children as a social group comparable to racism or sexism; one that legitimates and rationalizes a broad continuum of acts that in fact run counter to children's best interests. Perhaps it is not so much an issue of not taking children seriously, however, as one of where attention to children lies and what sorts of knowledge production about children is deemed relevant and recognizable. According to Young-Bruehl, "Reform is possible only if we acknowledge this prejudice in its basic forms and address the motives and cultural forces that drive it" (Young-Breuhl 2012).

Childism in international development

Is childhood studies then complicit in childism? Although our tendency may be to look inward at our own failures to advance the cause of childhood studies (Tisdall and Punch 2012; Boyden 2015),[6] we also have to put it in the context of broader institutional and intellectual barriers and resistance. Despite the advent of child rights-based approaches to international development, there remains considerable resistance to other childhood studies approaches in international development practice and policymaking. I posit that there are two reasons for this: the predominance of a particular kind of children's rights discourse and the persistence of quantitative, positivist research models as evidence base for policy formulation—both of which also have patriarchal and colonial underpinnings.

The Hegemony of Children's Rights Universalism

As mentioned above, children's rights have from the start been criticized as promoting a universalized Western-centric model of idealized childhood (Ennew and Milne 1990). Despite this criticism, international development targeting children is still dominated by Western-centric research (Nieuwenhuys 2013), sometimes prejudicially applying these models to children in the Global South (Valentin and Meinert 2009; Twum-Danso Imoh 2012). Childhood studies has had some trouble disentangling itself from this hegemony because of its rise at the same time as the CRC took hold in international development policy targeting children—"producing," as Sarada Balagopalan (2014: 8) points out, "a complex interrelationship between the open-endedness of academic interrogation and determinate policy concerns." Tisdall and Punch (2012: 254) have claimed that development studies has criticized childhood studies for its narrow conceptualization of the child, but I think it is very much the other way around: childhood studies, particularly the kind rooted in anthropological approaches such as ethnography, has consistently critiqued development studies for its narrow conceptualization of the child—which they base on the universalized child of the UNCRC but which therefore has little, no, or even negative resonance in developing country contexts (Cheney 2007). However, getting such "outsider" or non-practitioner arguments heard in the policy realm is quite difficult: acceptance of such principles of childhood diversity in policies and international standards, while ostensibly about the promotion of children's rights, more often serves the purpose of the nation gaining esteem within the international community (Cheney 2007; Balagopalan 2014). Moreover, policymakers have trouble incorporating the nuance of social research into policy—especially when such hegemonic, protectionist notions of children's rights have taken hold globally. This protectionism also confounds efforts to meaningfully prioritize children's "voices" and accommodate their participation in development policy and programming (Cheney 2014b).

Recent debates over the place of work in children's lives provide an example of how children's rights discourse has encouraged policymakers to dismiss evidence from years of scholarship. As the UN Committee on the CRC was preparing their "General Comment on the Rights of Adolescents" in 2016, over fifty leading childhood studies scholars, human rights practitioners, and child work advocates urged against issuing a blanket minimum age for work by binding the comment to the ILO Minimum Age Convention (No. 138). Drawing on their collective decades of research with working children, the group argued that such abolitionist approaches could in fact have a debilitating effect on reducing child poverty. They argued that age-appropriate work actually has positive developmental influences on children and must therefore be approached with much more nuance and attention to the structural determinants of children's work in different sociopolitical contexts. Instead of ILO Convention 138, the group called on the Committee to carefully apply the ILO Convention 182 on the Worst Forms of Child Labour, guided by consideration of the social, cultural, and economic circumstances of children's lives. Most important, the group asked that the Committee consult working children whose lives will most be impacted by their decisions. In an open letter to the Committee, the group wrote, "As working children's groups ... have made clear, their participation in a range of jobs, including many of those prohibited by policy makers, is often integral to their attempts to access education, livelihoods, and development plans as well as their socio-economic and citizenship participation in the broadest sense" (2016). The group was given the opportunity to briefly present these arguments to the Committee in Geneva, but the Committee decided to reference ILO Convention 138 anyway.

The Limitations of Positivist Research

One major contribution of feminist research is that "almost all sociological methods were subject to scrutiny and re-inscribed by feminism, even quantitative methods ... Part of the methodological attack was on sexism and positivism but also on the epistemological basis for knowledge: who can know, who inscribes, in whose interests?" (Skeggs 2008: 678). As mentioned above, feminist scholars have called out these biases for the adverse impacts they have had on knowledge production.[7] However, the contribution of situated knowledges has not quite trickled down to development policy that, while acknowledging the many ways in which women and girls are disadvantaged, does so on the basis of rather exclusive epistemological frameworks favoring quantitative research that tends to be more positivist in outlook. For example, developmental psychology has made inroads based on "age and stage" models that have been adopted by international policy formulation organizations mainly due to the "measurability" they lend to determining children's "readiness," "progress," or "failure" to take up their roles in human capital economic frameworks (Boyden and Dercon 2012: 23). This can be seen quite clearly in the World Bank's 2007 World Development Report, which explicitly, if problematically, links child development to broader socioeconomic development (World Bank 2006).

Moreover, international development is yet another male-dominated field where "evidence-based" research is often interpreted in terms of numbers and "hard" sciences—also seen as masculine compared to the "soft" social sciences such as childhood studies, which is largely rooted in the more qualitative and interpretivist disciplines of anthropology and sociology. Because qualitative research tends to focus more on social practice and processes of meaning making (Morrow and Crivello 2015), it is less valorized as revealing "Truth." Such positivist and quantitative tenets of research thus contradict those of qualitative and interpretive research (Alderson 2016)— perhaps precisely because qualitative, interpretive research is so well positioned to critique inclusion and exclusion in policy construction and its consequences, as well as daily development practices. Childhood studies developed from the premise that children were competent social actors in their own right, partly to counter the prevailing deficit and dependency models of childhood perpetuated by developmental psychology (James and Prout 1997). Yet the nuance such social research inquiry produces is still too often seen as a distraction by policymakers who require massive amounts of quantitative data and "representative samples" that can show them the "progress" and "effectiveness" of policy decisions that reinforce hegemonic human development discourses (Boyden 2015).

Political economic analyses have made some inroads in policy debates, but they still face resistance from positivists. A recent case-in-point arose around the Netherlands' discussion of banning foreign adoptions. My research had identified the growth of an "orphan industrial complex" correlated with the rapid proliferation of orphanages in Uganda, despite a decrease in the percentage of orphaned children (Cheney 2014a; Cheney and Rotabi 2017). This trend, along with other indications of force, fraud, and coercion in intercountry adoption, formed the basis of concern by the independent Council for Criminal Justice and Protection of Juveniles (RSJ in Dutch), which recommended to the minister of Security and Justice that the Netherlands prohibit foreign adoptions by Dutch citizens (*Raad voor Strafrechtstoepassing en Jeungdbescherming* [Council for Criminal Justice and Protection of Juveniles] 2016). Yet some developmental psychologists from Leiden University's Knowledge Center for Adoption and Foster Care (ADOC in Dutch), which has historically been funded by adoption agencies, countered with their research that had shown that adoption was in fact good for children.[8] While no one disputed their evidence, their assessment lacked important contextual evidence relevant to the argument. First, intercountry adoption is not the only route to family permanency for children in institutions; in fact, according to international standards set forward in the Hague Convention on Intercountry Adoption, it is meant to be the *last resort* for children in institutions to find permanency (Hague Conference on Private International Law 1993). Second, this narrow focus on developmental indicators did not address the question of how children were getting into orphanages in the first place—especially when it is estimated that approximately 80 percent of children in orphanages worldwide have living, locatable relatives, including parents. Third, intercountry adoption is just one end of the spectrum of activities in the orphan industrial complex that includes fundraising for, volunteer visits to, and establishment of orphanages for financial gain that are driving children into unnecessary and damaging institutionalization in the first place (Cheney and Ucembe forthcoming).[9]

This is a vital part of the story that cannot be told by experiments in developmental psychology. And yet Marinus (Rien) van IJzendoorn, a senior, highly decorated, developmental psychologist at ADOC, rushed to defend intercountry adoption by attacking the research on which the report was based—my own included. Van IJzendoorn claimed that because it was not narrowly quantitative (does not "put numbers in a row" or table), it was to be discounted.[10] Despite his assertion that only objective observation and statistical analysis provide clear evidence, van IJzendoorn went on to discuss only selected numbers presented in our chapter so as to distort the clear pattern of drastic increases in both orphanages and international adoptions.[11] Moreover, many of the ADOC researchers refused to acknowledge their positionality as adoptive parents of foreign children, claiming that this fact was scientifically irrelevant and had no bearing on their objectivity.

It is unfortunate that all too many policymakers reinforce this prejudice against qualitative research when ethnography, participatory research, and attention to positive deviance have ultimately enhanced interventions in policy and practice. As Morrow and Crivello (2015: 277) argue, "We need to get beyond the level of thinking that qualitative research is about 'stories' (which implies something fictitious or capricious), to thinking about systematic integration of qualitative and survey analysis." We might also challenge the implicit biases of quantitative research and encourage more reflexivity about the positionality of quantitative researchers.

Expanding What Counts as "Evidence" in Child-related Policymaking

Even if a certain level of navel gazing in childhood studies is warranted (Tisdall and Punch 2012), chastising ourselves for failing to make broader policy impacts will not help us make better inroads into influencing child-related policy. Childhood studies has made great strides toward theorizing childhood as a social variable equal to others, as well as developing a political economy approach that is especially salient to the contemporary global challenges of neoliberalism and austerity (Cheney and Rotabi 2017; see also Boyden and Hart and Spyros, Rosen and Cook, this volume). This is especially important for combatting what Rachel Rosen labels "the rising use of the trope of the child in a way that effectively blames women for the conditions of children's lives in the context of crisis and austerity, and the continued subsumption of children's lived experiences by their future promise, in social research and policy making" (Rosen 2017: 4). But in the short term, at least, we will unfortunately have to keep re-establishing our work's legitimacy and making a place for qualitative research more broadly—and child-centered social analysis specifically—in order to break down intersectional prejudices and resistances. The Young Lives project at Oxford University provides a relatively successful example. Young Lives is a longitudinal, international study of child poverty documenting 12,000 children in the Global South over a fifteen-year period in order to determine what drives and impacts child poverty so that policymakers may appropriately respond to alleviate it.[12] But Young Lives is a huge project that is not easily replicable without the political will to fund such massive, longitudinal studies.[13] Now nearing its end, the final results of the study and its policy impact will be indicative of how far childhood studies has come in influencing local, national, and global policymaking in relation to children's lives.

On a more modest scale, participatory research with young people is gaining gradual acceptance among the policymakers, largely based on childhood studies' challenges to practically enhance the meaning of "participation" in the CRC. But there are still many challenges to overcome, particularly in respect of childist attitudes and prejudices against children's capabilities; hence the need to move not only to a post-colonial position (cf. Balagopalan's chapter, this volume) but toward decolonization.

Decolonizing childhood studies

Decolonization is an epistemological approach informed by critical, feminist evaluations of positivism. Pioneered by Linda Tuhiwai Smith, this approach urges researchers to move away from racist and ethnocentric practices that could potentially also be exploitative toward more respectful, ethical, and sympathetic research (Tuhiwai Smith 1999). While decolonizing methodologies have been picked up by other social science disciplines such as feminist studies, they have not yet been widely applied in childhood studies (Cheney 2011). However, it seems high time to explore the potential of decolonizing research, policy, and practice in childhood studies.

Unlike postcolonial theory, which can uncover patriarchal and adultist social relations with its historically informed discussion of the effects of colonialism on the formation of subjectivities, decolonization acknowledges an "outside" to the binomial of coloniality/modernity (Icaza 2017) that allows for the re-imagination of these problematic social relations by reorienting the field from critique and deconstruction to critical engagement and scholar activism. Decolonization does this by asking us to reimagine knowledge production, representation, power relations, and personhood in ways that not only reverse but more fundamentally challenge hegemonic cultural assumptions that foster epistemic diversity by actively engaging in debates about what constitutes knowledge. In childhood studies, this could be achieved through a vitally inclusive *co-production of knowledge with children* that aims to resist or even rupture the status quo of adults as the primary holders of knowledge. In keeping with other decolonization movements, including decolonial feminism, childhood studies could strive not only to decolonize the curriculum[14] by diversifying its contents but also to actively question broader structures of research, policy, and practice to make space for epistemic diversity that will in turn help children's knowledge to be seen as more legitimate in the eyes of researchers, policymakers, and development practitioners.

Confronting Presumptions and Prejudices: Participatory Research with Young People

One effective way to enact decolonial principles for epistemic justice—redressing the silencing and sidelining of non-dominant ways of knowing to recover subjugated knowledges (Fricker 2009)—is through a critical approach to participatory research. We need to speak to power not only with research but also *within* research. Childhood studies, while highly interdisciplinary, has much of its roots in anthropological/ethnographic approaches that can lend themselves well to seeing research processes from various situated viewpoints. However, decolonizing childhood research means going beyond the discursive to the material deconstruction of coloniality (De Jong et al. 2019). Making this a reality will then necessarily involve rethinking and even redefining expertise. My colleagues and I have tried to do just that by devising innovative mechanisms for the meaningful participation of young people in research. This includes creating a vital space for participation by prompting adult NGO and research partners to critically reflect on their assumptions about young people and how those assumptions influence their abilities to work for and with children in non-regulatory ways (Gallacher and Gallagher 2008).

For example, the study I and my colleagues from ISS facilitated as part of an international nongovernmental organization's (INGO) project to contextualize their Comprehensive Sexuality Education (CSE) programming in Ethiopia and Uganda was youth led, *conceptually* in that young people's concerns drove the research and *logistically*, in that we trained youth peer researchers and supported them to collect data from various stakeholders. Importantly, it was also highly *participatory*, viewing young people as key actors in (rather than targets of) knowledge production about their sexual and reproductive health needs. The proposed project thus involved youth peer researchers in all stages: designing the research, generating research questions, identifying research tools, collecting data, reflecting on the findings, constructing the analysis, planning dissemination of the findings, and orchestrating advocacy programs.

The challenge was that although youth-focused policymakers and INGO partners claimed to be in support of young people's involvement, there was still considerable resistance to the project, especially where it concerned young people's competencies. Once we elaborated upon what *we* meant by youth participation, we discovered that the partners—both the INGO and their local implementing partners—had very different preconceptions about what "youth participation" meant. Many actually assumed that very minimal and tokenist involvement of young people would be sufficient to meet the criteria of "participatory" and thus were uneasy at the prospect of including young people as co-creators of knowledge. As researchers, we thus encountered voiced skepticism about youth's abilities and even resistance to the research design from the very organizations that had initially conceptualized and funded the project.

We therefore had to take a more activist stance: we held reflective, inward-looking workshops with local and international partners to critically explore their assumptions about gender, generation, and participation. This decolonizing exercise revealed some startling aspects of adults' attitudes toward young people—and how those influenced the kinds of interventions they tended to design for children and youth. We realized that their resistance derived not just from their preconceptions about young people (especially poor, young, people of color in developing countries) as vulnerable and incompetent to conduct quality research but also from their preconceptions about research quality and what constitutes valid "evidence." Again, this derived from a limited, positivist understanding of research as well as preconceptions about the exclusivity of research; that it is the domain of certain ages, classes, educational levels, races, and languages. Such preconceptions often serve to further entrench "gendered and classed [but also ageist] understandings and inequalities" (Edwards et al. 2015). Responding to research exclusivity led us to a decolonial approach by more explicitly challenging the prevalent "culture of expertise" within research that leads to presumptions that young people cannot contribute, nor handle, research responsibilities (Ngutuku and Okwany 2017). Instead, we had to guide them to an appreciation of the "other knowledges" that young people possess.

This experience taught us that opening a space for truly participatory research with children requires a decolonizing approach: Who else are experts in their own lives than young people? To combat adultist assumptions, we stood our ground by going back to research basics, emphasizing that different methods are appropriate for answering particular types of research questions: it is impossible to say whether a saw is a better tool than a hammer unless you have a clear understanding of the task at hand. For the task we were given, using a mixed-methods approach that honored young people's capabilities and expertise was most appropriate—and it explicitly challenged the idea that such types of evidence are not scientifically valid.

In the end, some of the strongest critics were quite pleased with the results. Advocacy meetings between the seventy youth peer researchers we had trained and policymakers further helped everyone involved open to the capabilities and views of young people—including the young researchers themselves, who had internalized adults' assumptions that youth had little knowledge to contribute.

Conclusion: A decolonized future for childhood studies?

In this chapter, I have provided some of my own impressions of the dilemmas of patriarchy and prejudice in academia and policy. Similar to the project described above, constant self-reflexivity is essential to achieving some form of decolonization in order to keep at bay the adult gaze and Western assumptions of childhood. Women's studies have managed to gain legitimacy in international development policymaking due to a "foundation in political activism, focus on diversity and social justice, and collaborative learning environments [that] have created academic communities for women to share their unique perspectives and connect their personal experiences with traditional scholarship" (Crouch 2012). Can we do the same for childhood studies? More research and reflection is needed; however, I do not believe this will be achieved via children's rights "as usual" but through emphasis on the decolonizing strategies detailed above—in our own studies but also in practice. While we need to keep chipping away at childism through academic critique of policy and practice, we also need to maintain reflexivity about academic institutional practice and strive to make space for epistemic diversity. It is difficult to envision, for example, the creation of a community of higher education that can truly be inclusive of children's experiences, but decolonization can only occur if we challenge institutions from the inside: if we can at least work toward the decolonization of assumptions and prejudices to let ourselves be better informed by children's actual concerns and lived experiences, then we have the potential to change hearts and minds at the policy level as well. First we have to clean our own house, though.

Another important question for childhood studies is what kind of institutional relationships we want with other disciplines and practices. Is integrating childhood across the social sciences curriculum just a matter of "add children and stir," or can it be inclusive? For women's studies, a focus on social justice—although it may have alienated them within the academy—has ultimately made policymakers sit up and take notice of women, girls, and broader gender issues, even if these issues are sometimes coopted by fundamentally exploitative neoliberal projects (Wilson 2015). A similar rooting of childhood studies in a more critical (Alanen 2011), activist social justice stance (which I separate from a children's rights stance that all too often reinstates a protectionism that alienates and excludes children) may help impact social policy. Decolonized research can provide an evidence base for more effective and inclusive interventions. However, we are severely constrained by neoliberalizing changes and the persistence of patriarchy in the academy. Although the #MeToo movement is challenging some of this more broadly by calling out daily misogynist practices,[15] we need to continue to reach across silos of research, policy, and practice and collaborate in order to address patriarchy and prejudice—but if we are to be successful, we also need policymakers and practitioners to meet scholarship halfway.

In conclusion, a decolonizing approach to childhood studies may help to reduce the childism that pervades scholarship as well as policy and practice, hopefully liberating those spaces for an acknowledgment of epistemic diversity. But to truly achieve epistemic justice, we have to keep encouraging critical reflection among academic and non-academic partners alike to create spaces for meaningful engagement of children in resolving the issues that affect them. Achieving that sometimes requires yielding our authority as adults and acknowledging children's expertise when it comes to childhood.

Notes

1 "For cultural studies (in addition to many other theoretical projects), the intervention of feminism was specific and decisive. It was ruptural ... As a thief in the night, it broke in, interrupted, made an unseemly noise, seized the time, crapped on the table of cultural studies" Hall (1992). "Cultural Studies and Its Theoretical Legacies," in L. Grossberg and C. Nelson (eds) *Cultural Studies*, New York and London: Routledge.

2 See also https://tcf.org/content/commentary/student-evaluations-skewed-women-minority-professors/

3 http://www.vsnu.nl/en_GB/f_c_ontwikkeling_aandeel_vrouwen.html

4 https://www.erasmusmagazine.nl/en/2015/11/19/deja-vu-nog-steeds-weinig-vrouwelijke-profs/

5 Personal communications with numerous colleagues, 2016–17.

6 This is something women are often societally conditioned to do, even within academia.

7 See also https://www.gopetition.com/petitions/seoul-declaration-to-advance-gendered-research-innovation-and-socio-economic-development-in-the-asia-pacific.html

8 ADOC was dissolved at the end of 2016 in the face of waning support from said adoption agencies, partially because of a decrease in intercountry adoptions.

9 Read my full rebuttal online: https://www.opendemocracy.net/beyondslavery/kristen-e-cheney/netherlands-proposed-ban-on-foreign-adoption-and-abuses-of-scientific

10 The blog, in Dutch, is available online: http://opvoeding-wetenschap.nl/2016/11/03/is-kind-buitenland-halen-nog-tijd/

11 https://www.opendemocracy.net/beyondslavery/kristen-e-cheney/netherlands-proposed-ban-on-foreign-adoption-and-abuses-of-scientific

12 http://www.younglives.org.uk/content/about-us

13 Core funding for the Young Lives project was provided by the Department for International Development (DFID) for the duration of the project from 2001 to 2017 but received supplemental funding from many other organizations throughout the project (http://www.younglives.org.uk/node/7494).

14 Cf. https://theconversation.com/africa/search?utf8=%E2%9C%93&q=decolonisation+curriculum

15 https://www.chronicle.com/forums/index.php?topic=252981.0

CHAPTER SEVEN

Children's Geographies and the "New Wave" of Childhood Studies

Peter Kraftl and John Horton

Introduction

This chapter offers a critical engagement with what has been termed a "new wave" of childhood studies (Ryan 2012). It proceeds in three parts. First, it outlines some central tenets of the "new wave": an eclectic, wide-ranging, perhaps "infra-paradigmatic" (Oswell 2013) set of approaches that has gained increasing traction in recent studies of childhood and youth—in geography, sociology, anthropology, education studies, youth studies, and beyond. Challenges of these tenets—typically derived from actor network theories, feminist new materialisms, and nonrepresentational theories—for subdisciplinary work in children's geographies are highlighted. Although wary of the disciplinary politics inherent in naming/claiming/shaming new "paradigms," and cognizant that these approaches are, although expanding rapidly, currently taking hold patchily rather than across childhood studies scholarship, we argue that the "new wave" offers some exciting beginning points for novel, interdisciplinary work on childhoods in diverse global contexts. Secondly, we highlight and develop a key critique of "new wave" scholarship in terms of the latter's persistent claim to overcome a division between the biological and the social that has for many commentators been a central tension within childhood studies. We raise fundamental questions for "new wave" debates: about the patchiness of inter-disciplinary dialogue;

about the centrality of biosocial dualism; and, about the positioning of *children and childhood*—and therefore how childhood studies constitutes "the child" as an object of inquiry—in theoretical positions that seek to transcend the very notion of the individuated (human) subject. Thirdly, we outline a suite of ways in which childhood studies scholars—and others— might engage critically and constructively with a "new wave" of childhood studies, via the key theme of *construction* and the example of a large-scale school building program in the UK. We thus propound theorizations of childhood that could offer a powerful set of approaches for animating research in relation to both longer-standing and hitherto-unexplored aspects of children's lives. Writing from our position as children's geographers, we weave arguments about space, place, scale, and spatiality throughout the chapter, beginning with a brief introduction to the subdiscipline in the next section.

Four demands: Contextualizing the "new wave" of childhood studies and children's geographies

For the past couple of decades, the subdiscipline of children's geographies has become well established, gaining influence within and beyond human geography (Ansell 2009; Jeffrey 2012; Holloway 2014; Kraftl et al. 2014). Children's geographers have developed wide-ranging contributions to scholarship on (for instance) social (Hopkins 2010), cultural (Horton 2015b), political (Kallio and Häkli 2013; Skelton 2013), economic (Hall 2015; Pimlott-Wilson 2015; Horton 2016), urban (Skelton and Gough 2013), and development (Ansell 2005; Evans 2011) geographies. These contributions have typically shared a number of underpinning commitments: to uncover children's voices and agency, particularly in terms of place-based concerns such as their mobilities or interactions with others in public spaces; to value the critical, political, and conceptual potentialities of their agency; to foster their participation in civic life; to critically attend to the *spatial* constructs (such as institutions and discourses about public space) which constitute children's lives (Holloway and Valentine 2000); and, to critically interrogate the different spatial scales through which children's lives are articulated— and, especially, how aspects of children's local experiences intersect with and produce wider-scaled policies and forms of political action (Jeffrey 2012). As such, the subdiscipline of children's geographies can be understood as part of—or, certainly, sharing connective, infrastructural influences with—a wider contemporary, interdisciplinary context often labeled the "New Social Studies of Childhood" (NSSC) (James and Prout 1997). While children's geographies and the NSSC have not always felt seamlessly interconnected (Tisdall and Punch 2012), their shared underpinnings surely mean that future work in children's geographies should attend closely to debates within NSSC, and vice versa.

The present "new wave" within interdisciplinary childhood studies (Ryan 2012) constitutes one of the most profound critical examinations of the founding principles of NSSC. We therefore argue that it is important that children's geographers and, indeed, all childhood studies scholars, should engage carefully and constructively with the critical demands emerging from this "new" interdisciplinary "wave." This "new wave" in fact represents a diverse body of scholarship, spread across several disciplines (but especially human geography, sociology, and education studies). This scholarship has emerged from, and in direct response to, some of the major, founding premises of childhood studies, which have centered upon the importance of social-constructivist analyses of childhood and the potentialities of children's voice, agency, and political participation (see Kraftl 2013a, for a more detailed critique of these premises). As we outline below, this "new wave" challenges some of the foundational principles of at least mainstream childhood studies scholarship, in terms of a series of key demands. In many ways, however—and this observation sits behind our ultimate hesitancy in using this term—although conceptually radical in some senses, this "new wave" also continues lines of inquiry that have been evident in elements of childhood studies scholarship. For instance, there are resonances with fairly early work the construction of children's bodies in legal and medical discourses (James and Prout 1997) and with ongoing strands of research on youth subcultures and children's popular cultures that emphasized how particular material or consumer objects acquired symbolic meaning in the articulation of youthful identities (Horton 2010). Yet, to differing degrees, "new wave" theorizations of childhood offer more radical conceptualizations of the child, which seek to depart from, if not (in their most extreme guises), dispense with the very idea that the child—as an individuated human subject—should be the primary object of analysis for childhood studies. For this reason, we develop an argument around the idea of both *decentering and recentering children* in the field of childhood studies. For some scholars, as we argue in the subsequent section of the chapter, this may not appear that radical a claim (Ryan 2012); for others, it may appear to run against the very idea of doing childhood studies and the wider political project of which that academic scholarship is a part. However, it is our contention that, in all its diversity, "new wave" scholarship offers a series of prompts, critiques, and jumping-off points that can complement and extend the theoretical, methodological, and ethical premises of childhood studies.

With the above context in mind, in this section, we outline some key demands from this emerging "new wave," with two caveats: that not all of the authors we cite necessarily badge themselves as "new wave" thinkers, nor is there any widespread agreement that there has been any "new wave" at all (although it remains a useful shorthand for this chapter); and that, given burgeoning work in this area, our review cannot be exhaustive.

A first key premise for "new wave" writers is that childhood is not merely a human *social* construction. As Prout (2005) argues, childhood experiences are comprised as much from nonhuman materialities—toys, stones, pets, drugs, food, desks, mobile telephones—as they are human social interaction (Kraftl 2006; Blaise 2013). Thus the "new wave" demands acknowledgment that social relations are always-already stitched together by nonhuman technologies, artifacts, and "natures"—from the stones children carry in their pockets (Rautio 2013), to popular cultural stuff (Horton 2010), to materialized manifestations of poverty and inequality (Katz 2004; Hall 2015), to the oft-present abject substances of dirt, excrement, and litter (Horton and Kraftl 2018), to nonhuman copresences ranging from the bacterial to the megafaunal (Taylor 2013; Taylor and Pacini-Ketchabaw 2015). This is not to downplay "the social" but to demand that childhoods should be conceived as "more-than-social" (Kraftl 2013a), and complexly co-constituted.

Second, as a result, "new wave" theorists have questioned the notion of "the child" as a sovereign, individuated agent, focusing analytically upon nonhuman *materialities* and the *body* (Blazek 2015; Hackett et al. 2015; Kelly and Kamp 2015; Esser et al. 2016). Their work draws influence from Deleuze, Latour, and diverse feminist new materialist scholars such as Grosz, Barad, Haraway, and Bennett (Taylor et al. 2012, 2013; Lester and Russell 2014). Their demand is to recognize that childhood is not only relational in the sense of intra-/inter-generational relationships between individuated "children" and "adults," but in the sense that human bodies (and subjects) are constantly being de/composed through energies, technologies, prostheses, and emotions that flow through them (Morales and Christensen 2014). In this vein, scholarship on (children's) play has been instrumental in highlighting the ethical demands of "new wave" thinking: for example, from assessing what else *matters to children* beyond traditional, representational concerns (Horton 2010; Woodyer 2012), to emphasizing "adult response-ability to pay attention to equitable distribution of resources that might create the conditions in which playfulness can thrive" (Lester and Russell 2014: 253).

Third, much "new wave" thinking is constitutively linked to an apparent "spatial turn" within interdisciplinary childhood studies: an emergent demand to understand spaces as dynamic, politicized and co-constructed via the embodiment, emotions/affects, and agencies of multiform co-present actants (Hackett et al. 2015). This apprehension of spatiality may seem somewhat commonsensical to many children's geographers, and here we offer a (gentle) critique of some aspects of scholarship in the wider childhood studies *oeuvre* that have engaged patchily and sometimes superficially with fairly long-standing theorizations of space, place, and spatiality in children's geographies. Indeed, this spatial turn shares a good deal of terminology and conceptual intent with well-developed, particularly nonrepresentational, approaches to childhood, developed by geographers

(Thrift 2000; Lorimer 2005). Within children's geographies, this premise was taken up through an emphasis *not only* on nonhuman materialities and the body, or straightforward acknowledgments of how "place matters," but through spatialized theories of everydayness, temporality, and affect (e.g., Harker 2005; Horton and Kraftl 2006a). For instance, children's geographers' work on memory sought to bypass debates about children as either "becomings" (future adults) or "beings" (rights-bearing individuals in-the-present) in several senses: by developing Deleuzian notions of becoming (Worth 2009); by examining how we might "access" childhood memories through ineffable, contingent reveries (Philo 2003); through nonlinear conceptualizations of the "ongoingness" of life-itself (Horton and Kraftl 2006b). Relatedly, geographical theories of affect were mobilized in understanding force-full dynamics through which children's lives and spaces may be choreographed (Youdell and Armstrong 2011) or the atmospheres that may be generated in educational spaces in order to promote particular behaviors (Kraftl 2006). However, although geographical work is often not necessarily substantially engaged in articulations of the "new wave" (a point to which we return below), we suggest that the "new wave's" spatial turn could mark an opportunity for productive interdisciplinary rapprochement: a demand to think together, and anew, about the ways in which spatialities matter for children's lives.

Fourth, among wider retheorizations of children's political lives (e.g., Kallio and Häkli 2013; Skelton 2013) the "new wave" has increasingly constituted a demand to explore how children's bodies are key loci for *biopolitical* intervention (Lee 2013; Youdell 2016). Resonant with work elsewhere, there has been particular attentiveness to how the "molecular gaze" (Rose 2007: 11) of the biological- and neuro-sciences might enable the governance of, particularly, *young* citizens. Children have been a focus for such interventions since the emergence of the psychological sciences in the nineteenth century (Gagen 2004; Wells 2011; Philo 2016). Thus, geographers and others have attended to how technologies and scientific knowledges have become imposed upon children in the exercise of biopower. These technologies range from "Mosquito™" devices, which emit a high-pitched whine only audible to young people aged under 25, and which have been used to disperse them from particular public spaces (Lee and Motzkau 2011), to neuroscientific advances that are increasingly shaping school curricula (Gagen 2015; Pykett 2015). Critically—for some scholars—"many present and emergent bio-political formations of childhood consist of novel and unpredictable connections among materials and processes, forces and events that are not best understood through bio-social dualism" (Lee and Motzkau 2011: 8). This philosophical-political questioning of *biosocial dualism* has been at the heart of emerging debates about the "new wave" of childhood studies (Ryan 2012). The underlying logic here is the claim that, since the advent of the NSSC, there has been a schism between "scientific" approaches to childhood (biosciences and developmental psychology) and "social-scientific" approaches (rooted in social constructivism). We return to this debate in the next section of the chapter, simply noting here that recent biopolitical scholarship has sought to transcend this dualism.

Emerging critiques of the "new wave"

While we call for geographers to engage with the "new wave's" demands, we also advocate careful consideration of nascent critiques of "new wave" thinking. We do not wholeheartedly endorse the idea of "a" "new wave" of childhood studies, nor agree that it has (yet) taken hold as anything more than an "infra-paradigm" within wider childhood scholarship (Oswell 2013): indeed, we signal some key critiques of—for instance—nonrepresentational children's geographies, which charge such work with an interest in banality at the expense of more enduring politics, exclusions and/or wider-scaled challenges facing children (e.g., Ansell 2009; Mitchell and Elwood 2012). We recognize the importance of these critiques, not least in spurring scholars to remain vigilant about wider implications of nonrepresentational work for addressing (for instance) children's place within structural politics of marginalization, inequality, and exclusion. However, this section reflects on a perhaps more fundamental appraisal of the very promise of "new-ness" presented in "new wave" scholarship, which, read in tandem with the previous section and the empirical analyses that follow, might offer further points of reflection for childhood studies scholars (whether they subscribe to the "new wave" or not). In two provocative papers, Ryan (2012, 2014) argues that:

> United by a core objective—to escape the constraints of bio-social dualism—the new wave of childhood studies instates a division between the strictures of past childhoods and an imagined future where boundaries are blurred. (Ryan 2012: 443)

Ryan argues, however, that the very premise of a biosocial dualism is false. He accepts that in childhood studies, there exists a persistent "wall of silence" between sociological and natural-scientific approaches, manifest as an absence of interdisciplinary research (Thorne 2007: 150). However, Ryan argues that modern Western childhood itself has never been split into these two realms. Focusing on Rousseau and other early childhood specialists, he witnesses instead a zig-zagging between the biological and the social through a series of frictions: through conceptions of "human nature" that view the child as a malleable "lump"; and through the tutor's shaping of an individual child toward the latter's ultimate self-mastery, albeit a shaping that works with the laws of nature. Ryan takes these historical precedents as evidence that childhood is, and always has been, a "biosocial" phenomenon (although Philo 2016 complicates this picture still further). Therefore, it follows that the critique of biosocial dualism is a straw one, with attempts to move "beyond" it confounded by long-established precedents.

Ryan's critique should encourage childhood scholars to carefully refine the ontological bases of a "new" wave of childhood theorizing. However, Ryan's assessments, and those of others cited above (e.g., Mitchell and Elwood 2012) themselves require some careful further scrutiny, since rather than foreclosing the debate, they might—in conversation with some of the wider literatures reviewed above—actually offer some productive ways to more carefully theorize childhoods. Here, we highlight four considerations that are not only pertinent to any "new wave" of childhood studies but to our ongoing attempts to critically reflect upon the field and the idea of "the child" as its focus of inquiry (especially given the ongoing influence of NSSC within large parts of the field).

First, and problematically, Ryan's conceptualization of the "biosocial" is resolutely human centered. It reinforces a Modernist, (neo)liberal conception of the Self as a sovereign agent. The realms of the "biological" and the "social" that are, apparently, counterposed in later work are confined to *human* nature and sociability. It is here that Ryan appears to rather misrepresent some "new wave" theorizations of childhood. This is because they do not only seek to move beyond the idea of the liberal subject; rather, they do not start with the human subject *at all*. They start instead with a conception of *life-itself*: of forces, movements and flows that may, if only temporarily, cohere as identifiable "subjects" or "objects" (e.g., Bennett 2010). This alternative ontology invites a sense of ever-changing constellations of vital stuff, in which, to make sense of it all, some (privileged) humans have the power to name certain bodies—as "schoolchildren" or "mobile phones" (Prout 2005).

Secondly, Ryan's emphasis upon Rousseauian models of development privileges a move "from" nature (the bio) to freedom (as a socialized being). If only implicitly, this view of the biosocial privileges the latter part of the dualism even as it seeks to efface it: it renders visible a move from nature *to* culture and, thereby, reinforces a second tenet of Modernist, liberal thought: human mastery over nature. Again, "new wave" scholars are not only critical of such a positioning of humankind, but begin from a different place. Politically, and philosophically, they position humans on a horizontal plane with other matter—the stuff we use, the stuff that stitches together society, and the very stuff of which we are composed. Ryan's conception of the biosocial—in its originary form—is rather overly determined by the dangerous promise of human mastery.

Thirdly, and moving away from Ryan's specific arguments, it is for the above reasons that, *if* the "new wave" is to gather momentum, the debate should probably move away from notions of biosocial dualism. The term has served both to confuse the issue and focus attention away from the more radical promises of especially new-materialist conceptions of childhood. It is here that the problematic lack of dialogue with wider fields of scholarship that resonate philosophically with "new wave" thinking is most evident. For instance, and to repeat a point made above, there appears to be little collaborative engagement with cognate "nonrepresentational" approaches developed in children's geographies. This is somewhat surprising, given ongoing claims around the "spatial turn" that we noted earlier. If, as we have already insisted, nonrepresentational (and other forms of) thinking do not start with dualisms *at all*, then we must initiate a shift in language that recognizes and names the more-than-dualistic potentialities of the "new wave"—perhaps through notions of "more-than-social" childhoods, which are attracting increasing attention (Kraftl 2013a). Thus, if any "new wave" of childhood studies is to live up to its promise, it must involve a wider array of extant theoretical work on childhoods than that which explicitly seeks to move beyond the "biosocial" dualism. Most tellingly, a more generous conception of a "new wave" would expand our conceptions of the *multiple* forms of relationality that compose children's lives (Hopkins and Pain 2007; Tisdall and Punch 2012; Christou and Spyrou 2016).

Finally, in reflecting upon "new wave" scholarship—and upon childhood studies more widely—we ask, once again, what is so *different* about childhood? Does it matter—within the internal logics of new materialisms— that children are *not* adults, *not* women, and rather, just human bodies that are intra-actively constituted as "smaller"? Does a focus upon children tell us anything different in terms of how we theorize new materialisms (and vice versa)? Even if children *are* singled out for particular kinds of bio-political intervention, how are these qualitatively different from those targeted at adults—and can "new wave" approaches help us to explain these differences, *without* careful recourse to cutting-edge bioscientific research? These questions demand considerable further thought—whether in constituting a "new wave" of childhood studies, whether in terms of interdisciplinary childhood studies scholarship, or whether in making the case for how childhood studies might influence wider debates still. Although we raise these questions to stimulate wider debate, we begin to broach these questions in the remainder of the chapter.

Reimagining (new waves of) childhood studies: The example of construction processes

In the final part of the chapter, we offer some initial responses to the above questions by outlining just one (of many) potential areas of scholarship that could be particularly productive for childhood studies scholars. This broad theme is not intended to be proscriptive, but offers a sense of how more-than-social studies of childhood might articulate with pressing global agendas in ways that—arguably—childhood studies scholarship has not done hitherto, especially in some areas of "new wave" research. It also offers—as a provocation for future debate—a sense of how both *decentering and recentering children* from our analyses might enable "new-wave-inspired" childhood studies scholars to *extend*, rather than evade, questions of politics and power (compare Mitchell and Elwood 2012). We cannot hope to fully answer the questions set out above, but hope that these questions—and our focus on construction below—prompt further reflections in reimagining scholarship in childhood studies, and in (re)considering how the child is constituted as the primary object of inquiry within the field.

Construction projects—from resource extraction to road, building and engineering construction—are responsible for approximately 50 percent of anthropogenically produced CO_2, massive-scale alteration of physical landscapes, and the pervasive presence of pollutants in ecological, geological, and hydrological bodies. Meanwhile, as scholars have long recognized, the social construction of childhood equates strongly to the institutionalization of childhood, which, in turn, is thoroughly materialized in institutional buildings—especially schools (Kraftl 2006). Moreover, by bringing these two strands of concern together, we know that many *children* are both relatively continuously exposed and *particularly* sensitive to a wide range of environmental toxins, pollutants, and nanomaterials, as well as to forms of exploitation, as a result of living or working in or near buildings and roads—not only during their construction but in the years afterwards (Tulve et al. 2015). Yet, within childhood studies, other than a few exceptions, there is scant research on children's engagements with (literal/material rather than "social") "construction," and that which does exist focuses on their *inhabitation* of individual buildings and *participation* in design (e.g., Thornham and Myers 2012; Kraftl et al. 2013; Parnell and Patsarika 2016). Thus, cognizant of huge historical, social, and geographical variations, we argue that childhood studies scholars could engage both more intensively and extensively with children's *broadly conceived* relationship with many aspects of construction.

At this point, as a step toward illuminating what we mean by "decentering and recentering children" from childhood studies scholarship, we introduce an example from our own research that invoked nonrepresentational, *geographical* theories to highlight the entangled spatial *scales* through which childhoods are literally and metaphorically constructed. We provide an overview of already-published articles about this research (e.g., Kraftl 2012; den Besten et al. 2008, 2011), and would direct readers to those articles in order to view detailed empirical evidence and literatures that we cannot include here for reasons of space. Between 2006 and 2008, the authors led an interdisciplinary research project that sought to explore children's participation in school design in the UK. Although superficially a fairly "traditional" topic for childhood studies (participation), the project needed to grapple with the multiple geographical *scales* through which school design was being imagined and constituted during the period in question.

To an extent, this required both a decentering and a recentering of children and young people in our analysis.

The project took place in the context of a series of nationwide, state-initiated programs of school building in the UK that ran during the period 2003–10. One key program, the *Building Schools for the Future* project, planned by the New Labour Government, foresaw the redesign or total reconstruction of each of England's 3,500 secondary schools (which provide for young people aged 11–18). Government policy saw the success of the scheme as resting upon the successful integration of a series of hugely complex institutional, financial, material, and cultural processes at several overlapping scales (see Kraftl 2012, for a detailed analysis). At the national scale, New Labour imagined "waves" of change that would completely revolutionize school buildings and leave a "legacy" for decades to come, in a program of school building that they claimed was the largest since the Victorian era. At the city scale, they wanted school buildings to become key nodes that—because of their design, their very newness, and the inclusion of complex public–private finance partnerships that would involve local state and business stakeholders—would spark social and economic regeneration in (especially) deprived local communities. At the scale of the school, they argued that school buildings should have multiple technological and affective effects—from the "inspiration" that would infect pupils upon seeing the new atrium for their school (national design guidance emphasized inspiring, flagship atrium spaces) to the "new"-style, technologically enhanced learning spaces and pedagogies that new buildings would enable. And, at the micro-scale, the Government emphasized the importance of "getting the details right, this time"—of ensuring that a bewildering array of design codes, health, and safety regulations and building technologies were successfully integrated into new school buildings. Significantly, New Labour claimed that it was *only* through the successful enmeshing of these differently scaled social, technological, affective, organizational and economic processes that *Building Schools for the Future* would be a success at a national (and even international) level. At the same time they also tied these multiply scaled processes to a (re)imagining of the twenty-first century, neoliberal school child, who would be technologically literate, a flexible, responsiblized learner, and able to compete on the global stage once an adult.

As geographers, we proceeded from the position that in order to more fully understand the opportunities and challenges facing children's participation in the design of any individual school, our methodology—and, especially, modes of analyzing and theorizing—had somehow to bear witness to the multiply scaled processes that we have summarized above. To do so would also enable us to initiate analyses not only of participatory processes in any given school, but to write a suite of papers that reflected on the wider politics, materialities, and affectivities of school building processes (and policymaking for children and education) in which they were inextricably entangled (again, see den Besten et al. 2011; Kraftl 2012). Therefore, combining an

Actor-Network sensibility (see Prout 2005) with critical discourse analysis, our research involved a close reading of government policy documents, national design guidance documents, and a detailed, laborious process of collating (literally) thousands of design codes, building regulations, and health and safety advice that were, in different constellations, constitutive of both individual school buildings and *every* school building in England at the time. We also interviewed professional stakeholders involved in the design, construction, financing, and management of new school redesign projects—from teachers to internationally renowned architects—and gained access to design materials and briefs for each school. Finally, we attended meetings, lessons, and "design days" in schools, using ethnographic observation and interviewing to engage directly with children and—ultimately—to "zoom in" on what *actual* kinds of participation were happening, how these were constituted through material engagements (such as model building), and what diverse groups of children, in diverse schools thought and felt about these.

On reflection, and in the context of this chapter, it strikes us that our project was, simultaneously, both *about* children (and childhood), and more besides. We are not claiming to have struck upon a model for a reimagined childhood studies wherein new materialist modes of theorizing remain attentive to more "traditional" concerns (like participation and social difference), and nor would we want to institute some kind of a break between "older" and "new wave" approaches, as we indicated above. Indeed, elsewhere, we and others have experimented with very different ways of attuning to intersections of materiality, affect, and social difference (Kraftl 2014; Lobo 2016; Pacini-Ketchabaw and Clark 2016; Horton and Kraftl 2018). However, we would make three observations at this juncture.

First, that this project—in attending to the complexly intersecting geographical scales of *Building Schools for the Future*—offers a snapshot of the importance of spatial thinking in and for childhood studies. As we noted earlier, the "spatial turn" in childhood studies has in some cases given rise to some fairly superficial studies that simply emphasize the local context of a given study, or make cursory remarks about the importance of "place." Yet what we are attempting to demonstrate in this example is the value that a geographical approach—in this case to a nuanced understanding of intersecting and recursively produced spatial scales—can bring to our analyses of nationally important phenomena like school building programs, which, as we argue further below, warrant pressing critical attention from childhood studies scholars.

Secondly, this project—like others we cite above—exemplifies the value of a more-than-social approach that is less tethered to the strictures of debates about biosocial dualism. As we have already noted, our analyses needed to witness the entanglements of materialities (pipes, wires, cables, chairs, toilets), affects ("inspiring" atria), regulations (the intimidating and astonishing array of legislation and risk mitigation pertaining to even small aspects of classroom design), complex local politics, and finances (the organizational machinations of public-private partnerships), the ambitions of policymaking, and bodies (the "actual" participation being done in schools). We argue that it was only through analyzing these manifold, more-than-social processes that we were able to undertake better-informed analyses of the positioning of both individual children in participatory processes and more widely of the figure of "the child" in early-twenty-first century neoliberal discourses in the UK.

Thirdly, then, during the project we had often to *decenter*—to divert—our analyses away from children. We spent many hours perusing and cataloguing the intricacies of English building regulations, assessing how they were combined to constitute the socio-affective-technical achievement of a "*Building Schools for the Future* School." We also analyzed many policy documents and pieces of design guidance that—although often about schools and/or education—actually (somewhat ironically) sometimes made little mention of actual, living children. However, as is evident from the above, these concerns were not separate from but (re)integrated with fairly traditional ethnographic techniques used to garner a sense of children's emotions, voices, and practical participation in school design. Thus, as Kraftl (2013a) argues, going "beyond" notions of voice or politics does not necessarily mean evading those concerns, nor even the introduction of radical, new research methodologies. Rather, such a move is—at least in part—a question of approach: of shifting viewpoints and, as we have intimated, of (at times) decentering children in order to *recenter* them in analyses that could, as a result, be all the more powerful. We would argue that a geographical lens is—in conjunction with other disciplinary approaches—vital to such an endeavor.

However, we would also argue that a move to decenter and recenter children and childhoods in our analyses could be more thoroughgoing still. At this juncture, we sketch some very brief suggestions for the kinds of topics and approaches that such work might demand. To begin with, childhood studies scholars might look beyond national school building programs to critically evaluate the circulation and entanglement of architectural technologies, (geo)political aspirations, and state/charity finance in the constitution of school building projects in contexts in the Majority Global South. For instance, the *Safe Schools Global Programme* aims to address how "worldwide, 875 million school children live in high seismic risk zones and hundreds of millions more face regular floods, landslides, extreme winds and fire hazards. Children spend up to 50 percent of their waking hours in school facilities, yet all too often schools are not constructed or maintained to be disaster resilient meaning children can't access a safe education" (https://plan-international.org/publications/safe-schools-programme#). Following innovative approaches of geographers such as Jane Jacobs (2006), childhood studies scholars might examine: how particular school-building technologies circulate around the globe and interface within local contexts;

the (potentially neocolonial) power relations inherent in "global" programs such as this; *and*, the assumptions that they make about children in any given context.

Beyond school buildings, we would also urge childhood studies scholars to critically analyze children's entanglements with construction in much broader senses still. There could be several fruitful lines of enquiry, whose specific focus will vary with geographical, social, and historical contexts. First, a focus on building work, such as the presence of children (whether formal or informal, and from visioning/design to physical labor) on building sites, road-building projects, and infrastructure development. Second, an exploration of the lives of children affected by the extractive industries, in particular the mining of construction materials—from their own work in such sectors, to the health and other effects of living nearby, to the support they provide for family members or communities engaged in such work. Thirdly, an emphasis upon children's work (in the broadest sense) outside the formal construction and mining sectors: in factories, in shops, and on the street, from the production of domestic ceramics to the manufacture of building technologies; and domestic "work," from decorating to maintenance and house-keeping. These lines of inquiry are particularly pressing in countries in the Majority Global South where children are more consistently (although again not necessarily universally) involved in such work, but also hint at the need for historical perspectives—for instance from historians and (the few) archaeologists of childhood—in unpicking the complexities of children's entanglements with construction.

Inevitably, these lines of inquiry do not obviate the need to focus on the staple concerns of children's geographers and others—immediately they bring to mind questions of children's (labor) rights and the gendering of work (Katz 2004). Critically, though, by carefully adopting (aspects of) the lens of "new wave" childhood studies, this work might achieve two things. On the one hand, it might enable academics and policymakers to attend to the manifold entanglements of human and nonhuman, at different spatial and temporal scales, gaining a much wider and much deeper perspective on what it means for *children* to be involved in construction work—in terms of their health, education, well-being, family lives, and economic status. For instance, in collaboration with environmental scientists, childhood studies scholars might examine the circulation of construction-related pollutants and nanomaterials through children's bodies and beyond. They might also compare the exposure of contemporary children to such materials with those of previous generations (using oral histories and, even, osteo-archaeological evidence to assess the exposure of earlier generations of children). We would then be better able to pose questions about, and to trace, the co-constitution and dis/entanglement of materialities and children's bodies, as well as their effects *on* children's bodies. Indeed, we might then think through how differently gendered, -aged, -raced, -classed, or –geographically positioned children's bodies are differentially imbricated within such processes, rather than assume that such effects will be universal. All the while, although each of these approaches might in varying degrees and styles require a *decentering* of children, they also require a resolute commitment to *retaining* or *recentering* a focus on children and (more-than-)social, multiply scaled constructions of childhood.

Conclusion

We have argued that the so-called "new wave" of childhood studies has led to, and has laid the ground for, some exciting, productive, diverse interdisciplinary scholarship, to which geographers—and theories of spatiality—have made important contributions. However, we have also expressed doubts—both about the naming of this "new wave," about its extensiveness and uptake beyond particular (although rapidly expanding) groups of scholars, and about its very newness. These center upon the articulation of a biosocial dualism, which much "new wave" scholarship purports to transcend, through a range of feminist, new materialist approaches. Our initial argument was that the figure of the "biosocial" has been a problematic one, and that—if it is to gain traction—"new wave" scholarship must dispense with this figure altogether.

The rest of the chapter centered upon some of the multiple possibilities for critically and constructively extending a "new wave" of childhood studies. We sought to imagine what might be the main accomplishments of any "new wave" and suggested that, notwithstanding their exciting potentialities, the current frames for debate in such a "new wave" could be both more reflexive and more ambitious, especially in terms of interdisciplinary engagements with work in children's geographies. Through a focus on the substantive theme of "construction," we have argued for both a *decentering and a recentering of children as the predominant objects of inquiry for the field of childhood studies*, which is cognizant of the more-than-social and multiply scaled entanglements of children and construction—and more besides. As we have argued, to do so is not quite the same as to emphasize the potentially universalizing and flattening relationalities of some brands of new materialism, but to be prepared, at times, to set our analyses *free* of a concern with childhood (and children) for us to *return* in a way that may be all the more powerful. We also argued that construction might be one key arena in which children are engaged, in diverse ways around the globe, but where their dis/entanglements therein have not yet been studied as systematically as they could be. Finally, and consequently, we have stressed that any attempt to engage the "new wave" must, at least at times, articulate pressing concerns—which are increasingly, and not uncontroversially, being couched as "global challenges" by large-scale inter/national research funding bodies, and elsewhere as "development goals"—in which *children's* health, well-being, and future prospects are often placed centrally.

Thus, we finish by asking what might be the new-wave *politics* of childhood. Work on the micro- and bio-politics of childhood—not least in terms of their complex, multi-scalar geographies—has begun to provide a powerful challenge to the centrality of "voice" and "participation" in childhood studies (Jeffrey 2012; Kallio and Häkli 2013). Yet a key question that arises from an unpacking of the individuated subject *is* a political one: to what extent can new-materialist (or "new wave," if we want to retain the term) approaches respond to and challenge neoliberalism's dogged commitment to individualization, "choice," and responsibilization in ways that extend beyond the ephemeral and the micropolitical? Thus, a key task for reimagining childhood studies remains one of examining—in the context of childhood experiences specifically, but of social difference, inequality and immiseration more widely—whether a "new wave" of childhood studies can offer a politics of and beyond childhood that is any more compelling or socially just.

PART THREE

Decentering the Agentic Subject of Childhood Studies

CHAPTER EIGHT

Panaceas of Play:

Stepping Past the Creative Child

Daniel Thomas Cook

Uncritical and univocal notions of play threaten the philosophical-epistemological scaffolding of childhood studies as a perspective and as a field. Many contemporary scholars, pedagogues, pundits, and activists locate in play that which they see as lacking in or menacing to children and their childhoods. From a nature deficit disorder (Louv 2005) to the commercial incursions into imaginative play (Elkind 2007; Linn 2006) to the loss of free time thought historically available to children (Chudacoff 2007), a strong strain of public and scholarly discourse finds children's play of the Global North in a state of decay. Foremost here resides a sense that play represents an original condition, perhaps a primordial urge, of human creativity now funneled into stifling, institutionalized, and commercial modes of expression. Just as play is presumed natural and naturally incorrupt, so too are children when engaging in it without instruction or without adult intervention. Play here stands as something in need of rescue from debilitating forces and conditions and, importantly, from adult imposition. To recover play allows the recovery of some true child, long sought after since the expulsion from the Garden.

Early versions of this chapter were presented at the Program and Children and Youth Studies seminar, University of Stockholm, Sweden, October 2015 and at the "Conceptualizing Childhood and Youth" conference, Brock University, St. Catharines, Ontario, Canada, October 2017.

Deep strains of thought and practice embrace such indiscriminating, redemptive narratives of children's play and, in doing so, (re)assign an essentialness to the child and to childhood. In many ways, theorizing the nature of play has become both a rather suitable substitute for theorizing the nature of the child and, as well, an acceptable vehicle toward that end. When conceptions of play (re)essentialize the child, the definitive problematic of childhood studies becomes compromised, weakened. That is, the "problem of the child"—of interrogating received notions about the nature, contours, and extensions of childhood—dissipates and dissolves in the confluence of the nature, reach and, particularly, the benefits of particular conceptions of play.

Global North's panics about the erosion or loss of children's play in recent decades (and longer) have been answered on the rhetorical level with an erosion of another kind—i.e., the erosion of the ambiguity of play itself. Key thinkers from Freud (1960) and Vygotsky (1978) to Huizinga (1950) and Erikson (1950) to Bateson (1972) and Sutton-Smith (1997) affirm the inescapability of encountering different orders of ambiguity when seeking to comprehend the characteristics of play and the various, often contradictory, meanings and experiences of players. As Sutton-Smith (1997: 5–7) points out, the variety of things referred to as "play"—from poetry to ritual to economic modeling and war games to sport and flirtation—itself delivers an order of fuzziness to attempts to determine whether comparable phenomena are being addressed. But, play's ambiguity reaches also beyond the multiplicity of its referents and into the dynamics of playing and playfulness. Theorists point to such phenomena as the necessity of paradoxical meaning (Bateson 1972; Vygotsky 1978), the "as if" quality conjured by inscribing a "magic circle" of ritual (Huizinga 1950) and the "hallucination" of mastery (Erikson 1950: 185) as elemental uncertainties integral to whatever play is and whatever play does. For these and other thinkers (Sicart 2014), the crux of the matter resides in the slippage of meaning, in the indeterminate framing of the play situation, in the porous boundaries between what is and what isn't play and in the negotiated, iterative identities of the players.

Within the contours of the contemporary ludic episteme, however, "play" sheds these levels and kinds of uncertainty so as to be put into the service of shouldering the epistemological burden of the "child." Instead of operating as necessary and generative ambiguity, play often and increasingly holds forth as an explanatory capability of its own. Key problematics regarding the shape and scope of children's imagination, agency, interests, powers, and abilities find hospitable analytic refuge, and a measure of emotional comfort, when transferred to the arena of play. As vehicles for learning, therapeutics, empowerment, sociability, creativity, and preparation for future occupations, ludic forms such as make-believe, schoolyard games, unstructured play, and tinkering, among others, regularly provide resolutions to pressing problems like commercialism, stifling school environments, over-scheduled lives, and media-saturated imaginations. A "flight from ambiguity," like that noted by

Donald Levine (1988) regarding social theory, characterizes current efforts to "know the child" through attenuated, essentialized, and sometimes rather clear-cut notions of the functions of play.

The case I make here argues that the contemporary inattention paid to various ambiguities of play ultimately subjects "the child" to definitional closure, thereby undermining the project of childhood studies, particularly through the figure of the "creative child." Play rhetorics (Sutton-Smith 1997) and discourses found across a variety of fields of study reveal a rather consistent tendency to assert play as a panacea to the substantive problematic of childhood and, as well, to the conceptual challenge "the child" poses—or should pose—to childhood studies scholarship and practice. Indeed, the child becomes the play in many cases, understood and approached as an efflux of rather ingrained, natural, given dynamics. Consequently, writers tend to rally around and laud the rather pleasing notion of an incessantly innovative, creative child whose liberation can be realized in and through play.

The discussion offered here suggests that perhaps the most enduring provocation facing those who pursue a childhood studies framework resides not simply in discerning which children to study or which methodological instruments to wield at them, but rather in determining the level of tolerance for epistemological uncertainty regarding central figure—the central problematic—of the field. The interrogations of play herein hopefully encourage such considerations so as to goad a re-imagination.

Spying the ludic episteme

Over the last decade or more, a number of scholars, activists, and practitioners have tended to converge around a handful of rule-of-thumb understandings regarding the nature, scope, and exigencies of play, of children's play in particular. Some writing with a popular—or, at least, non-academic—audience in mind, these works together give shape and outline to a contemporary ludic episteme by offering analyses of the history, location, purpose, texture, and possibilities of play, often with regard to US American contexts and understandings. In so doing, they posit, implicitly and explicitly, theories of children and childhood and, by extension, theories of human social ontogeny and ontology. A stout conviction about the basic constitution of the play-child dynamic binds these texts together as carriers of an abiding and consequential discourse which, following Foucault (1982), operates as a episteme—i.e., as an historically conjectured *a priori* constellation of knowledge which sets the conditions of its own possibility. For historian Howard Chudacoff (2007), children's play manifests as a vital urge in human beings. Given and natural, play stands as a nearly tangible entity, initially owned by children as an expression of their autonomy and original freedom (7), but which exists under constant threat of being confiscated, attenuated, or expunged by adults and adult culture: "In some circumstances adults used guilt and sin as means to regulate children's playful behavior; at other times they applied physical punishment or the threat of such punishment; and still at other times, they used instruction, persuasion or material inducement" (13). Pitched as a transhistorical, generational battle, the character of children's play—especially independent, informal play—arises from a subaltern position as oppositional, illicit, and unauthorized (16).

In the second half of the nineteenth century, children fought adult attempts to "domesticate" their play with toys and "acceptable" games and with efforts to contain pastimes within the parameters of pedagogical application in schools and the modern kindergarten. Drawing on a variety of historical sources, Chudacoff offers numerous examples of the ways in which children created play spaces in the interstices of the adult world—as did slave children, poor children, Native American children, and urban immigrant children. Chudacoff's children display incredible ingenuity in their constant effort to exert autonomy in the face of a ceaseless onslaught of adult maneuvers—big and small, micro and macro—to attenuate their worlds and control their actions.

The strength and resilience of this underground child culture found its match in the twentieth century with the "invasion of play culture" by social reformers like child savers and play societies and by accompanying commercial interest in "educational" toys. But, as his narrative enjoins, the battle was not over. For it was this same time period, 1900–1950, that stands as the "golden age of unstructured play." The flexibility of their play culture enabled children to claim both rural settings and urban spaces alike—fields and forests, streets, alleyways, and sidewalks—for their own inventive uses. These moments, actions, and locations, he laments, eroded with the onslaught of commercial culture after the Second World War whereby a complex combination of media, material goods, and increasing participation of mothers in the workforce diverted children from unstructured, inventive, and adult-free play. In the process, children's imaginations have been colonized: "No longer does a kid picture a fantasy world by looking at the clouds or indulge in mundane contemplation such as what one's thumb is supposed to do; instead, he or she obsesses over the life of some teen pop idol or focuses on destroying objects in a computer game" (212). Any solace for Chudacoff resides in his faith that "children's manipulation of objects for their own purposes creates true play value" (97–198), instead of the false, imposed values proffered by commercial concerns. Play here activates the agentive quality of human beings—beings who enter this world necessarily in a state of structural inequality—both because of and despite the apparently unavoidable dominance encountered whenever and wherever adults and children commingle.

Susan Linn, in *The Case for Make Believe* (2006), similarly understands play as a vital, endangered resource in children that nurtures creativity and the "capacity for meaning making" (13). Fantasy and make-believe play arise naturally in children when given the opportunity and are inextricably linked to learning, problem-solving, risk-taking, and the ability to reflect on their worlds. But "prevailing societal norms characterized by a commercially driven culture and bombardment of electronic sounds and images" threaten the survival of make-believe play to such an extent that Linn approaches the situation with the "kind of urgency that environmentalists feel about the rain forest" (13). Media characters, flashy technology, and "psychologically savvy marketing strategies" overly structure the imagination thereby stultifying children's vitality by creating dependence on external materials. What is needed, Linn inveighs, is for caring adults to enable children to engage in play "on their own" providing them the "gifts" of time, space, and silence (204).

For both Linn and Chudacoff, play evinces a thingness, something with a pre-existent, positive, life-affirming quality best realized by children in childhood. In Chudacoff's conception, play possesses childhood as much as children possess play, and this play has something of quantity, in addition to its qualities, which can be diminished and eroded by adults, adult culture, and adult institutions and practices. Unlike Chudacoff, Linn's players require the action of adults in a supportive, provisioning role to counter the corrosive aspects of popular/media culture and to give nature an opportunity to arise (Linn 2006: 219–221). At the same time, the character of play resounds in familiarity. Linn likewise locates humanness and freedom within the natural inklings of the child-in-play. It exists as extant, latent potential to be guarded, saved, cared-for, and preserved, like childhood itself (225).

In these treatments, play manifests not as a problem to be engaged or an enigma with which to grapple, but as a known entity with known attributes to be handled (or not) accordingly. Thing-like, it accords only positivity when treated according to its character. Any nastiness or negativity with play—especially for Chudacoff—is the result of the resistive position of children who are disobeying social rules and social graces to exercise voice and make themselves heard. As original and natural, play speaks of a deep, human spirit. Stuart Brown, medical doctor and founder of the National Institute for Play (US), likewise acclaims play as the "purest expression of our humanity, the true expression of individuality" (2009: 5). He considers the ludic impulse a "vital essence" and "the basis of civilization" rooted in the human (and mammalian) brain which enables people to experience a joy that is "our birthright and intrinsic to our essential design" (147). Parents, he asserts, need to recover memories of their emotional states of play from their own childhoods so they can "create a playful household" where "everything from education to chores will go better" (80). Brown does not consider that play may have harmful associations and that "recovered memories" of play can invite recollections of injury, humiliation, and fear. Indeed, situating play as an unequivocal good and as remedy—whereby any negativity resides as an outlier or externality—virtually ensures an uncritical perspective on what and who a "child" is, on the social-political constitution of childhoods, on the thrust and character of "development" as well as on the place of adults in the whole matter.

If play is part and parcel of "our" humanity, if it is a "mode of being human" as Miguel Sicart (2014: 1) offers, then logical consistency poses the conclusion that it must be functional, useful, and a positive good, at least on the margins, and thus worthy of boosterism. Thus, when Carlsson-Paige (2008) makes her case to "take back childhood," she understands it as a return to or recovery of what children "ideally" do naturally—i.e., making creative interventions on their worlds. Lawrence Cohen, in *Playful Parenting* (2001), argues that adults, having "forgotten" their own play, need to participate consciously in and produce playful spaces and interactions with their children—e.g., get on the floor, take up roles in pretend play, roughhouse with them—so they may embark upon a "long sought bridge back to that deep emotional bond between parent and child" (1). Unsurprisingly, media-originated images and stories "kill imagination" because they encourage children to "act out someone else's script instead of their own" (127). A similar habit of thought informs the prescriptions touted by Jones and Reynolds (2011) who see teachers as schoolroom "stage managers," storytellers, and players themselves. In so doing, teachers can scaffold children's efforts to realize what they are naturally—i.e., "master players who use materials imaginatively in sustained complex dramatic play" (17).

The panacea of play here derives from its imputed antecedent, original naturalness, and unabashedly positive function and so can be found discursively operative across sites of study and thinking about childhood. Children's natural propensity to create, pretend, and fantasize—particularly when imagined to be hidden and only in need of scaffolding or support to be realized —counteracts the bad play offered by media, entertainment industries, consumerism, the structure of education, and by ludically amnesic adults. Play can serve as a cure-all because it is positioned as the thing that is missing—often lost, forgotten, sublimated, or killed—and, hence, recovering play arises as tantamount to recovering the "child." The child and childhood become nearly isomorphic with the play proposed, with the solution it offers and with the solution that it is in itself. Play, in these renditions, manifests as unmitigated; its function and impact transparent.

Contradictions and conundrums: Elisions of voice, power, and agency

Enough discussion about children's play exhibits a boosterism to warrant concern. In such iterations, play reveals itself as a form of truth and as a truth-revealing dynamic. Play tells the truth in its enactment—the truth about the child, the truth about humanity. Hence, one needs only to provide the conditions to allow an underlying, latent verity to arise to the light of day. Yet, like each truth, the playful child swims in tautology and contradiction. Play manifests, at once, as both natural and constructed, as freely chosen yet requiring motivation and assistance, as powerful and empowering but diminished by external forces, as autotelic and, at the same time, teleological in purpose and reach. As noted, the ambiguity arising through such paradoxes and contradictions can fruitfully be considered as constitutive of the phenomenon of play, generally conceived (Bateson 1972; Sutton Smith 1997). The strong tendency, however, has been for writers to imagine one kind of play as all play—or, as all "good" play—and thus to imagine one kind of childhood. In selectively attending to those aspects which serve to bring into relief the kind of child and childhoods favored, many fabricate an ideology of childhood in the form of an ideology of the playful, thus creative, child. As in all ideological acts, the playful child suppresses alternative constructions and smooths over internal contradiction.

Truth-revealing discourses of play tend to crowd around a tautology of freedom and purpose which, in turn, unfolds as evidence of the existence of children's voice and power. The concept of play, for many, echoes the insights of twentieth-century Dutch philosopher Johann Huizinga (1950) who insists that, to count as a form of play, the activity must be undertaken freely. Huizinga writes that "all play is a voluntary activity. Play to order is no longer play; it could at best be a forcible imitation of it" (7), adding not only is play free but "is in fact, freedom" (8). Play, "never a task" (8), has to be freely undertaken in order to retain its joyous quality which underwrites the ability to lose oneself in the excitement, fantasy, and indeed rapture of play. Roger Caillois (1961), who otherwise challenged Huizinga on several key points, concurs here that "playing is not obligatory; if it were, it would at once lose its attractive and joyous quality as a diversion" (9).

The requirement of play's freedom—or, at least, its non-coercion—reigns as definitional to the concept. It carries also the additional requirement of being undertaken for its own sake or for its own ends and so without the burden of external purpose. For Huizinga, play makes its own reality—inscribes its own "magic circle" —which by necessity shuns the teleology and exteriority of the profane world. Play, he remarks, is disinterested and not ordinary, standing "outside the immediate satisfaction of wants and appetites" (1950: 9). Caillois considers this property a bit differently, putting it in Vebelenesque terms when he argues that, in play, no goods are produced and "nothing is harvested or manufactured ... Play is an occasion of pure waste" (1961: 5). A number of decades later Mihalyi Csikszentmihalyi (2008) famously referred to the quality of an activity which is an end in itself as *autotelic*, a key property of the "flow" experience.

Contemporary writings tend to recuperate the agentive, joyful, and creative child from these tidbits of play theory. Chudacoff invokes Mark

Twain's oft-repeated nugget of wisdom from his famous character, *Tom Sawyer*: "Work consists of whatever a body is *obliged* to do. Play consists of whatever a body is not obliged to do" (quoted in Chudacoff 2007: 1, emphasis in original). In so doing, he instigates a tight tautology between play, choice, and the child, whereby anything a child choses must, by definition, be play or, at least, eligible to be play. He adds that play would also have no "extrinsic value" and be voluntary and actively engaged in on the part of the player (Chudacoff 2007: 3). Brown (2009), after demurring on a single definition of play, lists some key characteristics including the apparent purposeless of play—i.e., that it is undertaken for its own sake—which is voluntary and has an inherent attraction to the player (17). Drawing on both Piaget and Vygotsky, Jones and Reynolds (2011) posit that, in play, children are "agents" (4) and are "at their most competent" (15). Indeed, how can it be otherwise? How can the child be anything other than an agent in and through play when the play arrives pre-defined as instinctual, voluntary, and non-coerced?

As the enactment and definition of the agency and will of the child, the existence of "play" connotes a sense of power, an ability to act with and upon the world. Often, this ability arrives as a form of creativity—i.e., an ability to envision new possibilities. Sometimes creative, make-believe play can serve protectively or therapeutically, as Clark (2003) discusses regarding children's practices in play camps which provide contexts to cultivate children's ability to pretend so they can actively engage with difficult or painful situations—to imagine ways out of them. In the main, though, "play therapy" currently manifests as an organized industry and a set of practices which promote individualized notions of play and the child, naturalizing and normalizing both in the process (e.g., see Camastral 2008; Gonzalez and Bell 2016). Many, like Landreth (2001: 3–9), conceptualize play as the "universal language" of children, emphasizing its autotelic, agentic aspects, and relate that play gives a child a "sense of control." Teachers, therapists and parents alike are urged time and again, perhaps paradoxically, to create unstructured contexts and unscheduled time—particularly in the out-of-doors (Louv 2005; Guldberg 2009)—so children can realize in play the power and agency they possess naturally but which is often denied to them *as children* in the rounds of everyday life.

Yet, those flexible subjectivities imagined as arising through ludic engagement both obligate and abhor the intervention of adults and the adult world. Children's power rests on the ability of adults to, at once, provide for play experiences and contexts without interfering with a natural process. The conundrum at issue here derives from a curious equivocation regarding children's play power when it comes to commercial-media culture. Even as writers extol the extreme, world inspiring, transformative force of children's play in one breath, many decry the near omnipotence of commercial-media culture over children's imaginative abilities in the next. Carlsson-Paige (2008) commends the "profound purpose" of pretend play in children's lives as a "vehicle through which they master difficult life events, and build new ideas" (53) but which is "stamped out by so many of the media and products marketed to children today" (8). Linn (2006), who exhorts strong faith in children's make-believe play, nevertheless finds that "(w)hen screens dominate children's lives they are a threat to creativity" (30). Even Brown (2009), who found play essential to being human, worries that the scripts, narratives, and characters of commercial origin can "rob the child of the ability to create his [sic] own story" and thus "(a) chance for imaginative flights of fancy is lost" (104).

In another corner of cultural life, children are not involved enough in "high tech" or, at least, not involved with technology in the right ways. In recent years, a "Maker" movement has taken hold in the United States and other places which emphasizes the hands-on building of physical things to boost imaginative learning (Willett 2016). Makers—like others—see in the child and in the child's play a kind of truth as the natural, extant, and ever-present antidote to contemporary ills. Children's play and playful exploration promise to provide the fount of salvation and the content of an imagined civilization to come, which will arise by constructing spaces where children can learn to tinker (see Gabrielson 2013; Honey and Kanter 2013; Thomas 2014). *Make* magazine, a key vehicle for the movement, expresses the point directly: "The urge to make is primordial and unstoppable" (quoted in Thomas 2014: 2). Here, Claude Levi-Strauss's (1966) notion of bricolage, of tinkering, comes roaring back—now writ into childhood, into all of humanity. For Levi-Strauss, bricolage was the way of "la pensée sauvage," that is, the savage mind. It was a way of apprehending the world through iteratively derived categories and, as some might now say, through a kind of "grounded theory." In Maker thought—which crystallizes a good deal of the contemporary ideology of children's play—the child returns as primeval savage, as Rousseau's child born free only to be manacled in the very processes of being and becoming but, importantly, who now has the keys (in play, tinkering, etc.) to unlock its own shackles.

As agency and will itself, play makes the child out as active, creative and powerful; yet, the very source of this power—of this ability to act upon and move the world—is not strong enough *in and of itself* to overcome commercial frames and interpretations. Commerce, in these narratives, wins every time and, recalling Chudacoff, has indeed created the childhoods whose play and creativity is at risk. Children apparently can play their way out of most anything except a Disney multiplatform marketing strategy. One way out for many of the writers considered here centers on separating children from the commercial-media-schooling environment so that the essential, generative core of an inner ludic *geist* arises and becomes manifest. Yet, in the effort to separate the good from the bad play, the authentic from the inauthentic, advocates keep one foot in the conundrum of children's power and agency and the other in the conundrum of intervention.

Stepping past the creative child

The troubling disambiguation of play evident across a variety of fields acquires authoritative ballast through the philosophical-legal elaboration' of its status as a child's "right." Article 31 of the United Nations Convention on the Rights of the Child (1989) provides for the recognition of States of the "right of the child to rest and leisure, to engage in play and recreational activities appropriate to the age of the child and to participate freely in cultural life and the arts" (54). At once confused and confusing, the UN gathers play, recreation, rest, leisure, cultural life, and the arts as a single and perhaps singular catchment, making of them the same type of thing, the same kind of activity or experience. Strung together as a configuration of equivalences—i.e., play is recreation, is rest, etc.—the unifying principle making them mutually correspondent unfolds in their negation. That is to say, these practices (or non-practices, as in "rest") can be understood by what they are not—they are not productive and not-instrumental and cannot readily be compelled. They may even be said, positively, to be pleasurable or to induce pleasure. In this way, Article 31 reifies long and uncritically held associations between play and work, and child and adult, as the simple difference between (recalling Tom Sawyer) obliged and unobliged activity.

In response to the apparently "poor recognition" by States of the rights in Article 31, the UN issued "General Comment No. 17" in 2013 to elaborate upon the "equally important … need to create time and space for children to engage in spontaneous play, recreation and creativity, and to promote societal attitudes that support and encourage such activity" (1). In this document, the UN Committee reaffirms vague, oft-repeated connections between spontaneous play, creativity, learning, development, and pro-social activity when "initiated, controlled and structured by children themselves." In doing so, the international body reasserts the wisdom of the age that it is adults, more often than not, who likely peril the natural impulses of children with "pervasive" control that "undermines the child's own efforts to organize and conduct his or her play activities" (2) or that detracts from the ability of children to be "free of any demands—basically to do 'nothing,' if they so desire" (UN 2013: 7; see also Lester and Russell 2014). Personal, emotional, and societal benefits flow from play when left unsullied by "exclusion, prejudice or discrimination" and kept "secure from social harm or violence" (UN 2013: 6)—as would, it must be noted, most any undertaking. Enabling or provisioning children's free, spontaneous, self-driven play will contribute to the creation of culture, the appreciation of nature, the therapeutic recovery from injury and will lead to cross-cultural understandings of religious and other difference—a panacea to be sure. Play, indeed, performs these feats because it is, as a right, "*by definition* in the child's best interests" (4, emphasis added). The Committee's "comment" completes the isomorphism, and does so with the authority of conferring a right, between the child and play.

Agentive, creative, immanent, auto-generative—here, in play, stands the child of public rhetoric, moral panic, and social action. This figure represents also the philosophical headwinds against which childhood studies must struggle if it is to sustain its distinctiveness as a framework and field of thought constituted in and through the critical problemitization of the "child" and all that effort entails. The general inclination I presently sense toward settling on a rather narrow a version of *pedi-ludens* portends to undermine the productive, necessary ambiguity of the "child" by substituting it with some known, essential, comfort of play. Goodley and Runswick-Cole (2010), for instance, smartly caution researchers to attend to their own presumptions about the value and use of "play" for dis/abled children as a normative ideal. Their answer to this problem, however, backslides into promulgating the notion of play as something to be "emancipated" from adults, and particularly from psychologists. Conceptually, analytically, and morally, in fact, there appears to be no separation between spontaneous play and the "child" in terms of voice, perspective, and agency and, hence, no space between the child and its "interest" in any of the approaches discussed. Resisting the conceptual closure of the child through play poses significant challenges when, as we have seen, the tide of presumption, belief, and desire on the part of many favors, indeed encourages, a posture of boosterism.

Confident in what play is and what play does, entities like the UN along with efforts like Playwork ("Play and Playworkers" 2017),the Alliance for Childhood (Alliance for Childhood 2017) and the Association for Play Therapy build bodies of conception and practice which ossify the child, play, and the child-play relation as a rather fixed systems or sets of relations to be tweaked to produce the conditions from which a relentlessly inventive, creative child is to spring forth. The Importance of Play Group (2017) explicitly cites the UN's statements as a call to "take play seriously" so as to "invest in Europe's future"—making capital out of a certain kind of play or of its presumed "outcomes." The rescue of children's play surfaces in position papers and special statements regarding the importance or essentialness of play to children by organizations and journals in a manner one might expect of policy statements about military intervention (see Isenberg and Quisenberry 2002; Milteer et al. 2012). Such efforts imperil the project of childhood studies not because creativity, exploration, and inventiveness are somehow undesirable attributes by themselves or that play has no role in their realization and expression; they imperil because they make and remake childhood into something which is to have an objective, a goal, in the first place thus ensuring that the child remains firmly emplaced on a teleological trajectory structurally similar to that advanced by a narrow developmentalist ethos.

In the same gesture, they advance an individually articulated, aspirational notion of personhood clearly in concert with a Global North, neoliberal,

Euro-American versions of subjectivity, ontology, and ontogeny. When Roger Hart (2002), a significant voice in children's studies, writes that "(a) child must be free to play ... (m)uch of what adults prescribe or schedule for children is not truly play" (135), he is simultaneously championing *a style* of childhood—one which is resonant with particular family structures, educational systems, economic relations, gender dynamics, and, as Foucault would say, forms of (self)governmentality. Here again one encounters play as epistemologically privileged over against the child. The child, hidden among the presumptions about individualism, comes to stand for that creed through the incitement to play and the complementary admonishment to adults to stand aside. For true play—a.k.a. the true child—to emerge and become manifest, it must be separated from social process, here represented as adults and parents.

Persistent focus on discovery and inventiveness heightens attention to children's individualities and, in so doing, detracts from considering ways in which play practices often speak to and participate in varieties of social reproduction. Indeed, most any careful examination of children at play, or descriptive research of the same, leads one to the quick realization that most of what children do (and adults also, perhaps) relies upon and moves from pattern and repetition in the form of gesture, sound, movement, and script. Children create little completely and utterly anew but, like everyone else, work with the worlds before them as materials for appropriation—as illustrated in research trained on the dynamics of literacy and play (Dyson 1997; Wohlwend 2011; Genishi and Dyson 2014) and on the use and re-use of popular culture texts and meanings in playground games (Willett et al. 2013; Burn and Richards 2014; Marsh and Bishop 2014). Indeed, it is difficult to think of play apart from its appropriative quality (see Sicart 2014). One must *play with* something, in order to transform it or resist it (see Tam 2012; Helgesen 2015). Yet, ensnaring all play as actually or ideally emancipatory or resistive likewise encloses the "child" into a singular requirement of creativity (see also Thomson and Philo 2004; Harker 2005).

Materials gathered by folklorists, anthropologists, and other ethnographers testify to the dynamics between reiteration and invention in children's schoolyard and playground play, where hand-clapping and rhyming games, dancing and feats of physicality (like skipping and jumping rope), and performances of all sorts—including screaming (Rosen 2015)—comprise vehicles for different orders of sociality (Opie and Opie 1959; Schwartzman 1978; Sutton Smith 1997; Beresin 2010; see Marsh and Bishop 2014; Burn and Richards 2014). Lanclos (2003), for instance, in her ethnography of Irish children's lives, discusses how play was used to reiterate and comment on several lines of social demarcation evident in and relevant to their worlds. She describes how play, playfulness, and play contexts of working-class school children in Belfast served as a means for the young people to work on interpretations of the divisions between adult and child, female and male, Protestant and Catholic. Children would at once reproduce, for instance, gender power dynamics in their play through exclusion/inclusion in games and activities and through preforming "domestic" scripts while commenting on them and making them visible (84–123). As well, they used rudeness in the form of scatological and sexual reference as ways to call attention to their facility with topics and knowledge forbidden to them as children, thereby marking a boundary and mocking it in a single gesture (52–83). Here, as elsewhere, the tensions, divisions, and textures of social life undergird and inform the substance of play, making play something which remains tethered to specificities of identity and context rather than transcendent of them to be found deep within the natural child.

The preponderant, contemporary ethos of childhood studies facilitates a preoccupation with the unremittingly inventive child. Borne of an intense desire to find immanent resolution to the perceived threats to and problems of childhood, many now appear to find solutions in a certain a kind of imaginative play found latent within each child to be reassuring (see Grindheim and Ødegaard 2013). Paradigmatic fidelity demands of child subjects to perform innovation. To posit or describe a child who behaves non-imaginatively—who acts in accordance with given understandings and expectations of home, school, gender, or race—is akin to suborning existential erasure. Childhood studies has come to require its subject and object not simply to have and employ voice and agency, as analytically problematic as these can be (see James 2007; Komulainen 2007; Spyrou 2011; Oswell 2013), but to do so with inventiveness and resourcefulness. In consequence, "play" habitually serves to rearticulate childhood in a narrative of progress (Sutton-Smith 1997), one animated by the figure of an incessantly busy, mobile, and creative child that is in the process of becoming. It is a figure deeply resonant with Global North, bourgeois, neoliberal aspirations for producing agentive, kinetic persons who must avoid becoming "stuck" (Rosen 2015)—of succumbing to mere "natural growth" (Lareau 2003)— whereby inaction appears tantamount to passivity.

This figure, as well, haunts the imagination of childhood studies holding forth as it does as something of an ideal subject and subjectivity. Nothing is as unrewarding intellectually in this current context than a child who does not stand out as a maker of her own world—as an individualized tinkerer. Indeed, the creative, assertive, and disruptive child in many ways constitutes the ideal child—the darling—of childhood studies; it is the child who we as scholars want to see and, perhaps, need to see in order that our studies, profession, and efforts retain meaning and purchase. Reportage about a reproductive or—God forbid—situationally passive child in childhood studies research carries the same kind of stigma as do "non-significant" findings in experimental research. Neither accrues much currency with regard to peer assessment. In the case of childhood studies, however, the violation may throw the shade of moral suspicion upon the researcher rather than simply raise questions about research design. Participating in uncritical, unreflective expectations about the nature of play can very well mandate that one *demands* creative agency *from* children and their life practices, thereby undermining the core project of childhood studies which is to engage unremittingly in the problemitization of the "child."

The import of interrogating the presumptions and contours of play rhetorics and discourses, of naming and giving shape and texture to a ludic episteme and of speculating about the kind of child privileged in these constructions themselves provide resources with which to engage in contemplating about new directions. Contemporary deployments of "play"—in the manner addressed here—enable activists and commentators to conjure the child of their own making, elide inopportune contradictions and make of play a kind of remedy to the child it presupposes. The analytical sleight-of-hand of showing "the child" while theorizing play performed by popular and academic writers alike may not be specific only to those who take play as their central focus. Indeed, those who understand themselves as participating in "childhood studies," and who do so across different fields of inquiry, may garner significant insight by remaining vigilant about how suppositions operative in one arena of thought can reappear as driving propositions in another.

No doubt, inventiveness and voice, agency and suppression, inequality and access, therapeutics and joy—all these matter regarding the play with, by, about, and for children and their childhoods. Indeed, it does not seem it can be otherwise. But, the figure of the playful child, dominant in the accounts above, stands in the way of childhood studies so long as writers and researchers content themselves with the pleasant reflection it offers. When play arrives predetermined as the answer, the child ceases from serving as an incitement to critical interrogation. Intellectual rigor requires not only analytic and conceptual vigilance, but also a readiness to embrace the ambiguities evident before oneself so as to enable a re-imagination.

Acknowledgment

Special thanks to Ellen Malven and Jessica Schriver for assistance in preparing this manuscript.

CHAPTER NINE

Queer Young People of Color and the Affects of Agency

Stephen Bernardini

Innovative scholarship emerging from queer studies presents a nearly inexhaustible source for re-imagining not only the study of childhood(s), but also "real-life" children—flesh-and-blood beings whose experiences have been so central to the birth of a formal study of childhood. Queer studies offers tools to (re)think and (re)create the theoretical, epistemological, and methodological approaches in childhood studies—and queer theory can gain much from adopting work from childhood studies, particularly with regard to qualitative and ethnographic inquiry. Like childhood studies, queer theory is a heterogeneous field with a rich, varied history of epistemological engagements and productive critiques of social and political life. As such, *queer* surfaces in a number of forms. Queer can emerge as an identity—a (young) person might identify as "queer," gesturing to a form of gender or sexual nonconformity. Oftentimes, people identifying as queer come to think and practice queer; queer people are often enthusiasts for queer practice and expressions. To think or practice queer is to explore the insidious causes and effects of normative forces inhering in social, cultural, and political atmosphere, and to offer new pathways to survive or resist said forces (Warner 1993; Jagose 1996). It is unsurprising then that queer theory centralizes the figure of the child in early key scholarship (see Sedgwick 1991; Kincaid 1992; Rose 1984) and that queer scholars[1] continue to examine how childhood inheres in norms associated with social, cultural, and political life.[2] Queer studies has also shown the rich strangeness inherent in the demand for children's development and presumed innocence. As Kathryn Bond Stockton (2009) illuminates in *The Queer Child*, childhood is rendered queer by adult presumptions, making what seems so "natural"—the child—paradoxically protected yet threatening, familiar yet alien. Here, the crossing of queer studies and childhood studies provides fertile ground on which to capture these effects. As child studies scholar Diederick Janssen (2008: 86) argues, "Lived childhood [...] destabilizes existing 'natural' gonadal, and adultist orderings of sex as reproductive, 'oriented,' preference-delimited, gendered, orgasmic, a-traumatic." Children and young people's lived experiences disrupt normative investments in linearity—in pathways guided simply toward one formulation of sexuality or one kind of future.

Research on young people's sexual practices and experiences (typically over 13 years of age) has focused largely on discourses surrounding risk—chiefly, sexually transmitted infections (STIs) and early teenage pregnancy—and how to avoid these "risky" behaviors. Youth and young people's sexual expressions are positioned largely as a problem with which adults must contend to ensure that "healthy" behaviors are privileged and other expressions marginalized (Shoveller and Johnson 2006). Discussions of children and childhood may appear in these cases to (re)inscribe feelings of innocence and, moreover, bolster the discourses surrounding young people's delay of sexual knowledge and practice until adulthood. The child, therefore, surfaces generally as an absent presence; a shadow forming as adult anxieties over sex and sexuality come to light. Moreover, a dearth of research on young people's sex and sexuality foregrounds issues of race, class, and gender and sexual nonconformity. As the matrix of such intimacies grows, scholars may attend differently to dominant notions of children and childhood. While younger-aged children are constituted by different types and intensities of sexual risks, the sexual practices and expressions of young people promise new ways to situate such manifestations beyond adult imaginings and anxieties.

Queer's destabilizing potential may generate a re-imagining of a concept central to child and youth studies: agency. Research on young people's agency typically follows a narrative that presents the problems or conflicts experienced by children and young people as remedied by agency and voice, often ending with an "upbeat note" (Lesko and Talburt 2012: 280). These accounts often reify agency as individualistic and unquestionably positive, and this is especially relevant (and potentially problematic) in work with queer young people[3] of color. Such accounts in childhood studies may reinforce neoliberal narratives of progress and dominant notions of Western-based childhood that such research seeks to interrogate and disrupt. Despite greater geographical diversity—perhaps even because of it—agency has become part of the "normative foundations of childhood research" (Alanen 2011: 150). Because queer theory situates normativity as a primary area of inquiry, queer critique is well positioned to investigate the normative force of agency in studies of young people. Bringing together queer studies with notions of agency, I use the experiences of queer young people of color to *queer* questions of agency. I want to speculate how queer might shift approaches to young people's agency, especially given the dense, complex affectivity embedded in visions of queer young people of color. As education and youth studies scholar Edward Brockenbrough (2015) states, "Situated at the intersections of multiple oppressions, the bodies of queer [young people] of color are already marked by crisis-oriented discourses on youth of color, queer youth, immigrant youth, poor youth, and other constituencies to which they belong that are considered *at risk*" (28; emphasis in original). Given these intersections, I want to consider queer relationships to affect[4] alongside queer of color critique to challenge current connections and imaginings of queer young people's agency. To do this, I turn to ethnographic work on Black queer youths' (ages 14–25) everyday experiences in city spaces to re-imagine agency in the face of structural vulnerabilities. These structural vulnerabilities include the compounding effects of homo/transphobia, racism, lack of educational and health resources, risk of impoverishment/lack of job resources, and violence—both interpersonal and systemic—and point to how these effects are imbricated in the intersections of queer youths' identities. I centralize feelings, discussions, and interactions that youth tie to complex spaces of queer intimacy: sex parties. Youth demonstrate that these provisional spaces offer complex amalgamations of risk, intimacy, desire, and community, and speak to a blurring of the affective and epistemological boundaries of vulnerability and agency. In such destabilized territory, I contend not only that sex parties shed light on cultural practices of marginalized groups but that these feelings, relationships, and survival practices bound to these spaces invite scholars and advocates to theorize differently about young people's lives.

Queerness, affect, and reflections on agency

Understandings of young people's agency involve intense affect and can shape the conditions that underpin common conceptions of children and youth: "Part of the operation of rationalities and technologies [of young people] is affective, evoking an almost automatic response to stock representations of gang members, innocent teens, or gangling geeks. Thus, educators', youth workers', and researchers' investments in particular rationalities and technologies are often felt ones" (Talburt and Lesko 2012: 4). Problematically, this affective work can anesthetize the very young people it seeks to aid. Raising critical questions about agency often appears as suspicion, as masking, undermining, or taking away children's agency. Certain forms of children's agency are then privileged and, subsequently, reproduced in research and advocacy work. However, important questions remain. What does agency serve to elaborate or extend? And for whom? One such critique has emerged in relation to the affective valence developed around certain conceptions of children's agency. "Agency can be accepted uncritically as being a positive[5] thing [...] children and young people's agency should certainly be a contested and scrutinised concept rather than one which is taken-for-grant, unproblematised, or assumed inherently to be positive and desired by all children and young people" (Tisdall and Punch 2016: 16). Tisdall and Punch (2016) begin to connect affect and emotionality to agency—the positiveness—and its unproblematized deployments. However, this argument can be extended further. Perhaps agency's presumed positivity simultaneously draws scholars to the term *and* creates the conditions whereby it can be taken-for-granted. This question (and challenge) of the ways of seeing young people also emerges in critical youth studies: "Can research, youth studies, and youth who do not fit an agentic, optimistic, can-do world have a place in 'our' future? What would we see, represent, or research if we were not remembering an imagined past or curing the present via the future?" (Lesko and Talburt: 288). Individualistic abstractions of agency tend to promise optimism, bringing positive representations together with reclaimed images and knowledges. Yet these dominating forms of agency risk reducing children and youth's experiences to normative representations that line up with neoliberal investments in their lives and in their futures (Asad 2000). Such critical examinations have generated new understandings to agency. For instance, one such collection poses the notion of "ambiguous agency":

> [Ambiguous agency] is typically seen to be not of the right kind [of agency] because it is not consistent with the liberal conception of autonomous agency, which presupposes a notion of the subject as "responsible citizen" … ambiguous agency is frequently subjected to processes of concealment or correction, or moulded to make it consistent with specific moral and social standards couched as being in the "best interests of the child." (Bordonaro and Payne 2012: 367)

Imbuing agency, specifically children's agency, with positive qualities risks reproducing norms, morals, and values that reify the very power relationships addressed in critical childhood studies. When recognizing children's agency becomes hagiography, there is increased risk that the complexity of children's experiences erodes, obscuring the structural mechanisms influencing young people's lives. To be clear: this is not to say that children and youth are not, *or cannot*, be agentic. Nevertheless, scholars must interrogate the production of knowledge surrounding agency even, and especially, in regard to marginalized groups, in order to question the affective power linked to methods of control and regulation.

It is at the meeting place of the conceptual and affective effects of uncritical agency where queer theory can be most useful. The work of Heather Love (2009) in *Feeling Backwards: Loss and the Politics of Queer History* resonates here as a cautionary tale for collective projects of queer futurity—as children and youth are often positioned as future-oriented, queer inquiry that disrupts this linearity can be particularly productive for theorizing about childhood and creating opportunities to recognize new forms of agency. Love (2009: 3) suggests that "the emphasis on damage in queer studies exists in a state of tension with a related and contrary tendency—the need to resist damage and to affirm queer existence." Love's point about the direction of feelings and the ways these feelings structure knowledge about gay life reflects this affirmative insistence on children's lives—that scholars must insist on ways that children are social actors to speak back to vulnerability, but their agency must be highlighted and affirmed precisely *because* they are vulnerable. Love's (2009) arguments regarding orientations in queer studies parallel dominant conceptualizations of agency in childhood studies as positive, optimistic, and future-oriented. That is, just as queer life is compelled to be reclaimed in the name of progress, overdetermining agency's positive valence can cloud the effects of vulnerabilities—areas that not only hold within new promises for agency but also point to structural inequalities.

Reflections of the theoretical considerations of damage and remedy emerge in the lived experiences of structural violence. Heather Love (2012) further argues for a (re)turn to a queer(er) method, moving toward more queer forms of analysis. Love (2012) writes:

> I want to recall a queer tradition that focuses on the lived experience of structural inequality [...] It's also true that I probably have less to say about crisis than about making do and getting by. Because of its emphasis on everyday life and intimate experience, the tradition I am pointing to can seem to lack a revolutionary horizon. *But for me this refusal of the choice between revolution and capitulation is what makes this tradition queer.* (Love, in Crosby et al. 2012: 131, emphasis added)

Love's (2012) refusal of choice between revolution and capitulation is a queer practice that offers a new method for situating childhood and youth. Can agency fit under the banner of "making do and getting by," or does ascribing agency to young people's experiences obscure the diverse social and cultural practices in everyday life? Love's turn to the quotidian realities of structural vulnerability and inequality positions queerness as a critical possibility *inside* an admixture of vulnerability and agency, while moving beyond the future-oriented narratives. This method complicates the victim/ agent binary (and victim→agent narrative) that directs many scholarly approaches in child and youth studies. Narratives of victimhood and agency—of damage and remedy—inhere in accounts of queer children and youth of color. As typical depictions of queer young people include youth at-risk or in crisis, efforts to locate agency to speak back to the portrayals of vulnerability and victimhood of queer youth of color become central (Blackburn 2007; Brockenbrough 2015). Yet, are current queer theoretical or youth studies conceptualizations of agency the only way, or "best" way, to capture these experiences? A queer(er) methodology like Love's holds the capacity to attend to the affective tendencies of knowledge production, and to focus on the lived realities of structural inequality in order to foster critical approaches to agency while documenting children's experiences. Using this approach, structural inequalities such as a lack of access to communal spaces, health resources, and public and street locales are not necessarily overcome, but re-imagined as elements that generate diverse self and space-making practices. Such queer approaches may break from the typical "upbeat note" and "can-do" emotional resilience (Talburt and Lesko 2012; 280) that risks flattening the present for future-oriented (adult) imaginings.

Another generative site for rethinking agency surfaces through queer of color critique. Cultivated in women of color feminisms and queer theory, queer of color critique examines the effects of norms by foregrounding race in studies of gender and sexual nonconformists to identify the specific strategies for endurance, survival, and resistance employed by queer people of color. In a foundational work, Roderick Ferguson (2004) argues that queer of color critique seeks to address the normative attachments of social life to nationhood and capital. Ferguson asserts:

> To address these formations as an accumulation means that we must ask the question of what possibilities they offer for agency. We must see the gendered and eroticized elements of racial formations as offering ruptural—i.e. critical—possibilities. Approaching them as sites of critique means that we must challenge the construction of these formations as monstrous and threatening to others who have no possibility for critical agency and instead engage nonheteronormative racial formations as the site of ruptures, critiques, and alternatives. (2004: 18)

Ferguson posits that formations foregrounding the precarious and threatening erotics of race and gender hold potential configurations of agency. This intensifying can fissure the normative dimensions of life, generating social, cultural, and political change through subjectivities positioned as "monstrous" or "threatening." If agency attaches to neoliberalism and normativity, it may also serve to reify heteronormativity. Queer of color critique continues to challenge the epistemological foundations of queer theory by centralizing the quotidian realities of queer people of color.[6] As anthropologist Jafari S. Allen (2013) argues, queer theory must grow its "optics, archives, and its politics to successfully *see* and *say* what is happening among Black sexual minorities and gender nonconformists" (554; emphasis in original). At present, queer of color analyses focused on queer youth of color remain scarce.[7] A queer of color critique in child/youth studies invites new theoretical and scholarly engagements with Black queer youth, centralizing the racial formations of young people and exploring the constraints in the face of structural vulnerability alongside youths' methods of survival, escape, and resistance. Because Black queerness is often imagined to emerge as "monstrous" or "threatening," and is, thereby, subject to pervasive public and epidemiologic surveillance, current imaginings of (queer) youth agency may be insufficient to name such forces or describe how queer youth of color navigate them at the level of everyday life.

Bringing together critiques of agency from child and youth studies with queer considerations of affect and queer of color critique cultivates a critical archive to explore the social, cultural, and spatial practices of Black queer youth. Examining the current (re)cycled imaginings of young people's agency alongside queer critiques of the affects of knowledge production and a turn to lived experience provide the conceptual framework for childhood studies to deviate from the overdetermined place of agency in child and youth studies. This orientation toward understanding queer young people of color provides a reflexive position from which to explore sex parties as a queer world-making practice situated in complicated arrangements of affect that, I argue, are not readily imaginable for current permutations of young people's agency. Put another way, delinking the overdetermined, future-oriented elements of agency as it is currently conceived allows for queerer moments of intimacy, belonging, and enduring that complicate and extend youths' experiences at sex parties.

Sex parties as queer sites of affect and agency

In my ethnographic research (Bernardini 2016) I sought to engage fully with the affective tendencies that characterized current (or lack thereof) visions of Black queer children and youth. My archive included an amalgamation of queer theory, queer of color critique, Black queer studies, and urban ethnography in order to reorient approaches to understanding race, gender, and sexuality constituted in, and in the face of, violence and (structural) vulnerabilities. For nearly two years, I used as a nexus an urban LGBTQ youth of color space, the Meridian Center, which granted me the opportunity to engage with over 100 respondents and conduct over 30 in-depth interviews. Through ethnography, I argued that the absence of rich, detailed portraits of queer youth of color virtually hinders efforts to engage in public praxis, and that without the inclusion of youth in the matrix of accounting for a racialized queer life we will continue to be left to ideological typifications, which inform the constructs of both those who are hateful and those holding genuine motivations for justice. Tracing these affects and effects, Black youth revealed critical agency that could not be captured sufficiently by typical notions of youths' agency, and which surfaced through gender and sexual subjectivities and in provisional movements and communities that were highly structured in a network of relationships with the institutions serving youth in the city. Here, the inclusion of young people was not simply a matter of finding voices to speak back to ideology. Elaborating the phenomenological and affective registers of ideology helps identify how structural inequalities or vulnerability congeal at the level of everyday life, and points to sites of tension, disruption, and creativity forged under such constraints.

Black queer young people revealed in their discussions and interactions the nuances of creating and navigating sex party spaces. Youth reported finding these spaces at houses throughout city, but also discussed some sex parties that took place in hotel rooms. Sex parties were typically found by word of mouth through friends, or through online advertisements and friends' posts on websites and mobile phone applications (such as Grindr, Adam4Adam, Black Gay Chat [BGCLive.com], Facebook, and, most frequently, Jack'd). Sex parties are gatherings where queer young people may engage in various kinds of sexual and intimate practices, and appear as a significant, if contested, part of the cultural landscape of city-dwelling queer young people of color. The scant literature[8] on sex parties frames these spaces as places of increased concern surrounding high-risk sexual practices (Mimiaga et al. 2010; Solomon et al. 2011). Some attention here is expected. However, the relationships and experiences fostered by sex parties show a much more varied space that grants city-dwelling queer youth of color provisional queer sites for relationships, belonging, and intimacy. When I inquired as to the difference between bathhouses and sex parties, and why a person might choose the latter, Trent (25), the youth group facilitator, elucidated:

[Fieldnote Excerpts]

"Well, with a bathhouse, it's right out here and I work and walk around this area," Trent said while he gestured toward the window. "I can't be seen strolling out of a bathhouse at 2:00am and see people I see everyday, cause they are gonna know what I was doing [...]. With sex parties, it's more informal and no one is really gonna question what I am doing walking out of a house."

Rowan (17), a queer youth in the group, appears to corroborate Trent's comments, "A bathhouse is private, but not really. You gotta come out on 30th street and everyone can see you. It's just like, you could walk by a house where there are sex parties and never know what the fuck is going on in there."

Both Trent and Rowan point to the inherent surveillance they feel on the street in relation to the bathhouse and its location within the city, and note how sex parties serve as an alternative that escapes this gaze. Surveillance operates on multiple levels: consider Trent's anxiety that he would see someone he worked with or knew from the organizations with which he worked, and peers or family that could be around the city. Trent and Rowan also reveal a sense of shame not necessarily attached to the spaces and the activities therein, but in contrast to what others would think seeing them walk out of a bathhouse versus walking out of a home or hotel. In contrast, Trent and Rowan make the distinction between a bathhouse and a sex party by the provisional, informal, and relative innocuity of the house on the city street. In this way, sex parties offer a potential escape from surveillance, but one that is bound to structural inequality. That is, Trent and Rowan use these spaces as sites of refuge to sidestep not only the policing of queer young people's sexualities, but of the inherent suspicion surrounding queer intimacies more broadly.

Black queer young people reported gathering at sex parties to explore intimacy beyond the surveillance that shaped much of themselves and their social geographies. These spaces were complex, multifaceted sites of both (sexual) vulnerability and agency, which created an affective connection for intimacy, belonging, and survival. As this conversation about sex parties continued, youth discussed the moral obligation of friends to protect or police others' behaviors, including what responsibility one plays in another's sex life, particularly at a sex party. The general atmosphere at the start of the conversation seems to be that a friend should "step in," especially if that friend knew someone was HIV positive, but by the end appears to be more of an individual responsibility:

[Fieldnote Excerpts]

"Yea, that's like, his [my friend's] business. And if those guys are grimy and going to sex parties, like what do you expect? Stay in your own lane and do you." Other youth, particularly Hugo (22), agree with Reese's (18) assertion that people choosing to go to a sex party are responsible for their own actions and bodies.

Reese continues: "Well whatever [...] if you do *that* and you thirsty (horny) and you a dirty bottom faggot, like this is what happens. Why is it your job to step in?! That's awkward anyway."

The topic of sex and the word "risk" comes up a lot in relation to sex. Many others claim that sex is always risky and never safe, with Ashton (20) commenting that sex is "essentially a gamble."

According to Devin (17), sex parties are considered "high risk" because of the drug use, alcohol, and "stuff" [sex] going on at sex parties.

Trent, pulling out his wallet, removes a condom, stating, "Well, I always have one of these on me. But usually, a sex party, the host will have like a bowl of condoms and some liquor. Like, that's part of it."

[...] When prompted, youth in the room suggest that sex parties are a negative thing, but Trent challenges the youth, saying young people of color particularly should think about them as "sex positive" (his term) spaces. He clarifies, "There's not a lot of places where guys in the city can like, go, hang out, and have sex with men without it being a big deal. It's a space for us."

"That's true. For real, though," says Riley (16) in his low-pitched, scratchy voice.

Dwane (19), wearing scrubs from a recent shift at work, raises his hand and says, "Yea, [sex parties] don't all have sex. You can play video games, play games, just drink and chill. You don't need to fuck. But like, that's why you are there, ya know? Sometimes that stuff is just a break between nuttin' [orgasms]. You need a breather." The room erupts in laughter at Dwane's last comment.

Chuckling, Laurence (18) interjects, "Yea, but like, if it's just ya'll, especially if you are friends, just sittin' around in your underwear playing games, like … [*Laughing*] like why bother?"

Jumping to Laurence's point, Elijah, a trans-identifying youth, asks, "What's like the difference then between like that and a sex party? Like that just sounds like a house party."

Vonn (20) stops everyone from talking and details that there are different kinds of sex parties: "Yea some you don't know anybody and you walk in, drop your clothes off in a trash bag, pay fifteen bucks, and just go in to fuck. Others you can like hang out with people. It depends … "

Zoe (16), a queer-identifying youth speaks up, saying "I have been to one, but it was in like a nice hotel room. These sex parties are usually in sketchy neighborhoods. Like, that's a difference, too." People in the group nod in agreement with Zoe's point.

"Yea that's why people usually don't go alone," Rowan adds.

Trent: "Yea, like I barely seen anyone show up to a sex party alone. You usually bring a friend or friends."

This intense conversation demonstrates the world-making potential bound to sex parties, while highlighting the complex, affective trouble of "high risk" spaces that hold different possibilities for intimacy and belonging. Devin addresses the initial, more "high risk" element of holding and attending a sex party. Reese is also critical of these spaces and the potential risks he attaches to them, making a judgment linking "risky" sexual behavior with gendered positionalities. Trent, however, challenges these positions. He grounds the importance of sex parties as "sex positive" spaces, as provisional spaces where queer youth of color can meet, talk, and hang out, but also have sex without the shame and stigma that is attached to certain other places in the city. Despite immediate connections made to "high risk"—due to alcohol, drugs, and sex—Trent and other youth note the importance of friendship in helping to take care of each other during sex parties. Additionally, Trent reveals that the host of sex parties usually makes condoms available for the sex party. This comment regarding condoms suggests an element of care taken by hosts and attendees of sex parties. Additionally, sex parties, in Trent's eyes, fulfill a communal connection ("a space for us") the "us" in this case being young Black queer men. Dwane corroborates Trent's claims, suggesting that sex parties also emerge as spaces youth can go to simply "hang out," and adding that these places promise other forms of intimacy. In this regard, seeing sex parties as simply sites in need of intervention because of sexual risk erases the culturally grounded meanings attached to these spaces. Sex parties provide a partial and contingent context for queer youth of color to make decisions about intimacy and relationships. At the same time sex parties do not completely erode the interpersonal and structural vulnerabilities youth face. Indeed, the blurring of vulnerability and agency opened up by sex parties provides the conditions for young people to build community and relations of intimacy that might otherwise remain unavailable. Moreover, sex parties appear irreducible to binaristic visions of victim/agent or narratives of "stock images" of queer young people. A form of agency emerges in the creation and negotiation of relationships linked to sex parties, and complicates the positive, optimistic, and individualistic vision often promoted in the study of young people—especially in the case of sexual health. Sex parties challenge dominant notions of sexual health that inhere in images of Black queer youth, at the same time that these youth utilize and reject elements of such discourses to reimagine forms of intimacy within structural inequalities.

Trent's claim that sex parties are "sex positive" spaces is an almost unfathomable remark for the youth, but one that crucially points to understanding how Black queer young people create queer geographies of intimacy and belonging that are important for enduring the effects of structural inequalities. In a conversation later that same week, Damarco talked to me more about sex parties as "sex positive" spaces:

[Fieldnote Excerpts]

It's tough to say that they are sex positive. Like, I thought Trent meant that they were HIV positive or something *(Laughs)* [...] For real, I didn't know what he was saying at first. But I do kind of get it. Being Black and gay, it's really hard to meet people sometimes. Like other Black, gay, queer, whatever, people like me, you know? I meet people, we have some good conversations and discussions sometimes, and then sometimes we fuck and I never see you again after the party. And that's it.

Damarco (and other youth) framed sex parties as sites of refuge, intimacy, and community surrounding hardships at the intersections of racialized queer identities. Damarco's comment that he thought Trent gestured to HIV speaks to the epidemiologic saturation that haunts sex parties and youths' lives more generally. That "positive" codes as infection rather than a sexual space of community or intimacy suggest the extent to which these youths' sexual subjectivities are sites of control and intervention within dominant discourses. In this part of our conversation, Damarco links the discussions at the sex party, and the provisional relationships (sometimes sexual) that are formed as part of his sex positive framework. The promise of enacting desire and pleasure, "high-risk" or otherwise, is sutured to other relations of belonging, friendship, and intimacy. Yet the relations in which Damarco engages are sometimes fleeting, but offer the possibility of often-inaccessible sexual connections. Damarco contends that he is uncertain about sex parties being sex positive. Or, perhaps, Damarco gestures to a larger structural level that inhibits feeling positive about sex and sexuality; youth spoke often about the control and anxiety surrounding their sexual relationships. The structural inequalities surrounding lack of culturally informed health resources and sites of sexual community work in part to produce the conditions for the emergence of sex parties. Yet, the uncertainty and risk of sexual contact with strangers appear to provide the framework for other kinds of relations of belonging to open up in more ambiguous, yet powerful, forms.

The communal and spatial queer possibilities offered by sex parties force questions of "stock images" of queer young people of color, while demonstrating the need to take seriously the gender and sexual practices that run counter to innumerable efforts to discipline youths' experiences. A nuanced picture at the intersections of Black/queer/young blossoms from a failure to attach easily the affective tendencies associated with youth and youth studies—those optimistic, positive, resilient images that risk blocking significant potentialities for intimacies and pleasures at the level of the quotidian. This, in turn, challenges prevailing ideologies tied to epidemiologic views of queer young people of color as paradoxical persons of risk and at-risk, blurring these constructions through culturally situated inquiry. Sex parties, and the interactions that take place within, suggest a range of feelings under a framework of "making do and getting by" in the face of the material conditions of youths' lives. Queer and sexual geographers have examined such spaces, and link questions of becoming to questions of movement, place, and belonging, particularly linked to the affect generated in queer spaces (Browne 2006; Browne et al. 2009). Moreover, such spaces can promise joy, pleasure, and exuberance in the temporary escape these sites actualize, or even promise; queer survival and optimism need not be mutually exclusive here. Spaces like sex parties suggest new formulations of agency that can emerge in these provisional, generative spaces in the face of structural vulnerabilities, and in contexts where queer youth of color face multiple, overlapping levels of racism, homophobia, and transphobia from within and outside of their communities. I contend that queer formulations of this sort do not reveal "some mythically pure form of agency or will but rather model other modes of being and becoming that scramble our understandings of place, time, development, action, and transformation" (Halberstam 2005: 187). It is in this regard that I argue that queer theoretical work offers methods for re-evaluating agency by turning away from the mythical and to the material—to the everyday interactions and relationships that not only tell us how communities adapt and reshape vulnerability, but allow for rethinking of theoretical insights into understandings of people, places, and lives. To be clear, queer youth of color possess agency. Yet these agentic practices run against the grain of notions of agency that are emblematic of the fields of child and youth studies, those in which "the child" more broadly is typically situated. Queer theory helps elaborate key questions surrounding agency: Does referring to the actions of queer youth help extend or undo agency, or does the overdetermination of agency obscure more granular components of queer life? I speculate that uncritical forms of agency more often produce the latter effect. As child and youth studies scholars suggest, if agency is cycled repeatedly, then attaching the term to both the extraordinary and the ordinary masks these distinctions. The question then becomes not what is agency, but what is *not* agency? Tracing the latter question would lead to queerer methods of engagement with young people's practices and relationships. Currently, there is no homogeneous form of a queer methodology (see Nash and Browne 2012). However, a queer(er) methodology in child and youth studies might focus on the power relations that produce ways of seeing and saying what appears—or what can be imagined as possible to appear—as agency, while exploring queer theoretical work on gender and sexual nonconformists as embedded within this framework. Love's (2012) contention about the everyday experiences and intimacies in the face of structural inequality moves toward this queer methodology. Such approaches, however, may offer new frontiers that critically examine and destabilize orthodoxies regarding ethics, consent, kinship, and "the field" in studies of childhood. Queer studies offers a mode of inquiry and engagement to explore and examine the "stuff" that is masked or left behind by agency's capture.

Conclusion

Queer theory allows scholars in and beyond the field of childhood studies to (re)imagine the conceptual, epistemological, and affective elements of agency. That agency endures as a mantra-like call should invite questions of its taken-for-granted status in child and youth studies. This question is especially imperative for queer young people of color who are so often caught on the horns of the victim/agent dichotomy—a problematic structure that elides the range of detailed, material conditions in queer youths' experiences. What I have called for here is a consideration about directions queerness might take us through studies of children and youth in ways that seek to widen the breadth of the field in a manner that is untethered from typical notions of agency. Queer studies invites new engagements with children and young people as the conditions of contemporary life shift. That is, as the terrain of children's material worlds shifts, so too must scholars' tools for interrogating young people. A re-imagining, a queerer positionality, might appear not through looking forward, but through reconstituting those elements that studies of childhood have left behind; not as a transformative revitalization, but a rather ordinary shift toward notions of vulnerability, violence, becoming, and negative affectivity that direct us toward queerer forms of childhood and youth. As queer of color analysis demonstrates, ethnography can capture everyday kinds of movement, becoming, and gestures in ways that traditional queer theoretical work lacked. This gap led me to utilize ethnography on an under-theorized and under-researched area—queer young people of color—to destabilize ways of knowing and intervening on youths' lives. Both qualitative and cultural studies of children and youth need to remain reflexive about knowledge production on children and youth, or risk generating scholarship that reinforces normalizing values and moral judgments through the very terms (like agency) that seek to define and encapsulate children's experiences. Such conceptual maneuvers may ultimately undermine young people's creativity—not in some innocent or idealistic form—but in the necessary and inventive practices of everyday life that risk being homogenized by the terms used to define such expressions. The failure of the material conditions of childhood to endure in the present will most certainly shift the ideas associated with progress, development, health, and family life, while also reorganizing the regulation of these conditions. As such, I desire an expanded sense of the parameters of agency. Scholars of childhood must continue to capture the complexities of children's lives through research and creative projects that explore the various, complicated, paradoxical affects and effects bound to agency. However, the affective impulse to "fix" images or ideas of young people through agency must be questioned, and a space of re-imagining must seek to escape and/or challenge these affective demands. This position marks a significant shift in research with young people—defined, or defining themselves, as vulnerable—and is vital to expanding conceptions of agency.

What might we reimagine beyond that comfortable affective terrain?

Notes

1 This chapter is not an exhaustive account of the meeting between queer theory and childhood. See Abate and Kidd (2011), Bruhm and Hurley (2004), Halberstam (2011, 2012), and Pugh (2010) for some examples.

2 See Lee Edelman's (2004) polemic, *No Future: Queer Theory and the Death Drive*, for a key text on this issue.

3 "Children," "youth," and "young people" are used interchangeably throughout this chapter. Although these terms have their own respective histories and

epistemologies, I believe that the implications for agency in this chapter extend to conceptions of "child" and "youth" (albeit with different feelings and intensities).

4 Affect has a range of conceptual and definitional ties. Scholars of childhood have explored affect in a Deleuzian framework (Lee 2001; Prout 2005) and this area is certainly key to re-imagining childhood studies. Here, my use of affect reflects Ann Cvetkovich's (2012): "I tend to use affect in a generic sense, rather than in the more specific Deleuzian sense, as a category that encompasses affect, emotion, and feeling, and that includes impulses, desires, and feelings that get historically constructed in a range of ways" (Cvetkovich 2012: 4).

5 Uncritical deployments of agency may create the conditions for it to appear positive and, thereby, linked to happiness. In this sense, I am cautious of agency, considering queer theorist Sara Ahmed's (2004, 2010) work on happiness. Ahmed (2010: 38) suggests, "In other words, when we are affected in a good way by what is attributed as being good, we become the good ones, the virtuous and happy ones. Happiness allows us to line up with things in the right way."

6 See Allen (2011), Bailey (2013), Johnson (2011), Manalansan (2003), and Muñoz (1999) for key ethnographic explorations in queer of color critique.

7 See Brockenbrough (2015) for a possible framework for using queer of color critique to explore the experiences of queer youth of color, particularly in educational studies.

8 A notable exception is Marlon Bailey's (2016) work on "raw" sex and intimacy with Black gay and queer men, some of which takes place at sex parties.

CHAPTER TEN

Performative Politics and the Interview:

Unraveling Immigrant Children's Narrations and Identity Performances

Stavroula Kontovourki and
Eleni Theodorou

Introduction

This chapter contributes to the discussion on children's agency in childhood studies by suggesting that the notion of agency as it unfolds at the research moment should be dismantled, especially when connected to interviewing practices that promise to expand the space for children's voices to be heard. To do so, we deploy the notion of performativity to consider the ways in which immigrant students constituted themselves and others as particular types of school subjects during individual, semi-structured interviews; and, to concurrently reflect on our own responsibilities for structuring their agency and hence contributing to their subjectivation. We thus argue that children's agency should be neither reconsidered as some*thing* that can be found, exercised, or possessed nor even problematized as complex, particular, and contingent. Rather, it could be thought of as an incomplete and inconclusive process that unfolds at the interplay of different, often conflicting, rationalities whereby children as agents are constituted and, potentially, concurrently confined. We thus aspire to shift the discussion on children's agency in childhood studies not simply from the *what* (agency is) to the *how* (agency is produced, facilitated, or conditioned) but also to the implausibility of agency as a theoretical construct and an analytic tool.

Coming to these points was akin to a journey through multiple readings of data collected as part of a qualitative study that examined immigrant children's experiences in Greek as an Additional Language (GAL) classes in the Republic of Cyprus and which rested upon ethnographic methods of data collection, including interviewing with ten children of differential immigrant and academic experiences. As we engaged with multiple readings of the data, we gradually came to see the space of the interview (jointly shaped by both us as researchers and children as participants) as a space of performative acts which could not have been sanctioned or acknowledged as legitimate performances in the space of the mainstream classroom. And the more we were eager to see the possibility for children's agency in these data, the more we saw the constrictions and power dynamics which formed both children and us as performative subjects. Our latter reading of data is thus intended to illuminate the indeterminacy of the research process, the unfinishedness of children and adults as research(ed) subjects, and the complexity of agency as a present in action rather than a feature, a property, or process. Striving among the heterogeneity of agency and also realizing that possibility and constriction might concur, we conclude that the very notion of agency might be implausible and ask whether it is time to start considering the complications and implications of a "post-agency" era. The dismantling of agency implied in this "post" adds on critiques of humanist agency as the essentialist capacity of an autonomous individual to act witnessed in childhood studies and beyond (e.g., Bordonaro and Payne 2012; Oswell 2013; Wyness 2015), but is also in sync with the call for the radicalization of research in the social sciences (e.g., Barad 2003; Lather and St. Pierre 2013).

Children's agency and performativity

We embark on this examination of children's agency acknowledging that its conceptualization reflects and is marked by shifts witnessed over the past few decades in social sciences, particularly in sociology and anthropology, in the way the child has been conceptualized. Such shifts give way to what has been termed the "new sociology of childhood" (Prout and James 1997; James and James 2004) that emerged in response to critiques of deficit and restrictive understandings of children as less competent than adults and as beings-in-the-making (James and James 2004). Among the basic tenets of this epistemological shift has been the recognition of the child as a competent human being (rather than becoming) and as an agent. As the new sociology of childhood broke new ground in our understanding of children's worlds and of children in the world, the child-as-an-agent has come to be something of a field mantra juxtaposed to (earlier) more passive conceptualizations of the child as bound by structure.

This preoccupation with agency in childhood studies reflects a broader interest in agency in the social sciences (Ahearn 2001; James et al. 1998) as well as a political project among social scientists for empowering the "weak" (Bordonaro and Payne 2012). The conceptualization of the child as "being" rather than "becoming" sparked several ethical and methodological discussions on children's agency and what this might mean for children's participation in the research process. Many of these discussions centered on the child's ability to voluntarily decide to participate, on the child's competence to do so in ways aimed by the researcher to respect both the individual and the categorical child, and on issues of representation as linked to children's voice (e.g., Bell 2008; Christensen 2004; Thomas and O'Kane 1998). The dominant working assumption behind conceptualizations of agency as a property of the child-as-being is that of one's (intentional) capacity to act (Wyness 2015).

More recently, however, the notion of children's agency, and its implications for research with children, has come to be problematized following critiques on the heterogeneity and vagueness of the term, and the morality that it presumes (Bordonaro and Payne 2012). The heterogeneity of definitions of "agency" in childhood studies may be easily seen in the ways agency has traversed through approaches which embraced it with a naiveté that equated it to free will and/or resistance to more complicated notions of it as a plural, as socially mediated, structured, and constricted, and as collectively or relationally negotiated rather than individually originating and possessed (Oswell 2013; Wyness 2015). Still, Bordonaro and Payne (2012) posit, undergirding these understandings of agency, even if (more) nuanced, are (mainstream) moral definitions of agency as inherently positive and normative assumptions of childhood as a place of innocence (Duschinsky 2013). Such conceptualizations of children as inherently innocent and agency as inherently positive become problematic in cases where children are engaged in acts that are seen as morally questionable in a particular context or appear to reproduce matrices of oppression or resist social interventions aimed at children's "best interests," prompting some to speak of "ambiguous agencies" (Ahearn 2001; Bordonaro 2012).

Post-structural approaches to agency have also chimed in this criticism to emphasize the fluidity and unpredictability of agentive acts. Hence, for researchers engaging with post-structural understandings of children's agency, complexity, fluidity, and incompleteness lie at the heart of understanding children's performances—be it in the case of high school girls who "do smart girlhood" in Canada by repositioning themselves as agentic subjects in an effort to resist constricted and constricting constructions of their subjectivities at school (Raby and Pomerantz 2015); or in Indonesian children's subtle acts of subversion of the nation-building project as performances, discourses, and rituals aimed at the inculcation of national identity took on different meaning for their performers (Moser 2015).

This notion of the subject-child-potentially-agent aligns with a Foucauldian perception of power as not some*thing* that one possesses, but rather a present in action(s) within action(s), "the multiplicity of force relations immanent in the sphere in which they operate and which constitute their own organization" (Foucault 1977: 92). Precisely because it operates in action, in fields of relations, power is unfixed, simultaneously productive and constricting (Foucault 1977). Hence, by looking at discourse as a form of productive power, one then is able to approach subjectivity, namely the constitution of the subject, as the twofold process of *subjection* and *subjectivation*: as subordination to someone else's control and an embracing of those conditions that form one's existence (Foucault 1982; Butler 1999).

From a performative perspective, individuals are constituted as subjects in performative acts: in discursive practices that constitute what they name and in the continuous/repetitive addresses that permeate those (Butler 1997a; Youdell 2006, 2012). Engaged in repetitive, stylized performances, the individual cites and ultimately embraces the normative discourses that come to constitute one's sense of "core" identity, as if this existed prior to performance or any operation of power (e.g., Butler 1999). Such embracing is both necessary and constraining for individuals' recognition, and thus constitution as subject within matrices of intelligibility—namely, those conditions of possibility against which particular performances are recognized as legitimate while others are seen as pushing against or traversing particular norms (Butler 1999; Youdell 2006).

From this stems an understanding of agency as possible to take many different forms: as possibilities of re-inscription, of resistive performance, of rupture, of mutation, of slippage, of imperfect reiteration, of failure to perform as expected, of opening to redefinition, and of performing differently (e.g., Butler 1999; Holt 2004, 2010; Youdell 2006). That these possibilities exist only in performance necessitates that agency is searched for in the quotidian, mundane workings of everyday action not so much to identify or confirm children's capacity to act but to connect that to the fleeting yet structuring conditions of children's intelligibility as subjects. The identification of those is complicated when taking as granted the possibility to concurrently perform multiple, potentially conflicting and contradictory, discursive formations (Holt 2010); the differential ways in which these performances are perceived by different audiences (see e.g., Youdell's 2003 discussion of Black students' intelligible performances as members of student subculture that was also the moment of practice for their constitution by school organization as a challenge to authority); and, the very idea that children's desires are implicated in the process (e.g., Burnside 2015; Robinson and Davies 2008). As per Butler (1997b), this constitutes "an agency of a desire" (p. 9), an ambivalent notion of agency, constrained by no teleological or moral necessity that may nevertheless aim at the dissolution of the subject.

Drawing on these perspectives, we talk of *performative politics*, namely, the possibility that dominant meanings of being are re-inscribed *and* unsettled in subjectivating processes (Butler 1999; Youdell 2006). This offers an opening into approaching the question of children's agency through highlighting the omnipresence of the political in immigrant children's subjectivation in schools. We proceed with this exploration by delving into two instantiations at the research moment: in the first instantiation, we discuss immigrant children's subjection and subjectivation at their concurrent resistance to and embracing of the school discourse as forms of agency the meaning and effect of which is difficult, if not impossible, to grabble. In the second instantiation, we turn the gaze unto ourselves (not only at children) as performative subjects, who shaped the interview context in ways that both restricted and enabled certain possibilities of (children's) performances of selves.

Situating our discussion

The data which serve as a springboard for the discussion to ensue are part of a small-scale exploratory qualitative study that sought to examine processes of social and academic integration of immigrant children in the Greek Cypriot educational system and particularly, in remedial sessions in GAL. Mainstream education and remedial teaching in Greek as an Additional or Second Language (GAL/GSL) constitute the core of intercultural education policy in Cyprus which, on a rhetorical level, advocates the inclusion and respect for all children, regardless of cultural, ethnic, or other characteristics (Theodorou 2014a). At the time of the study, the remedial teaching policy operated as a pull-out program whereby those considered as "other-language"[1] children were extracted from the mainstream classroom to receive classes in GAL for an assigned number of teaching periods a week, calculated yearly as per each school's reported needs.

This policy came about as the result of the incoming of a large number of immigrants from countries of the former USSR and Asia over the past few decades in Cyprus which has traditionally been an exporter, rather than an importer, of immigration. Recent reports locate the presence of non-Greek Cypriot children in public primary schools at 15.8 percent of the student population (MoEC 2017). According to the MoEC's 2016 Annual Report (2017), the five top countries from which immigrant children in Cyprus originate are Georgia, Rumania, Greece, Bulgaria, and Syria. Intercultural educational policies and practices have received quite the critique among local researchers in Cyprus who have pointed to its discriminatory, exclusionary, and assimilative effects (Hajisoteriou 2010; Zembylas 2010; Theodorou 2014b). Immigrant children's position has been generally explored through the elicitation of others' perspectives—e.g., mostly Greek-Cypriot students' constructions of themselves and others (not only children but also adults) as ethnically defined, raced, and classed subjects (e.g., Philippou 2009; Spyrou

2013; Zembylas and Lesta 2011). However, the very institution of remedial teaching, let alone immigrant children's lived experiences therein, had received little attention at the time we engaged in this inquiry (early 2013), with few researchers soliciting children's voices and performances across school contexts, including but not necessarily focusing on remedial teaching classes (e.g., Theodorou 2008; Kyriakou 2015; also, Charalambous 2015 as an example of study on remedial teaching).

Instantiations of performative politics

The school we visited was a suburban primary school (grades 1–6) with approximately 350 students. It was fairly multicultural and multilingual, with forty-two languages spoken collectively by students in its setting. A total of twenty-seven periods/week were designated centrally by the MoEC for the provision of remedial GAL teaching during the school year of data collection (2012–13), which the school opted to organize in sessions formulated based upon children's age and perceived ability in Greek. In addition to our observations of remedial GAL teaching sessions (total number of twenty teaching periods), we conducted interviews with ten children, six boys and four girls, who attended such classes. Our research participants shared six different ethnic and linguistic backgrounds as well as variegated circumstances and trajectories of arrival in Cyprus. Specifically, at the time of the interview, two students were short-stay visitors, four were recent arrivals (one was a political refugee, three were migrating as economic immigrants), three were living in Cyprus for over a year, and one was born in Cyprus but to non-Cypriot parents. With the exception of the latter child born to non-Cypriot parents, five of the nine children, all of who were recent arrivals, had reported to have Cypriot fathers who, however, had not been living with their immigrant mothers. In terms of their remedial instruction experience, four of them were placed in the intermediate-upper-grade beginners class, another four in the early beginners' class, one in the intermediate-grade advanced class, and one in the upper-grade advanced class.

As one of us (Stavroula) entered the field, we were unsure what to expect from it as our previous attempts in other settings to study the issue of remedial teaching of GAL and children's experience therein were met with resistance from school administrations. We had gone into this endeavor well aware of the way the official discourse constructed GAL learners as culturally, linguistically, and academically deficient by subjecting them to culturally and linguistically assimilative practices which exclusively centered on the (lack of the dominant) language marker (Zembylas 2010; Theodorou 2014a, b). We anticipated that these experiences of subjection would be reflected in children's narratives of what we had assumed would be less-than-meaningful experiences in GAL remedial classrooms. It turned out that our experience with children in the field both confirmed and discredited these assumptions, exposing all at once our naiveté as adult researchers and the indeterminacy of research as a fundamentally performative process.

Situating the Performances: The Constitution of Immigrant Children as School(ed) Subjects

Through official intercultural educational policy, the instructional material produced for the purposes of GAL teaching, and the school teachers' perceptions and pedagogical practice the immigrant child was marked as lacking. Constructed in negative rather than affirmative terms—as "non-Greek speaking" ("other-language") vs. "X-speaking"—the immigrant child was constituted as a subject whose intelligibility in the particular school and institutional setting depended on his/her ability to speak (only) Greek. The institutionalization of monolingualism contributed to its normalization in the school setting thereby rendering monolingualism a constituent of the normative discourse of studenthood which served to foreclose immigrant children's performative subjectivity of the student proper. The excerpt below is illuminative of such processes of foreclosing:

> Student: Now when I talk in class, *they make fun of me but not so much*.
> Stavroula: Hmm ...
> Student: Because *now I know Greek*.
> ...
> Student: *I write and read without difficulty now*.
> Stavroula: OK
> Student: I speak Greek and *I have many friends now*.
> (Student 10, individual interview in Greek,
emphasis added)

Student performances over the course of the interview, such as the one above, were replete with references of either lamenting their inability to speak Greek or displaying their newly acquired ability to speak it. As children repeatedly referred to the importance of speaking Greek their statements served to (re)produce the hierarchical dominance of the school norm. Hence, this child's narrations revealed the pervasive dominance of the normative discourse through the way one's subjectivity was constituted in acts of locution which served to (re)affirm it: "Because *now* I *know Greek*." The reiteration of this utterance is an integral part of the performative act whereby the individual strives in the context of the interview to constitute itself as a subject. It is through engaging with, embracing and replicating the normative discourse expressed through its desire to *be*, that the (non)subject is subjected to discursive power but also seeks to be rendered intelligible and thus recognized as a subject by others (see Butler 1997b): "I speak Greek and I *have many friends now*."

Attempting a different reading of this performance, we shifted our attention not to the immigrant child as (only and ever) an (im)proper-student-subject, but to the interview process as space for/of performative acts examining how the context of the interview might have foreclosed or enabled particular performances of subjectivities. Seeing the child as a-subject-in-the-interview, the expression of desire for the norm becomes a situated act which occurs in part *because of* the interview rather than irrespective of it (see Kesby 2007). As such, this child's performative subjectivity may be read as a feat of resistance or even an agency of desire whereby the child-in-the-interview traverses, to the eyes of the interested-researcher-audience, his/her constitution as the (im)proper-student-subject by conferring seemingly unnoticed dents in stylized repetitions rather than violently fracturing the dominant discourse. Perhaps such performances were facilitated at that point in time and in that particular setting by the interview operating as a space which sat between official and unofficial school practices; with a person that was and was not a school(ed) subject—a non-knower for whom children could perform differently in the dual sense of performance: as both a possibility for re-inscription (again, as resistance to, deviance from or a performing differently of their constitution as deficient learners), and as theatrical—a performance which presupposes an audience (imaginary or real) and which falls constantly under (re)interpretation.

Hence, in the interview context, we argue, immigrant children were able not only to bid for their recognition as subjects/students proper through their stated knowledge of the marker language, but were also able to potentially resist their construction as linguistically and culturally deficient by subverting the repeated history of their performances as academically deficient, even if that subversion, once again, depended on embracing the norm:

> Stavroula: OK. So what … Alright, let's see. So you're in fourth grade here. And how do you spend a day in class? What do you usually do in class?
>
> Student: For math I don't read, all the numbers are the same. It's pretty easy to understand. Gymnastics is really easy. For Greek I really don't know if there's something I can do. The teacher tells me and I do that. And for Religion I can read half the time and concentrate the other half because it's a bit easy to understand. History, I don't read because my friends help me with that and that's quite easy. And Geography I do sometimes. It's like Religion. Sometimes I read, sometimes I don't. And what other classes are there? Science. I don't read through that because it's easy to understand. Life Skills sometimes I read, sometimes I don't.
>
> (Student 1, individual interview in English)

Constructing a successful academic identity in school subjects other than Greek disrupts children's rendering as subjects who cannot be. What is then read as agentive about this performance is children's (re)claiming of a social position through the portrayal of different-than-assumed competence either in Greek or a different subject area (as above)—a performance which would not have been recognized, or even possibly allowed, in the mainstream classroom.

Such fluidity, and perhaps inconsistency, in immigrant children's performances renders the indeterminacy of their performances as key condition to engaging with the query of what one is to make of the notion of children's agency, especially when children's acts are seen to contribute to the sustenance of practices and discourses that work to suppress them. Evident in the statements of Student 10 and lurking in between the words of Student 1 above is the normative discourse of proper studenthood in which academic competence and Greek fluency are part and parcel of the same construct that renders children intelligible as subjects in the school setting: here, the local context of the particular school yet as informed, shaped by, and mediating official policies inscribing the non-Greek-speaking, non-Cypriot student, and their position in school. This norm is not being challenged in the way that this child discursively constructs his/herself. On the contrary, it is further consolidated through the repetitive utterances regarding one's knowledge of Greek and "ease" of understanding the school curriculum upon which a successful performance of the proper-student-subject depends.

Reading such performances as political acts opens up possibilities for analyzing children's subjectivation and agency when the personal (desire) coincides with the institutional/social (normative school discourses). It, thus, complicates understandings of children's agency, as it raises questions about the meaning of performances that extend and reinforce normative school discourses at the same time that they are intended to traverse them. What are we to make of children's performances as language learners and school students when those subject and subjectivate them in accord to the rationalities that permeate a space like school, where being a student proper surfaces as an object of desire even if this erases particular children's histories and present experiences?

Kesby (2007) suggests that we see children's agency not as a fixed entity but as being achieved through engaging with available resources, with the school-in-research but also the interview space and the research methods employed being parts of these. If children's reproduction of normative discourses is linked to the limited availability of resources around them from which they could draw, what is then the ethical and methodological obligation for researchers working with children to facilitate the achievement of children's agency? In what ways could/should such obligation be fulfilled through the use of which research methods and tools? What kinds of questions does the fulfilment of this obligation on behalf of the researchers raise considering the power dynamics between adult researchers and children participants, and the risk for manipulating, patronizing, or imposing new subjectivating discourses and practices unto children? It is with these questions in mind but also with an acknowledgment that children's agency—in childhood studies and in social science research more broadly—is linked to the researcher's ethical obligation to have children's voices heard (e.g., Wyness 2015) that we proceed to discuss the complications thereof. As we unpack the interview as a performative space, we thus argue for understanding the ambiguity and impossibility of agency at the research moment.

The Interview as Performative Space and Children's Agency Therein

In our attempt to destabilize the power dynamics between us (the Greek/English-speaking Cypriot adult researchers) and the participants (non-Greek speakers with varied knowledge of English, immigrant child participants), we designed interview tasks like drawing, photo-elicitation, and sorting of materials, in order to solicit children's voices yet without necessarily relying heavily on the verbalization of thoughts, experiences, and ideas. Despite our intentions, our second current reading helped us realize that our own performances as adults, researchers, others (to the children and to the school) had constituted not only immigrant children but also the very process of research in particular, perhaps restrictive, ways.

Of most importance is the realization that the student proper, and particularly the prioritization of Greek as the condition of children's intelligibility as school subjects, was reiterated through the statements we had chosen in order to provide children with categories and features to talk about children in general, themselves, and finally children in the remedial classroom (all of which stemmed from relevant research and our own prior experience of researching [with] immigrant children; see e.g., Theodorou 2008): *Cypriot, non-Cypriot, speaks Greek, does not speak Greek, speaks many languages, has travelled a lot, has many friends, reads and writes without difficulty, asks for help in class, everybody wants to be their friend.* To our direction that they grouped the statements in ways that made sense to them, children responded in differential ways that signified both openings and constrictions in the ways they constructed categories but also subjectivated themselves. For some, construction of themselves was connected to features like traveling a lot, speaking many languages, everybody wanting to be their friends, and having many friends (e.g., Students 1 and 7); for others, such features were conditioned:

> Student: There's a group [of cards] that's like me in [country of origin] but not here. It's this one. Lots of people want to be my friend.
> Stavroula: So in [country of origin] what? Many people want to be your friends? But not really here [Cyprus]?
> Student: No. Well, because lots of people know Greek and I don't really ask them, because I don't know enough Greek to ask.
>   (Student 6, individual interview in English)

This child's performance of social status and thus recognizability in school, as this might be instantiated through popularity and friendship, is directly linked to and compromised by her limited knowledge of Greek. There were indeed moments when boundaries were pushed to also include features like traveling a lot, speaking many languages and having many friends (Interviews 1, 4 and 9) or when that very child in the remedial teaching contradicted children's constructions of themselves, as if they did not see themselves as "remedial classroom students." However, it was through children's depictions of "children in the remedial classroom" as *non-Cypriots, non-Greek speaking* and *in need of help* (Interviews 1, 2, 3, 5, 9, and 10) that the student proper was repeated and thus stabilized as the norm. The multiplicity of performances and the contradictions within and across children's performances as school subjects could not flee away from centering knowledge of Greek as key to their subjectivation of students—a centering which was indeed put forth by the same activity we as adult researchers had initially designed with the intention to traverse it. And perhaps it was also put forth by the more subtle ways in which our own identities and restricted knowledge of languages (Greek and English rather than also other languages spoken by child participants) not only framed our communication with the children and thus their performances as literate beings and school subjects, but also reiterated aspects of the student proper that children appeared to concurrently traverse, resist, and desire. In a sense, this recognition dovetails with commentaries on structured agency, complicated agency, mediated agency, relationally negotiated agency—all of which reaffirm its multiplicity in meaning, form, and effect, and also point to what we presume as the impossibility of agency at the research moment.

Discussion

The current analysis sets out as an exploration into the notion of performative politics in the context of the interview through interrogating the readings of our data, the readings of their readings, and the data generative processes themselves. We came to this task engaging with the question of children's agency to the extent that, following post-structural lines of thought, we saw agency as intricately connected to the project of subjectivities. And we ended it with a struggle to grasp what we have come to see as the implausibility of agency as it has been currently defined: as structured, as constricted, as mediated, as unpredictable, as fluid, as complex, as resistant, as compliant, as ambiguous, as individual, as relational, as desire, as imperfect reiteration, as reinscription, as resignification, as ... evidently implausible: a construct that we may have to accede that it may well have reached its limits. We believe that this is so because:

Reading immigrant children's performances during interviewing as political acts, led us to see their *agency as constricted*: as they re-constructed (in the meaning of repeating) the student proper by reciting the conditions of their intelligibility as school subjects, their attempts to perform differently were confined within limits set by them, us, and others, rendering agency more akin to acts of unsettlement rather than rupture. Immigrant children's desire to be recognized as students proper was indicative of how they resisted not so much to the discursive norms that defined them, but their position therein. Thus, we asserted that, to be intelligible as school subjects, immigrants *needed* to recite discourses that made sense within the very context where they performed (the school, the remedial teaching classroom, research itself) (Youdell 2006), echoing Butler's (1997b) *agency of desire* and *imperfect reiteration*. By doing so, we posited, they attempted to re-signify themselves as non-deficient school subjects by risking their very existence as (other) subjects therein, thereby reading children's *agency as re-inscription* and *erasure*.

Still, we said, what this points to is the conceptualization of children's agency as a constant and concurrent struggle of resistance within discourse, albeit each time with *unpredictable and unpredicted outcomes*, effected through desiring the conditions of one's own subordination (Butler 1997b); in this case, through acknowledging and embracing the need to know Greek and, thus gain recognition as student proper, but in unforeseen ways and with unpredictable success. This calls us to rethink arguments in childhood studies on the necessity of providing tools and opportunities to children to engage in reflexive and critical or resistant agency as ways to destabilize power dynamics in the research process (see e.g. Kesby 2007; Wyness 2015). Concurring with Gallacher and Gallagher (2008), we argue that such understanding of children's agency in research rests on the supposition of a certain form of consciousness that risks denying the indeterminacy of research as a process of subject formation. Embracing this indeterminacy refigures broader discussions on the child as being or developmentally becoming to a becoming that is always already unfinished and uncertain, a challenge to "understandings of humans—adults and children—as singular, autonomous agents: identifiable subjects imbued with agency" (Gallacher and Gallagher 2008: 510).

Linking this to ethical and methodological considerations of children's agency at the research moment, we thus reflected in this chapter on our own actions and decisions. We acknowledged how we might have always already contributed to the construction of the student proper in unseen ways but also sought to take note of how the space of the interview provided openings to the re-subjectivation of children, through the same methods that constricted their performances. By giving them the opportunity to talk themselves into existence in subject-areas beyond Greek or in their previous schools, for example, the interview allowed many of the immigrant children to perform differently. As that different would compare to the prioritization of academic language as central to the constitution of school discourse, questions are raised on how constrictions and possibilities foreground the *fluidity* of children's performances and their shifting nature (Barron 2007) in research. That we could not escape our own performances of self or that those were possibly read by our own audience (children-in-research) in ways that prompted the re-iteration of the student proper add to the uncertainty that permeates children's agency and subjectivation in the research process.

Addressing these concerns necessitates that we become aware of our ethical responsibility of recognizing children's agency as necessarily bound to normative meanings of being that are nevertheless never immune from resignification (Youdell 2006). Such discussion of ethics would evoke the messiness of research as extending beyond ready-made, established categories and as necessitating researchers becoming comfortable with uncertainty and discomfort (e.g., Holt 2004). Connecting this to the acknowledgment of the relationality and contingency of research, as well as of the possibility of fallibility and mess, renders ethics in research a matter (of also) acknowledging that research happens in non-ideal ways (Horton 2008). We see this as leading to acknowledging the indeterminacy of research and the impossibility that the researcher herself can be a knowing and knowledgeable subject (Scheurich 1995).

It is in this sense that we see the performative space of interviewing as necessarily political in the ways it is designed but also in the ways it is repeatedly represented. In writing this chapter, we "forced" ourselves to read this politicality differently and re-pose questions anew. Rather than look for ways to ameliorate a rather fixed vision of the power imbalance between adult and child in the interview process, we asked: Can we ever really? Rather than trying to measure the power of/within subjects, we sought to unravel its omnipresence in human (inter)action. And rather than taking for granted the notion of the agentive child, we interrogated what the meaning of such agency might be, what sort of forms it might take, and what kinds of openings might facilitate and potentially, concurrently hinder, its achievement.

In childhood studies, some of these questions and concerns have lingered in the acknowledgment of a shift from the "what" to the "how" of agency. That our readings of our data led us to a multiplicity of "whats" and "hows," to more questions rather than answers in regard to what agency might mean, prompt us to further ask whether the very notion of (children's) agency needs to be dismantled. Such dismantling would work on two planes: a rejection of key ontological and epistemological premises upon which research in childhood studies has rested, and a radical re-theorization of research itself. The former has been an issue of discussion in childhood studies and social sciences, more broadly, in the form of challenging the humanist understanding of agency as an individual's capacity or freedom to act (e.g., James and James 2012; Wyness 2015). Researchers like Youdell (2003, 2012) have discussed such notion of agency by suggesting that what is perceived as agency should be linked to individuals' constitution as subjects amid power relations and discursive practices; and, we have attempted to do so with our own readings of the interview data.

The dismantling of agency is further evidenced in suggested definitions of agency as an "entanglement of flows," as intra-actions of multiple people and things whose meaning and existence do not pre-exist their encounter (Mazzei 2013: 733; see also Barad 2003; Lather 2013). Identifying themselves as "post" or "new" theorists (as in, e.g., post-structural, post-humanist, new materialist), scholars have suggested that such flow implies a temporal emergence, a potential continual transformation, a difference and differentiation that is yet-not-thought. This, as St. Pierre (2013) asserts, causes the collapse of boundaries between being and knowing, between ontology and epistemology, and renders representation unthinkable. For childhood studies, even the connection of agency to children's voice (e.g., James and James 2012) and the researching of those through participatory methods of varying types and degrees (Gallacher and Gallagher 2008) should be rethought: the notion of voice still implies a disconnection between children's experience and their ability to represent it, while participation would only make sense as the coming together of humans and nonhumans with histories and in spatialities that equally participate in the encounter in unforeseen ways and that create openings to think of the world anew.

A dismantling of this type points to a set of impossibilities: to an extreme, the opening of possibilities in seeing agency as the entanglement of flows actually makes it impossible to see. That is, such explosion of agency might cause its implosion, rendering it a non-object of study. Even if we get comfortable with such discomfort (Holt 2004), we come across a second impossibility: that of actually engaging (with agency) in a research inquiry. For some, this hints to the need to radically rethink research processes and methods, as opportunities to experiment with standard practices in order to think of thinking as creation, of analysis as resisting habitual ways of reading the data or as an enactment among researchers-data-participants-theory-analysis, of interviews and interview transcripts as a "collision of forces" (Mazzei 2013: 737; also Lather 2013). In a sense and without necessarily aligning ourselves with such "post" inquiry, we engaged in this through our multiple readings of data; perhaps unintentionally, perhaps partially, perhaps unsuccessfully. It is for this reason that we succumb to our inability to offer a more concrete suggestion on how discussions on children's agency may be framed in a post-agency era and are instead left with the urge to ask: If such shift implies the dissolution of the child-as-agent, of research, and even of us, as researchers, what are the risks, possibilities, politics and the ethics of making this move?

Note

1 *Other-language children* is the term encountered in official policy texts such as circulars and governmental publications at the time of the study. We use this term in our text when referencing the official policy context. Else, we employ the term *immigrant children* to refer to non-indigenous members of the student population.

PART FOUR

Engagements with Political Subjects and Subjectivities

CHAPTER ELEVEN

Who Is (to Be) the Subject of Children's Rights?

Matías Cordero Arce

This chapter deals with two different but interrelated issues: who *is* the subject of children's rights, which is an empirical question, which will be dealt with briefly, and who *should* be the subject of children's rights, which is a normative question, and the main issue at stake here. I will begin with the issue of who is considered a legal subject in general, with no qualifications concerning age, then delve into the debate prompted by the nature of the legal subject, and finish by addressing the question of the child legal subject. This endeavor is motivated by the aim of developing better tools and concepts for the study of children and their rights, and of putting those tools and concepts at the service of the wider field of childhood studies and of children themselves (Cordero Arce 2015a).

The legal subject and its critiques

In our Western legal systems, spread worldwide through colonization and globalization, when we talk about the subject of rights (the legal subject), we may refer to a biological human being, as the interests' theorists do, and in this sense all children are always legal subjects (and so, *objects* of legal protection); we may also refer to a pure legal artifice, shorthand for *whatever* is a rights-holder and duty-bearer, which is meaningful and necessary when talking of legal subjects such as corporations, municipalities, etc. (see Naffine 2003; Parcero 2007); but the most common use, which is also the pertinent one when discussing children's legal personality, is to refer to "a competent adult human being" (Feinberg 1974: 44); that is the kind of being of which it is usually meaningful to say she or he has rights (Parcero 2007: 127). By "competent" it is implied someone with the capacity to designate him or herself as the author of his or her acts, i.e., an *agent* (Ricoeur 2000: 2–3), a *rational* being "who is at full liberty to choose the kind of life he or she wants to lead, and is therefore responsible for his or her actions and omissions" (Lindroos-Hovinheimo 2015: 690). In this third sense the legal subject does not differ substantially from the moral subject.

As put by Nino (1989), in a definition that encapsulates well the liberal understanding of the subject of rights, she or he is someone not tied to any end, an originating source of valid claims, and responsible for her or his aims. The legal subject is capable of "choosing ends, adopting interests, forming desires," and is prior to those ends, interests, or desires, that is, separated "from the causal flow in which these empirical phenomena are immersed" (Nino 1989: 110). The subject's identity is thus impervious to whatever ends, interests, or desires she or he has. This is why adults are said to have *individual autonomy* (see Nino 1989: 120–130): in freedom understood as autonomy, it is "self" (*autos*) which gives itself the law (*nomos*) (Douzinas 2000: 235).

The legal subject thus conceived was already criticized as an "isolated monad" by Karl Marx (2009) in 1844, the Marxist critique pointing out

> the formal nature of the legal subject, its "freedom" from the substantive realities of social life, and the way that it defines most of the "real" inequalities into the residual capacity of private life, thus favouring the particular interests of one class while operating under the banner of universality. (Boyle 1991: 519)

The legal subject has attracted increasing criticism ever since, by communitarianism, the ethics of care, feminist jurisprudence, and other developments on identity stemming from philosophy and the social sciences. These critiques have been mainly aimed at such subject's petrous ontology, at its alleged but undesirable and impossible *independence*. Michael Sandel (1984), a leading figure in the communitarian tradition, described it as an "unencumbered self," Norbert Elias (1982) talked of the *homo clausus*, and Raimon Panikkar (1982) defined a society made up of such subjects as a mere aggregation of individuals who have no bonds with each other, nor with nature. The ethics of care, founded precisely upon bonding (Gilligan 1982), arose as a contradictor to that gelid society and its indifferent individuals, to the fact that "legal metaphysics has no time for the pain of real people" (Douzinas 2000: 240).

The legal subject is unencumbered, closed within himself,[1] isolated, and indifferent because he suffers an excess of reason only paralleled by the shortage of everything else that defines humanity; he is an abstract, disembodied, and decontextualized individual (see Douzinas 2000). But then, the alleged rationality and free-will that make up such supposedly autonomous being have also faced severe scrutiny from psychology and philosophy. The psychological critique, stemming from the psychoanalytical tradition inaugurated by Freud, points to the "consciousness-eluding, unconscious driving forces and motives of individual action" and "demonstrates that the human subject cannot be transparent to herself in the manner claimed in the classical notion of autonomy," which "invalidates the idea of autonomy in the sense of the controllability of our own doing" (Honneth 1995: 261). On the other side, the language-philosophical critique, advanced by Wittgenstein and Saussure, among others, points to "the dependence of individual speech on a pre-given system of linguistic meanings" (Honneth 1995: 261), that is, to the fact that whatever we say, and mean by what we say, is always dependent on the meaning-possibilities of our previous, given, tongue. These two critiques reveal that there are "forces" present in each of us which might not only be impossible to control, but, even further, impossible to detect (see Honneth 1995).

Engaging with the critique

So, we are left with a very unappealing subject of rights; a disembodied and selfish *pure reason*, which itself is not quite reasonable. And yet, we cannot and must not dispense with it, nor can children.

To understand why, it is necessary to underscore that the legal subject is just a *representation* of flesh-and-blood human beings (see Nino 1989: 47), and a representation that highlights only the aspects which are relevant to the legal field. We have to distinguish between the everyday use of the word "person," and its use within the legal field, as in "legal person" or "legal subject" (which for the purposes of this chapter I make the same). So, for example, if the sociological subject is the person as *agent*, who is also subject to a structure, and the psychological subject is the person as maker of *behaviors* and bearer of *mind*, the legal subject is the person as *rights-holder* and *duty-bearer*. And even if in all three cases we may be referring substantially to the same human being, each concept works formally, methodologically, and in practice at different levels; each "person" is molded by its respective discipline and is thus a circumscribed *persona* (i.e., mask) that human beings are made to wear when analyzed from a certain disciplinarian—theoretical and practical—perspective.

But why does jurisprudence need such an ugly rights-holder and duty-bearer? We will see that it does not need to be *that* ugly, but, it cannot part with some of the basic characteristics so harshly targeted by its critics.

If, as is the case, our societies need rules in order to organize its members' conduct, then, they also need to subscribe to the view "that man [sic] is, or can become, a responsible agent, capable of understanding and following rules, and answerable for his [sic] defaults" (Fuller 1969: 162). As put by

Neil MacCormick, autonomy is necessary to any idea of normative order: "Only an autonomous being can respond through acts of volition to the requirements of a normative order" (1997: 229). Law requires not only autonomous, but also identifiable and stable subjects "in order to attribute blame, responsibility or rights" (Mohr 2007: 123); subjects whose wills bind them and who can be held accountable for their acts and deals; subjects whose signature in a contract does not fade and whose imprint in a crime scene cannot be deleted. If we accept the view that a legal order implies, explicitly or implicitly, to accept some principles of conduct, and to abide by them, then "we also have to accept as its consequences certain ideas of separation between persons, continuity of personal identity through time and the possibility of ascribing normative consequences to decisions, despite their causal determination" (Nino 1989: 47). So, even if the psychological subject were to be defined as more unfree than free, or the sociological subject pictured mainly as an effect of structure, the fact is that the legal system as we know it *needs* an autonomous, free-willing legal subject for responsibility to be possible, and thus for the system itself not to collapse.

However, within the legal discipline we must not rely uncritically on such a legal subject. Elsewhere (Cordero Arce 2012, 2015a), I have argued for (children) legal subjects that seize their rights as tools of empowerment. Our aim, inevitably *political*, we must remember (Cordero Arce 2015a, b) should then be to dig into those theoretical approaches that strengthen the footing of such legal subjects as full-fledged rights-holders *and duty-bearers* (we shall see below the importance of emphasizing "duties"), but without neglecting the sound critiques with which the legal subject has been faced.

As said above, the ethics of care has critically focused on the rights discourse. But the ethics of care is inspired in experiences of actual people, interacting face-to-face with concrete others out of sincere care. Therefore, those experiences can hardly become generalized as normative standards for all (being, the vast majority of those "all," unknown others) because, if they so were, the virtuous care toward a loved one would most certainly degenerate into a patronizing vice toward multiple unknown ones (see Mendus 2015: 651). Besides, as Mendus adds, "here, what is desired is not sympathy from those who are better off than ourselves, but rather a recognition of our claims of need as claims of justice, not as requests for compassion or sympathy," that is, a recognition of those care-receivers as rights-holders. And so, goes on Mendus, the danger is "that a focus on care, far from supplementing considerations of justice … , may in fact drive them out and thus reduce what are properly claims of right to pleas for generosity."

A similar logic serves to question the recent capabilities approach as a move forward in the understanding of rights as empowerment tools. To situate rights at the center of an ethical theory of freedom and capabilities disregards the political history of human rights that has always been closely tied to struggles around legitimacy and just rule. Rights do not simply state strong moral entitlements that we owe to individuals; they are in the first place claims to justice and legitimacy that enframe our collective existence. (Benhabib 2013: 42)

In the 1840s, John Austin, the renowned legal theorist, criticized International Law by terming it "International Morality" because in it there was no real possibility of claiming between sovereign nations (Austin 1885). We should warn, once again, of the danger of turning the powerful discourse of rights into merely an ethics.

To find a strong footing for the legal subject, that at the same time engages with the critiques mentioned so far, we have to look somewhere else, and realize, first, that one of the greatest *political* acts of law "is the making of a legal person (simply put, [she or] he who can act in law) and, in the same move, the making of legal non-persons (those who cannot act in law …)" (Naffine 2003: 347). To be, or not to be a legal subject is a matter of power: "One of the prime effects of power [is] that certain bodies, certain gestures, certain discourses, certain desires, come to be identified and constituted as individuals" (Foucault 1980: 98).[2] Second, and this is especially relevant to children as will be seen below, we have to realize that once someone becomes a legal subject, the abstraction, disembodiment, and lack of context that are of her or his nature *as* legal subject are only a matter of formal discourse: the legal subject is always stained by those with the power to so do, that is, by those with the power to define who is to be a full-fledged rights-holder and duty-bearer, and who is not.

The point I want to make is that legal subjecthood—*to be* and *how to be* a legal subject—is an open possibility, a floating signifier; that this *abstraction* allows to be filled in multiple ways. Just as liberty or equality (see Cordero Arce 2015a), legal subjecthood is a contested definition that represents some and not other flesh-and-blood human beings, and which defines those who are represented in diverse, often hierarchical, ways.

For those human beings who are legal subjects, to be one is to be both a "vehicle of freedom and agent of morality" on the one hand, and subjected to, shaped by and called to account before the law on the other (Douzinas 2000: 216). "Uniting subjection and freedom stands the law," says Douzinas (2000: 222). But the hermeneutic relation between those two poles, the hierarchical organization of them *vis-à-vis* each and every legal subject, is a matter of power, of the power to fill in the abstraction implied by legal subjecthood. We are talking of the inevitable political nature of legal subjecthood, so it is imperative to bring up citizenship when discussing it.

Just as citizens, that is, as *political* subjects, the subjects of (human) rights do not designate a definitive collectivity. "Legal subject" and "citizen" are surplus names, names that set out a ... dispute ... about who is included in their count. Correspondingly, freedom and equality are not predicates belonging to definite subjects. Political predicates are open predicates: they open up a dispute about what they exactly entail and whom they concern in which cases ... Political subjects build such cases of verification. (Ranciere 2004: 303–304)

And *citizenship* builds the case for that form of organizing and defining freedom and subjection in which the subject

is no longer the man [*sic*] *called before the Law*, or to whom an inner voice dictates the Law, or tells him that he should recognize and obey the law; he is rather the man [*sic*] who ... "makes the Law", i.e. constitutes it, or *declares* it to be valid. The subject is someone who is responsible or accountable because he [*sic*] is legislator, accountable for the *consequences*, the implementation and non-implementation of the Law he has himself [*sic*] made. (Balibar 1994: 11)

The rights that make up the Law, although attributed to individual legal subjects, are *always* defined and conquered collectively. To understand legal subjecthood as citizenship means precisely, as Balibar explains, that *individual* autonomy is *collectively* constructed through the struggle for self-emancipation, that citizenship is incompatible with any form of subjection, and that "the value of ... agency arises from the fact that no one can be liberated or emancipated *by others*, although no one can liberate himself [*sic*] *without others*" (Balibar 1994: 12, and see Cordero Arce 2015b: 299–307).

Now, it must be stressed that to talk of "power," "struggle," or "conquest" is not to talk necessarily of sheer, brute force. Words, discourse, "reason," are all vehicles of power. The legal subjects conceived as citizens (hereinafter, *subjects-as-citizens*) rise powerfully when they claim a *justification* for being treated in such or such way, a reason why liberty and equality are being denied or not sufficiently assured to them. The discourse of human dignity can be traced centuries back precisely to "protests against forms of political domination that did not regard those who are subject to such rule as persons to whom the exercise of political power had to be adequately justified." (Forst 2010: 721). The struggle for rights is thus also a struggle for reasons, for a new common sense in which a once excluded group stands up to demand a deserved status (Habermas 2010) with which it will no longer be possibly excluded from the realm of full legal subjecthood.

Not only rights and its subjects, then, but also the dignity through which the latter win the former, are relational concepts, that stretch beyond the limits of the "autonomous" individual. Dignity is no longer conceived as stemming from a personal recognizable characteristic, capacity, "good" of the human being (most usually, "reason"). Rather, dignity is now manifested in the collective struggle *with* co-oppressed others *against* an oppressive other, and, as Forst (2010: 734) adds, in the subject as someone who has to give reasons *to* others, while at the same time being entitled to expect reasons *from* others. The legal subject is thus *embedded* in contexts of communication as well as interaction (Benhabib 2013: 39).

An emancipated and emancipatory (child) legal subject

With the UN Convention on the Rights of the Child (CRC), children have been invited to join the "club" of legal subjects, however, their subjecthood, the kind of subjects they are within the hegemonic discourse inaugurated by the CRC, is very disheartening. As put by the former Chair of the UN Committee on the Rights of the Child, sadly, but very precisely, children are represented as *mini humans*, who thus have *mini rights*.[3] In the organization and definition of the poles of subjection and freedom of which we spoke above, children are placed in the pole of subjection, subjection to *proper* legal subjects, that is, to adults (and so paternalism, under a cloak of euphemisms—v.gr. art. 12 CRC). In the hegemonic discourse of children's rights the child legal subject represents something more than a mere biological human being, that is, more than a mere object of legal protection, but definitely something less than a full-fledged rights-holder and duty-bearer, who still is, by definition, only the (male) adult (see Cordero Arce 2015a: 292–296, 2015b: 186–222).

However, a mounting children's movement spearheaded by the organized movements of working children and youth in the majority world has began shifting the understanding of the child legal subject toward that full-fledged rights-holder and duty-bearer, that is, toward the *subject-as-citizen*. Children have shown to be agents and to be able to define and conquer their rights, thus achieving in fact, and in law, the category of *subjects-as-citizens*. Such a concept of the child legal subject has opened emancipatory possibilities to children worldwide, which shows the sway in the rights discourse between the pole of subjection (hegemonic discourse, paternalism, *rights-as-control*) and the pole of freedom (emerging child legal subject, *rights-as-emancipation*) (see Cordero Arce 2012, 2015a, b).

What will occupy us in this last section is how to engage with the critiques and approaches exposed in the previous sections when dealing with this emerging emancipated and emancipatory child legal subject, because taking children's rights seriously (Freeman 1992, 2007) implies nothing other than taking the child legal subject seriously.

Adult Legal Subject—Child Legal Subject

We know that the (children's) rights discourse is "the currency in use" (Freeman 2011: 377); we have not devised another way to forcefully instantiate human beings' (including children's) claims of justice. And we also know that legal subjecthood is just a representation of flesh-and-blood human beings, which highlights only the human aspects relevant to the legal field (as rights-holders and duty-bearers). However, we must bear in mind that the rights discourse stemmed from the model of the "competent adult (man)," and still founds itself upon that model. The legal subject represents, conspicuously, the rational adult (man). So, if we wish to take the *child* legal subject seriously, to begin with we must acknowledge that we are representing her or him with the gender-loaded, adult model.

No matter how much the movements of working children have advanced the concept of the child legal subject as citizen, children remain an oppressed minority worldwide, not the least because of how they are depicted by Law. The continuous violation of their rights suffered by children *as children* compels us to expressly take into account the power differentials that result from social stratification based on lower (i.e., *lesser*) age when discussing the child legal subject and her or his rights. And this means that children's legal studies must embrace the corpus of anti-discrimination law and the legal-theoretical struggles fought on behalf of other oppressed minorities, such as women, black people, LGBTs, or people with disabilities.[4]

The quest of feminist jurisprudence to rebuild a legal subject who does not have *man* as the measure of humanity (MacKinnon 1991) is especially fit to inspire children's legal studies in rebuilding a legal subject that has neither the *adult* as such measure. This makes it imperative to include *adultism* as yet another system of oppression in any and every intersectional analysis, and, inversely, to analyze the place of children in society always from an intersectional perspective; say, approaching this child as a black, rich, heterosexual, blind boy; and that child as a white, poor, lesbian, visually unimpaired girl (see Cordero Arce 2015a, b).

Now, considering children *as children*, the pressing question we need to begin dealing with is which is the middle path between *sameness* (children are *as* human as adults) and *difference* (children are not adults, and adults are not the norm for defining "the human"). The following two subsections might hint toward an answer.

The Child Legal Subject and Her/His Duties

The fully independent legal subject, already critiqued in the previous section, is further held to account by the place of children's duties inside children's legal frameworks such as the ones enshrined by the African Charter on the Rights of the Child and the Bolivian Code of Children and Adolescents, by contrast to the CRC, which draws a pre-social "child," without present responsibilities (e.g., art. 29.1.d CRC).

The African Charter on the Rights of the Child explicitly talks about children's responsibilities (see art. 31). As ruled by Chief Justice Pius Langa (2008: 26) of the South African Constitutional Court: "The notion that 'we are not islands unto ourselves' is central to the understanding of the individual in African thought."

Underlying the responsibilities toward their families and society of Article 31 lies the central position of the extended family which is "the glue binding social, economic and political life in African tradition" (Sloth-Nielsen and Mezmur 2008: 173), preventing "the atomization of individuals into socially unviable, unconnected and ultimately disintegrated structures" (Sloth-Nielsen and Mezmur 2008: 174). In this scheme, in which duties are expressly regarded as *legal*, and not merely moral, "[by] providing for children's duties towards their families, ... the child is not merely an object upon whom protection and welfare is bestowed, but an actor, a subject, upon whom the responsibility to promote the overall well-being of the family unit is placed" (Sloth-Nielsen and Mezmur 2008: 175). The child legal subject is represented not merely as "a dependent," but also as someone upon whom others also depend; not just as someone in need, but also as someone needed by others. Assuming responsibilities and fulfilling their duties, the child legal subject participates in a relevant way in the social life.

In the same vein, the recent Bolivian Code of Children and Adolescents lists children's duties, which include, among others, the duty to assume their responsibility as *active subjects in the construction of their society* and the duty to know and defend their rights and respect the rights of others (see Article 158).[5]

In making the child legal subject a rights-holder *and also a duty-bearer*, these charters are headed toward acknowledging children's full-fledged legal subjecthood. And it should not sound paradoxical that legal subjecthood is enhanced by constructing a less "independent" legal subject. Already in 1861, John Stuart Mill, an icon of the liberal rights tradition, argued that the subject of rights is fully such only when allowed to take part in the affairs of her or his society, to become *responsible* for the destiny of her or his society:

> Wherever the sphere of action of human beings is artificially circumscribed, their sentiments are narrowed and dwarfed in the same proportion. The food of feeling is action; even domestic affection lives upon voluntary good offices. Let a person have nothing to do for his country, and he will not care for it. (Mill 2015: 211)

Subjects-as-citizens have thus a basic right *and duty* to democratic participation, a right to count and a duty to be held accountable; *subjects-as-citizens* have a basic right to be *necessary subjects of their present communities*.

And yet, the current subject of children's rights, that mini-human with mini-rights, represents equivocally a necessary subject of the *future* community (a future worker, a future citizen, currently developing and socializing), and/or a necessary *object* of the present community (the ultimate, and most vulnerable, source of *adult* meaning) (see Cordero Arce 2015b). The right to be a necessary subject of the present community implies transcending these representations and (re)turning the representation of their legal subjecthood to children themselves, right here, right now.

Autonomous Interdependence

As we have seen in the previous section and subsections, legal theory, political philosophy, and jurisprudence, as well as legal and political struggles often crystallized in proper legal charters, have lately all shown a tendency to fertilize the seemingly independent legal subject with an *interdependent* approach, which intends to transcend the atomization brought about by modern individualism.

In what concerns us here, there is a collectivity that stands out in these emerging understanding of the legal subject, namely, the children organized in movements of working children and youth (NATs) who have been struggling for decades now for their acknowledgment as full-fledged rights-holders and duty-bearers, *subjects-as-citizens*, legal subjects with the right to define their own subjecthood. The NATs are treading a difficult path but they find a strong footing in the approaches we have described as providing it, which are themselves empirically validated precisely by struggles such as the one undertaken by the NATs. They are defining and conquering collectively their rights, collectively constructing their individual autonomy, and assuming the responsibility of their own emancipation—from the category of mini-humans—in democratic collaboration with other children[6] and adults. By constructing a strong subjecthood for themselves in collaboration with adults, they are problematizing the unproblematic arrangement of childhood and adulthood in watertight compartments, thus blurring the petrous borders of the (adult) legal subject, who cannot be defined as independent anymore, nor as the measure of the "human" behind the legal subject. The NATs are demanding a justification for being excluded from work, and in countries like Bolivia, as shown by the recent Bolivian Code of Children and Adolescents (see Liebel 2015), they have not rested until proving that there is no such justification. They have thus redefined what the child legal subject is—someone entitled to work with dignity—and what work is—a realm not only of adults. The NATs are assuming to be already responsible subjects regarding their families and communities, that is, to be rights-holders *and duty-bearers* (see Cordero Arce 2012, 2015a, b).

The NATs are making the case for children legal subjects understood as necessary subjects of their present communities. Children who work are dependent on their families, *just as these are dependent on them*, so talking of (in)dependence is in itself highly misleading. It is not that children are independent per se, which they are not, but that neither are adults, no matter how much adultism tries to construct them as such (see Cordero Arce 2015a, b). Thus, the NATs are charting the course for a new legal subjecthood, which represents neither independence nor dependence, but *autonomous interdependence*. Here, interdependence does not annul the legal subject, quite to the contrary, it boosts her possibilities of furthering her rights, only possible through collective intergenerational struggle. That is why it is an *autonomous* interdependence, because the individual (child) subject is not pushed down by belonging to a community, but lifted up. Borrowing Bhaskar's concepts, family, community, and society are "a necessary condition for, and medium of, intentional agency" but intentional agency, children's will of their own, is also "in turn a necessary condition for the reproduction or transformation" of family, community, and society (see Bhaskar 1993: 154). *Autonomous interdependence* represents the meeting of "care"—dependence, relationships, duties—and "justice"—independence, autonomy, rights.

I can think of two important objections to the preceding scheme. First, what happens with those who simply cannot join the struggle for their rights; are they also full-fledged legal subjects? And second, how do we deal with a legal subject that purportedly is emancipated through oppression (i.e., work)?

On the first objection, once established that the struggle for rights is a *collective* struggle, the fact that within a certain collectivity there are those that do not participate directly or actively in the struggle for their full citizenship, say infants in the case of the collectivity of NATs, is relativized. And this is so because their lack of material participation in the struggle does not prevent them from belonging to the collectivity, that is, from participating of the identity of the collectivity which is immerse in the struggle, and thus of the rights and status conquered by the collectivity. I am speaking of a "general or generalizable will" (Hallward 2010: 121), meaning, a stated or alleged will, so it must be presumed that those who do not participate directly in the struggle enjoy their conquests nevertheless. This should not be taken as another, maybe subtler version of paternalism, because paternalism implies decisions taken by *some* (adults) concerning *others* (children) who are conceived, by definition, as *completely others*. On the contrary, here we are talking about a new subject, a political "us" which, at least in theory, should part from the essentializing and hierarchical distinctions implied by paternalism. We are now talking about *children* (and adults) fighting for *children* (and adults) who cannot fight. There is a radical difference between talking on behalf of *an-other*, and talking on behalf of *ourselves*. That is why the collective action of that plural subject strengthens the foothold even of its most "unable" members,[7] because it acts in order to straighten the inclined plane which serves as platform for the oppression of the whole collectivity (whereas paternalism presumes the need of that inclined plane, presumes that reality itself is tilted, being adults above, and children—the *others*—below). And, it must be stressed, we are talking here of the possibility of *materially* participating in or subscribing the struggle for a higher status (full-fledged subjecthood), which, compared to paternalism, narrows considerably the hypothesis of one will substituting another. Paternalism, we must remember, talks of a *conceptual* impossibility to participate, and thus pathologizes the whole collectivity of children (see Cordero Arce 2015a, b).

Regarding the second objection, the answer was roughly given, though not developed, by Marx himself:

> The right to work is, in the bourgeois sense, an absurdity, a miserable, pious wish. But behind the right to work stands the power over capital, the appropriation of the means of production, their subjection to the associated working class, and therefore, the abolition of wage labour, of capital and of their mutual relations. (Marx 2003: 63)

One could think that a possible way of resisting the exploitation derived from capitalist work is narrowing as much as possible the entrance of *everyone* to the labor market. The NATs, not all of them paid workers, but all of them inevitably imbricated in the predatory process of capitalist globalization, have chosen another way. They assume that leaving the labor market is just changing one way of subordination by another (Elson 1982: 495), that is, the subordination to the employer by the subordination to one's parents' economic wants (themselves subordinated to the exploitation of an employer), with one difference: the subordination of the child worker opens the possibility to act with an economic, *material* agency that her removal from the labor market precludes. In other words, the path chosen by the NATs shows that moral autonomy seems a chimera when anchored, *by definition*, in material heteronomy; it shows that not everything is lost when one receives a salary, that by expropriating surplus value the employer does not necessarily expropriates the dignity of the worker, who understands her work as a position from where to fight for more and better dignity. As said above, dignity stems precisely from the collective struggle for recognition. Because, either children and their families resist passively, until there is arguably nothing left for which to fight, or they raise their voices and tread the path of active resistance. The NATs rise and struggle against those who in any way reap the benefits of their own lack of benefits; they rise as much against (Eurocentric) adultism, which forbids their work, as against capitalist exploitation, which denigrates their work. And they claim, as the *subjects-as-citizens* they already are, their right to work with dignity.[8]

Concluding Remarks

The *autonomous interdependence* displayed by the NATs' struggles sows the ground for an understanding of the legal subject that makes it neither a dependent (object) nor an independent (isolated monad), and which by so doing does not prevent her from being a full-fledged rights-holder and duty-bearer. On the contrary, it shows that the only possibility to be such full-fledged legal subject is through *autonomous interdependence*. The hermeneutic coming and going from dependence to independence is displayed as autonomous interdependence and it is from that standing that children legal subjects are starting to define and conquer their rights. Now, children are in the midst of a steady yet emerging struggle, so there is still a problem of normative legitimacy with the whole legal system *vis-à-vis* them, at the local, national, and international levels. I have discussed that elsewhere (Cordero Arce 2015a: 296–305), and it is definitely a pending and pressing issue, as is also how to fertilize the endpoint of the legal itinerary with the same outlook, that is, how to fertilize adjudication, which still clings fiercely to the narrow independent representation of the legal subject.

I said above that a hint toward the answer to the question of transcending the "sameness" and "difference" dichotomy could be precisely the conception of a dutiful, interdependently autonomous legal subject. This conception is much closer to a legal subject that could represent both adults *and* children. But is still insufficient, among other things, because it does not respond to questions such as adjudication. There is much struggle to be undertaken, but there is as much theorizing to be done as well. And in order to make theoretical space for the emerging legal subject we have been describing, we adults and children need tools with which to start loosening the petrous individual legal subject that still reigns in adjudication. Alan Norrie (2004) advocates for permeating jurisprudence with what Roy Bhaskar terms *dialectical thinking*, as opposed to analytical thinking. The latter thinks distinctions and connections as separate, so it is by definition the province of the adult autonomous individual, whereas the former is precisely "the art of thinking the coincidence of distinctions and connections" (Bhaskar 1993: 190). So, even if in cases such as adjudication we currently cannot do or act without the legal subject as we know it, at least we can begin *thinking* the subject dialectically. Thinking dialectically means thinking the coincidences of, the *continuum* between, independence and dependence (legal subject and "legal collectivity"), adulthood and childhood, law and struggle for law (see Cordero Arce 2015b: 349–355), rights and duties, and, what may be perhaps most important to children, and should become at least as important to adults, work and play (see Cordero Arce 2015b: 361–367).

Acknowledgments

I wish to thank Maggy Barrère and Teresa Picontó for their sisterly support regarding my research, Arthur Glass for an enriching conversation about the issues discussed in this chapter at its very inception, and Dan, Rachel, and Spyros, editors of this volume, for their insightful comments on the draft. But most of all, I wish to thank my wife, Ainara, for *Being*, there.

Notes

1 I use the masculine pronoun because the legal subject thus understood represents also, by default, a man.

2 On law's *anthropogenic* power, the case of corporations speaks clearly of how power can turn a *thing* into a (legal) *person*.

3 In http://www.crin.org/resources/infodetail.asp?id=24180, accessed 26 November 2016.

4 I discussed the issue of children as an oppressed minority discriminated on an age basis in Cordero Arce (2015a: 305–314).

5 In http://www.migracion.gob.bo/upload/l548.pdf, accessed 28 November 2016.

6 I say "democratic" because the work of girls and boys in the *public* space already presupposes an equalization of the gender differences between them, since it relativizes the essentializing division between the "private woman" and the "public man," helping to free the girl from the domestic sphere which is by definition a space of oppression. And in the case of the girls organized as NATs, the public space is actually their "natural" place, because the "public" is *the* place of the NATs as social movements (Cussiánovich and Méndez 2008: 26). As González (2010) shows, there are reasons to believe that the action of the NATs, as *public* and also as *collective*, that is, as organized around a unifying *ethos*, a common identity and project, is a huge step forward toward the equalization of gender differences between girls and boys (for further discussion see Cordero Arce 2015b: 307–355).

7 On the issue of fetal personhood, see Borgmann (2009), for a possible starting point toward unlocking a deadlocked debate.

8 An analog struggle is "ensuing in those localities where gay rights activists are applying pressure for the right to marry. Marriage can be subjected to a withering critique as a transparently ideological institution, but in this case too the importance of reserving a vocabulary of 'rights' as a legal subject transcends those objections since the political objectives of securing gay marriage rights outweigh any hesitance about the identities presupposed by marriage" (Wicke 1991: 467).

CHAPTER TWELVE

Reimagining Disabled Children within Childhood Studies:

The Challenge of Difference

Mary Wickenden

Introduction

This chapter sets out to consider the representation, inclusion, and participation of disabled children[1] living in diverse cultural contexts globally. This necessitates a focus on difference and how children perceived as different are understood. Disabled children fall under the purview of two intersecting arenas interested in their perspectives and their lives, namely Childhood Studies and Disability Studies. This book sets out to reimagine childhood studies, and in this chapter I focus on disabled children specifically, as a subset within the larger group of "all children." There is reimagining to be done for these young people, as much if not more than is needed for children generally and within the academic arena of childhood studies more broadly. To date disabled children have not been routinely included in the discourses in childhood studies, and I argue that this is because the discipline has an ambivalent attitude toward difference despite its aspiration to talk about all children and childhoods. Perhaps the difficulties around the embracing of disabled children into the fold are actually one example of a greater difficulty that childhood studies has with diversity? Indeed this uncertainty mirrors wider dilemmas about the focus and direction of childhood studies and whether it aims to privilege unifying grand narratives about childhood or embrace and explore childhoods (James 2010).

I will focus particularly on difference and how this is dealt with in the two arenas of disability and childhood studies. Closely related to this is the way that the concept of inclusion, as an aspiration for all, is imagined to be best operationalized. Both difference and inclusion have received a great deal of attention and generated much rhetoric recently. Clearly they are implicated in each other, the acceptance of difference being implied in the practice of inclusion. However, although inclusion as a policy is now accepted and promoted globally and across sectors, whether and how it plays out as a practical reality for people who are different is less clear. Both difference and inclusion need careful interrogation in relation to disabled children. I see the concepts as in need of reimagining if disabled children are to be consciously considered, treated equally, and really welcomed within the larger structural group of children and youth.

The contested issue is not that disabled children are perceived to be different in some particular ways, as this is seemingly undeniable and unavoidable, but what this usually means for them. Childhood studies allies are as guilty as others of imbuing particular types of differences with perhaps undue significance and this attention usually being stigmatizing. This results in these individuals being excluded and devalued as people. I advocate that ideally disabled children would just be regarded as children, more like others than they are different, but this is probably utopian, so as a compromise, a strategic type of essentialism would allow the recognition of their "differences" only in order to make sure that they have the resources they need to order to "be the same," that is, have the same opportunities as others. As Thomas Jefferson famously said,

> There is nothing more unequal, than the equal treatment of unequal people.

This was an early and very prescient recognition of the need for differentiated and affirmative action to iron out inequality. As someone who works internationally as a researcher and practitioner with disabled children, in both the so-called "Global North" and "Global South," I will take an international perspective. There are both similarities and differences in the dilemmas across diverse cultural and economic contexts about how disabled children are conceptualized and in the way that childhood studies and disability studies might interweave and be applicable to them. Overall, I argue that disability advocates' and scholars' experiences of dealing with difference may have useful lessons to share with those in childhood studies.

Disability reimagined

The disability movement (Oliver 2009; Barnes 2012), with the evolution of the "social model" of disability in the 1980s, argued that people with impairments (various differences of body or mind compared with idealized norms) are not inherently different from others. Rather, they merely represent some types of human diversity, but they are denied citizenship and inclusion in a range of ordinary activities, as a result of society's habitually negative response to them. Thus, they are "disabled" BY societies. This treatment is not as a direct consequence of their functional difficulties with moving, seeing, hearing, thinking, or behaving like others, but because of embedded structural exclusion. Human beings, it seems, habitually respond to people who are different by "othering" them.

The emergent "social model" of disability argued that ideally, given a society which treats them as equals, people with impairments would not be "disabled" by their differences. Over time, disabled activists and scholars have developed a number of iterations of this approach, although it has not been without its critics (Terzi 2004; Shakespeare and Watson 2010). In essence, the argument is always for the inclusion of disabled people in all aspects of everyday life and for their right to choice, control, and independence. This has moved the discourse away from the previous "individual," "medical," and "charity models," which saw the "problem" as being located in the person, emphasizing their differences, toward recognition of their essential humanness and sameness (Watson 2012). However, it is also increasingly recognized that having an impairment does impact on people's lives in important and undeniable ways. It may cause pain or tiredness, or a need for particular equipment, an adapted environment, extra support, more time to do things, and so on (Thomas 2007). However, disabled people say that their differences are not usually or necessarily the most important and defining aspects of them. As disability has slowly been incorporated more into discussion about identity politics alongside gender, sexuality, and race, there has been increased recognition of the intersectionality between these fluid descriptions. People need to be responded to as multifaceted and complex individuals, rather than being defined by one particular aspect of them, which happens to be marked (usually negatively) by society (Davis 1995). Perhaps like the other identity categories, the problem within disability discussions is that it is still too often seen as a polarizing status (either disabled or not). In contrast, for most disabled people and certainly in my experience for disabled children, their disabled identity is only part of them. Its presence and importance as part of who they are vary for individuals between situations and are often not the most salient and prominent aspects of them (Shakespeare 1997; Bekken 2014).

Rising activism in the 1990s and 2000s by disabled people globally culminated in the UN Convention on the Rights of Persons with Disabilities (UNCRPD) (UN 2007). This has been moderately successful in pushing forward changes in perceptions about disability and influencing policy and practices globally. Disabled people are now recognized, in theory, as equal citizens and there is a gradual rise in "inclusive" approaches to services such as education and health and in community development (Singal and Muthukrishna 2014; Hashemi et al. 2017). Structurally then, disabled people have become a more vocal, recognized, and cohesive group, although there are rivalries and factions within the movement. Comprising around 15 percent of the global population, they are a large minority group, found in broadly similar proportions everywhere (WHO 2011). Opportunities for disabled adults to have a say about their lives have increased, although this varies across contexts. However, there has been criticism that the way the rights are recognized and realized for disabled adults in the CRPD is not paralleled for disabled children (Lansdown 2012; Sandiland 2017).

Parallels between disability and childhoods concepts and movements

The disability movement alongside its academic cousin "Disability Studies" and the arena of "sociology of childhood" have much in common, both having spearheaded radical changes in thinking in their fields. Both arose in the 1980s and have linked advocacy, rights-focused and academic branches, although relationships between these are sometimes uneasy in both cases. All have similar broad aims of increasing recognition of their constituents (disabled people or children and youth, respectively), arguably aiming to change their status in society by democratizing, de-exoticizing, and humanizing them (Shakespeare 2013). In parallel, both movements continue to argue for increased consultation with, acknowledgment of the structural importance of, and the potential contribution of their members in communities and to culture. They challenge views of disabled people or children as mere minority players, who are always cast as net beneficiaries or consumers rather than active contributors in their families and society. Both groups are people who have traditionally been disregarded (in community action and research) and who often remain voiceless. When their interests have been included in planning and policy, this has been on their behalf, by consulting proxies such as carers, parents, teachers, and others. They are seen as groups who are vulnerable and in need of support, rather than capable of being consulted as equal citizens. In both cases there have been debates and uncertainties about the extent to which they can be true rights bearers or about how they can exercise such rights (Sandiland 2017).

Like childhood studies, disability studies as a cross-disciplinary arena is well established, but suffers from ongoing dilemmas about its allegiances, focus, and purpose (Thomas 2010). It has moved from being seen as naturally most allied to health sciences, to allegiance with sociology, politics, and policy-related disciplines, both within national boundaries and beyond them globally. Similarly there have been developments in ideas about how research should be carried out, with moves toward equalizing of power gradients, increased use of participatory methods, and involvement of children or disabled people in research and service evaluation, as well as policy formation and planning (Stone and Priestley 1996; Kirby et al. 2003; Hunleth 2011; Ansell et al. 2012; Punch 2015). Thus, it is clear that there are many parallels between the two study areas and similar dramatic shifts in conceptualizations and theorizing about both disability and childhood (Oliver 2009; James et al. 1998).

Notwithstanding the progress made in relation to theorizing disability and in policy and practice around ensuring the rights of disabled people, this has not so far considered disabled children enough. Disabled adults have through their strong self-advocacy gained recognition as citizens (IDA 2016), but this is clearly more difficult for disabled children to do (Ghai 2001). They remain largely a marginalized and excluded group, experiencing a range of inequalities and disadvantages. Estimates for the proportion of disabled children in populations range from 5 to 10 percent depending on exact definitions (UNICEF 2013). Because of the power dynamics around being both a child and disabled, they are to a large extent an invisible, silenced, and excluded group (Corker and Davis 2000; Tisdall 2012; Sabatello 2013).

The calls within childhood studies for the recognition of children and young people as autonomous beings who are social agents in their own right echo that in the disability movement. Another similarity is the ongoing discussion about the applicability of the term vulnerable for either group (Brown 2011). Disabled people, children, and even more so disabled children notoriously dislike being seen as weak or as younger than their chronological age. They hate being infantilized, patronized, or regarded as incompetent, as well as resisting other overgeneralized assumptions about what their minority social status implies about them (Wickenden and Elphick 2016).

Clearly then there are many parallels between the disability and childhoods movements. In a sense, both have shifted from focusing on nature toward culture. They have moved, at least to an extent, away from essentialized views (of children or disabled people) toward a more socio-political consideration of their structural status in society and have argued for recognition of their pre-existing but arguably under-recognized rights within universal treaties and through the implementation of the two conventions of relevance to them (UNCRC 1989; UNCRPD 2007; Lansdown 2012; Sandiland 2017). Thus, the two advocacy movements and their more theoretical academic arms (childhood studies and disability studies) have achieved shifts in perceptions, consequently influencing thinking and policy toward more equality and inclusion. Evidence of impact on individuals' lives is less clear. Although disabled people and nondisabled children are now more often consulted and their perspectives acknowledged, at least superficially, some activists argue that in both arenas this is still often tokenistic. Disabled children however seem to provide extra challenges especially in some settings, where embedded assumptions about their capacity mitigate against their inclusion, and so they are particularly excluded and overlooked (PLAN International 2013; Bekken 2014; Curran and Runswick-Cole 2014).

Dealing with difference

Alongside the similarities between theorizing about childhoods and disability are some common challenges, both fields having difficulties in deciding whether to focus on grand universalizing narratives or on the diversity of the lives people lead (e.g., about childhood versus childhoods, disability as a concept versus individual experience). There is often some confusion and discomfort when discussing nonnormative understandings of people. Both childhood studies and disability studies have perhaps "run out of steam" and have recently been challenged as being reductive and insufficiently nuanced (James 2010; Watson 2012; Shakespeare 2013). They are particularly challenged when it comes to extending their theories beyond the minority world of the Global North to applications in the majority Global South, where arguably differences between people appear too big to incorporate into existing models. Theorizing made in the metropole and in Northern academia becomes problematic when attempts are made to apply it to broader contexts, where types of children and childhoods, responses to difference, and experiences of disability are hugely varied and neat generalizations do not apply (Campbell 2010).

There is often a troubled relationship between academic arenas and advocacy movements or practice settings in the real world. The accusation of practitioners and activists about theorists is that they sit in their ivory towers and know nothing about ground-level realities. Thus, childhood studies authors who emphasize the idea that children have or should have "agency" are criticized by practitioners who know that children, like adults, are subject to powerful structural factors around them and that sometimes opportunities for them to be influential or to choose anything are extremely limited (Tisdall and Punch 2012). Klocker (2007) describes the "thin or constrained agency" that child domestic workers in rural Tanzania have. Like the sometimes unrealistic childhood scholars, disability theorists are at times similarly accused if they deny the impact of impairment effects (both negative and positive) on individuals' lives. In addition, in the Global South a severe lack of services and assistive devices (e.g., wheelchairs, hearing aids, etc.) are important exclusionary factors. Thomas (2007) argues that to fully understand the experience of disability, the impairment effects must be recognized. This is in addition to exploring the negative attitudes and responses of others to people and hence the force of stigma and social exclusion on their capacity to be agentive. There seem to be difficulties with recognizing difference, without this automatically leading to negative consequences and challenges in dealing with it in practical ways which are judgment neutral.

There is plenty of anecdotal knowledge and now mounting evidence that disabled children are very marginalized in mainstream discourses and research about children, as well as in real-life situations (Feldman et al. 2013). This invisibility is pronounced where there are other disadvantageous socio-economic forces, such as poverty, low class or caste, very unequal gender relations, low levels of education, poor healthcare, etc. (UNICEF 2011, 2013). Disabled children will often be at best "at the back of the queue" or more likely not in the queue at all, in relation to family, community, and government priorities. The relative levels of oppression and invisibility do vary, with some impairment groups being more regularly and severely affected. For example, children with cognitive, communication, behavior, and complex impairments are much more likely to be excluded than those with physical, visual, and milder difficulties (Jones et al. 2012). These latter groups are less stigmatized and seen as "easier to include." Crucially perhaps, they are seen as less different, more "normal," their differences being easier to relate to and thus they remain beings who can be adapted to and interacted with. Importantly these children may be more able to resist the oppression they encounter because their communication skills are unaffected by their impairment. Given opportunities, they are more able to self-advocate.

This contrast in societal responses to children with various kinds of impairment was highlighted for me recently during an INGO lead project in Tanzania. Here we had planned to work with and consult disabled children about a program that was introducing inclusive education into local schools to increase disabled children's opportunities for schooling. My expectation before arriving was that we would meet children with a full range of different impairments. In fact our pre-planning discussions had emphasized this. However, the local team had only recruited children with milder difficulties and the "easier to include" types discussed above. It emerged that the inclusive education program was really only working with these groups. So, a hierarchy of exclusion which has been described within the disability literature was playing out here. The children with severe or "difficult" differences were differentially excluded. Here some kind of unwitting categorization of acceptable and unacceptable difference was at play.

Disabled children as children

When we reflect on how disabled children as a subgroup are viewed within the larger group of "all children," there are some awkward contradictions and discrepancies which often go uninterrogated. The discipline of childhood studies usually claims to reject purely developmental views of childhood, emphasizing the variability and individuality of different children's competencies and preferences at different ages and in diverse situations. It traditionally criticizes developmental psychology and related fields for overgeneralizing knowledge about how children learn and develop (Burman 2008). Unfortunately, however, childhood studies allies doing research with or about children have not been sufficiently open to including disabled children in their work, and here perhaps we can see a chink in their supposed "anti-developmental" stance. They traditionally reject age-based judgments, but in apparent contradiction they seem unconsciously to make value judgments about particular kinds of capacities and skills. So, children who cannot talk, read, or write might be seen as not able to be included in their projects. Their defense for excluding disabled children often implies that involving them will be too complicated, that they wouldn't be able to join in, and that they (the adults) are not specialists in disability. This may be implicit and unconscious when disabled children are apparently unthinkingly discounted as possible participants, or they may be more explicitly deselected by the selection criteria and methods used. For example, if recruitment of children is through schools, then many disabled children (especially in the Global South) will automatically be left out as many do not attend school; and if "school-like" activities dominate the methods, this will also exclude them.

Thus, childhoods researchers are invoking the very developmental approach that they criticize, by being very conventional in their expectations, assuming disabled children's incompetence, and denying them participation. A truly inclusive approach to childhood studies would assume that disabled children are competent albeit different and that they have a right to be included alongside their peers. It is not a matter of ignoring or denying difference but of acknowledging it in matter of fact ways, providing appropriate support and reducing as far as possible any negative judgments about the person's worth. Clearly then, it is the adults' responsibility to make the necessary adaptations to enable disabled children to join in, not the child's job to adapt. Disabled children themselves are usually very practical about the kinds of help they need. Thus, "accessibility" entails not only the easy-to-imagine adaptation of the physical environment to allow children with mobility impairments to move around (ramps, rails, etc.) but also positive attitudes, accessible information, and adapted communication formats (pictures, symbols, sign language, braille, etc.). It also means being able to adapt to disabled children's different styles of participation (Wickenden and Kembhavi 2014). Here we can see that dealing with difference is sometimes challenging for childhood researchers, even when, or perhaps because, their rhetoric is a universalizing one about "all children." The nuance and practical minutiae of how to include everyone is trickier than the rhetoric, and the stretch of the term "all" needs to be expanded, perhaps beyond people's current imaginations!

It seems that despite some sustained criticism of developmental models in their purest form and the accusation that they often fail to recognize contextual and cultural diversity, the normative rhetoric remains very powerful (Rogoff 2003; Burman 2008). There remains a strongly idealized expectation about what children should be like and what they are able to do at different ages, irrespective of contextual factors. Thus, the child development roller coaster is a hegemonic one, and it is assumed that children will be similar globally in many ways, despite some nods to cultural variation (Engle et al. 2007). Hence, a child who is deemed to be "different" in particular ways and is labeled disabled is essentialized; this category of difference and its implications become self-fulfilling prophecies (Hacking 1999). For example,

He uses a wheelchair, so he won't be interested in sport

or

She has learning disabilities so she won't be able to read.

There is in a sense a moral judgment made about their value as a person once the label "disabled" is applied. Consequently the child's rights and status as a citizen become diminished and assumptions about who they can be or what they can do follow.

In many settings where poverty is widespread and resources are scarce, the exclusion of disabled children (e.g., from school, community activities, and sometimes even within families) is common (Filmer 2008; UNICEF 2013; Kuper et al. 2014). They are not expected to participate and often lack the kinds of support they need to make decisions or join in alongside other children (Franklin and Sloper 2009; Witchger et al. 2014). If a strongly developmental normative stance pervades, it may be society's negative response to difference which is at the root of their disadvantage, rather than the perceived costs involved, which are just a surface representation of this deep-seated attitude. Disabled children are also at increased risk of various kinds of violence (physical, emotional, sexual) (Jones et al. 2012). If a child looks or behaves differently, their personhood or even their humanity is denied and then somehow ill treatment is allowable and goes unchallenged. More broadly their diminished status difference means that they are subject to endemic structural violence (Farmer 2005).

Disabled children's identity

Clearly, having an impairment and consequently being labeled as disabled is only one form of difference that might attract attention, wanted or unwanted. Other socially significant differences include gender, race, ethnicity, religion, class or caste, and so on, all of which are increasingly regarded in nonessentialist and nonbinary ways. This approach would also be helpful in the disability field.

Disabled people often say that they want to be recognized as having many identities rather than there being too much focus on their impairments, which they are sometimes aware frighten or alienate people and mask other aspects of them. For example, in my UK study (Wickenden 2011) a teenage boy with disabilities said,

> "Don't be scared of me, talk to me" (age 14)

One of the girls expressed exasperation at not being seen as a person:

> "See me not the chair!" (age 11)

Here she is really complaining about being objectified, the impairment becoming the person, not allowing her to be anyone else. Clearly then people who are seen as different in particular ways. They are at the whim of others and their propensity to see that difference as either shocking, difficult, and embarrassing or alternatively as ordinary, interesting, and part of human diversity, which can be embraced and accommodated to. Although we can describe these responses to difference at an individual level, it is easy to see that they can easily escalate and become habitual and reinforced at societal levels. Arguably routine aversive individual responses drive the widespread institutionalized stigma and oppression that are still commonly experienced by disabled children and adults.

Only a few studies have asked disabled children themselves about who they think they are and how they would like to be seen. These show consistently across cultures and contexts that overwhelmingly the children emphasize their similarities to other children, often in an age-referenced way, as in these examples from my UK work with children with severe physical disabilities and no speech:

> "I'm a normal teenager" (14-year-old girl)

So they are, in a sense, bound by developmentalism too, and additionally do not question the category "normal." However, by this they seem to mean normal in a social relational sense, so even if your body is different you can be a "normal" person. For them it is more about being socially like their peers rather than scoring the same on a developmental checklist that observes motor function or clarity of speech.

They also often position themselves in relation to their families:

"I'm just one of the family" (13-year-old boy)

They sometimes affirm their right to be different and simultaneously the same as others. As Jenna, a very sociable and "chatty" girl told me using her communication aid,

"I am interestingly different" and "I like to gossip" (15-year-old girl)

Here then her self-perception is that of a "normally sociable" teenager, not as somehow who looks, moves and talks very differently. Disabled young people tend not to emphasize their impairments or disabled status, except to talk about the practical needs they have for accessible environments, equipment, adaptation communication, extra support, etc. as Sarah (a 12-year-old) said,

"I am only disabled when I don't have the help I need"

However, they tend to regard these topics as rather boring. It would be a bit like talking endlessly about the color of your eyes or your shoe size! These young people tell us more about the ways that they are like others, than the ways they are different (Singh and Ghai, Watson 2002). The way that adults (and sometimes other children) often focus on their perceived competencies or incompetencies and the automatic coupling of this with agency is something they find frustrating and diminishing. Judgments made about who can join in based on supposed capacities need to be troubled (Skelton 2008). The extent to which children labeled disabled can be agentive is thus more likely to be a consequence of the responses of those around them than directly linked to their type and severity of impairment. Klocker (2007) and Robson et al. (2007) suggested "thin" or "constrained" agency and a continuum of agency are applicable here, although they have not as yet been applied to disabled children's situations.

Disabled children need to be seen as children first, their "differences" being only one aspect of their identity. In my interactions with many of them in various cultural contexts (UK, East Africa, South Asia), they are surprisingly consistent in asserting their "normality" as people and their desire and expectation to do what other children do (Wickenden 2011, 2014, 2016). As disability, difference and inclusion are all relationally generated; interactions between adults and disabled children need to be supportive and accepting, expecting disabled children to be significant people and to do things like others (Thomas 2007). However, an acceptance of a diversity of ways of doing things is needed. Thus, they may play football, but it might be wheelchair football. Many disabled children report that they are constantly on the edge of what is going on, not actively included, because the appropriate adaptations have not been organized. As one 17-year-old English boy with very severe physical impairments told me:

> "I am very good at watching, because I spend a lot of time on the sidelines"

Their disabled status makes these individuals liminal beings, neither completely in nor out of the situation. They are cast as indeterminate "others," where children and adults around them, unless they know them very well, are not sure what to "do about" them and how they can fit in, because of their perceived difference and assumed incompetence. In fact most disabled children can be included in most of what other children do, if the right kinds of practical accommodations are made and more importantly if those around them have positive responses to them (Wickenden and Kembhavi 2014). However, an emphasis on "doing" has to be carefully modulated so that those who because of severe impairments don't want to or can't "do" very much are still affirmed as people who matter. A range of different ways of participating needs to be valued and recognized. As a disabled girl I met in Uganda said when asked about her aspirations:

> "I want to be someone who can BE someone"

So this is more about being than doing. Positive, affirming, and even celebratory attitudes modeled by adults can strongly influence how other children respond to their disabled peers. Lobbyists for inclusive education argue that one of the benefits of this approach is that children, who learn together from nursery onward, accept diversity as "normal" (Singal and Muthukrishna 2014). However, we would probably want to problematize the term "normal" here (Davis 1995). Unfortunately, an essentialized dichotomy between "disabled and normal" is still very much the most common parlance, even among professionals working with children.

What do we mean by inclusion?

Inclusion has become a mantra in recent years, most notably with its widespread use in the recently reset global targets for international development, the Sustainable Development Goals (SDGs) with their laudable strapline "leave no one behind" (UN 2015). The espousal of the term "inclusion" can be credited mainly to the effective lobbying of the disability movement globally (IDA 2016). However, one can question both how the concept is generally understood and whether it can or really will be enacted in such a way as to impact on those who are most excluded. What kinds of inclusion are really imagined and are they possible? What would be needed to make them happen? People with some types of difference are perhaps more easily included than others.

Policies and structures can be put in place to establish the right to and expectation of inclusion for all, but in practice, there are a range of personal responses to people who are different (children and adults), who are seen to flout the conventions of "normality." The goal of and the challenges in achieving an inclusive society have implications for many groups of people who are perceived as different, including those of non-preferred genders, races, sexualities, classes, etc. Those labeled disabled are one of the largest groups experiencing exclusion. Some astute commentators argue that the very need for an active process of social inclusion reveals a status quo that accepts some people as outside the society (Campbell 2010). Why were they ever seen as out? Those who now have to be included usually know that they have been assigned inferior status. They may have internalized this oppression and so have low self-esteem and expectations of what they could be or do (Mason 1990). In my experience children labeled disabled are often unaware in their earlier years of their diminished personhood. It comes as a shock when as older children they discover that their difference has a deep significance for others, leading to a different social status. They did not know they were "outside the circle," and that they should now be invited in. Until this revelation, they thought they were in and are often puzzled about why they are regarded as out!

Links between childhood(s) and disability studies

Relatively fewer authors have addressed the relationship between disability studies and childhood studies or the way that disabled children should or could be included in discourses about children more broadly (Tisdall 2012). Connors and Stalker (2007) proposed the need for a "social model of childhood disability," their argument rightly being that there has been too much focus on the impairment aspects of disabled children's lives (e.g., often about service provision) and not enough attention to their everyday life experiences in social settings. These authors' motivation is an understandable one, to highlight the particularities of disabled children's lives as opposed to disabled adults or other children. Influenced by Thomas (2007) they argue that we should consider the "barriers to being" and "barriers to doing" that children experience, as well as direct impairment effects. However, for me their model is too segregating and potentially "othering," given that their research findings echo mine: disabled children want to be seen as the same, as not different from other children. They don't want to be seen as exceptional but as ordinary, therefore a separate model for them seems counter-intuitive. Similarly but again for me unsatisfactory is Curran and Runswick-Cole's (2014) suggested concept of "disabled children childhoods" as a discrete entity. Again their aim, like mine, is to highlight the group's experiences as in need of recognition. However, by delineating a separate type of childhood, they are potentially exacerbating the differences between and overlooking the commonalities with other children. Usefully, Watson (2012) points out that we need better theorizing about disabled children which would draw more productively on both disability and childhoods theories. As a move in this direction, ideally, I would like to see models of childhood which are able to accept a much greater diversity of children and childhoods, rather than proposing separate subgroups defined by one or other type of difference, which may not be the most salient to the individuals. Perhaps then we need not so much a "social model of childhood disability," but a social model of childhood? Sandiland (2017) has made a similar suggestion. This would recognize more fully the barriers to agency and participation faced by many children in diverse contexts, including not only disabled children but those from any marginalized and vulnerable groups who are negatively socially marked and stigmatized.

Conclusion: What could reimagining do?

Over time, both the "not so new" Sociology of Childhood (Tisdall and Punch 2012) and the now well-rehearsed Social model of Disability have become sacred cows. But perhaps they lack the power and flexibility to be usable tools for the analysis of the widest range of issues related to children, childhoods, or disability globally (James 2010; Shakespeare and Watson 2010)? Both have been accused of failing to address diversity sufficiently and being overly reductionist or too universalist so that they are not applicable in many situations. Particularly, both struggle to be relevant across many Global North and South, culturally and socio-economically diverse, contexts. There are commonalities to be found among all children everywhere but they seem to become bland or unsatisfactory easily. Theories from the two arenas have not so far been satisfactorily combined to reflect on disabled children's lives, taking into account the ways in which they are the same, as well as how they are different from other children. A strategic essentialist approach which only recognizes difference in order to provide what is needed to make children equal (i.e., by accommodating to their needs) would be ideal. Then the negative aspects of being categorized would disappear. Perhaps such a fundamental attitude change is utopian however!

Sandiland (2017) in his review of the UNCRC and the UNCRPD suggests that the former could learn from the latter, although perhaps this is unfair because of the chronology of the two treaties. He argues interestingly that there is not enough consideration of relationships between actors, about participation and about power gradients. Similarly then contemporary childhood studies could learn from the current disability arena about widening consideration and acceptance of difference and diversity.

Childhoods thinkers need to be able to imagine a broader range of different types of children as valid and of interest. Disabled people (including children I have talked to) often say that they want to be seen as ordinary, rather than exceptional. The affirmative model of disability which essentially promotes acceptance and celebration of difference makes a useful contribution here (Swain and French 2000; Cameron 2008). A move toward such positive action seems a fruitful route to pursue. Here then individual differences are seen as a natural part of human diversity, although heroic notions and mawkishness need to be avoided.

Childhood studies has so far had rather superficial and limited ways of looking at difference. Disability scholars, activists, and allies have of necessity considered this more and for longer and with a number of different lenses. Specifically then, childhood studies could reimagine disabled children, recognizing them as more like other children than they are different, seeing them for who they are and who can they be, rather than privileging what they can or cannot do. There is a human propensity to gravitate toward people who are like ourselves which is demonstrated by social psychologists (Brewer 1999). We need to find a way for people who seem very strange to be seen as less so and for them to be recognized as more the same than different. This may involve practical adaptations to the environment, but probably more importantly it is a matter of attitude and mindset.

There is a need for a flexible, accepting, and nonbinary approach to human variation and difference, so that boundaries between so-called disabled versus nondisabled (or normal) people as well as between children and adults are fuzzier and viewed as less important. Finding commonalities between people is more important than categorizing differences. If childhood studies theorists and practitioners recognized and legitimated a greater diversity of types of children, childhoods, and ways of participating globally, this would be major progress (Twum-Danso 2016). Disabled children would be then acknowledged as a group with particular types of differences, needing specific support, but not diminished status as people. In essence we need reimaginings about the validity and contribution of different children as well as about different childhoods. After all, disabled children tell us that they are just different in the way that they are the same as other children.

Note

1 I deliberately use the term Disabled Children throughout rather than "Children with disabilities" which is favored in many international contexts. Although I understand the "children first" sentiment of the latter usage, I prefer to align with British social model of disability thinking, which favors using "disabled" child, person, woman, etc. This recognizes and emphasizes that it is the society that disables the person, rather than their difference being an inherent aspect of them. Disabling is therefore something that is "done to" them rather than something they have inherently.

CHAPTER THIRTEEN

What Space for a Children's Politics? Rethinking Infancy in Childhood Studies

David Oswell

In many ways childhood studies from the mid-1980s onward was so keen to institute children as political subjects that it presumed an idea of politics but failed to really question what a *children's* politics might be like: how do children actually create, construct, and do politics? But also how do we, as researchers and others, recognize when and how children do politics? Often political action and activity have been seen as synonymous with social agency and interaction (e.g., Mayall 2000; Danby and Baker 1998) or considered through a model of participation (e.g., Cockburn 2012; Hart 1992; Thomas 2007). Writing "children into the script of social order" (Mayall 2000) was a statement based on the empirical observation of what children were actually doing in their everyday lives, but it was also a political and programmatic declaration. The social life of children was seen as conceptually equivalent to the political life of children. Moreover, it was such a view of children—one that both saw children as political subjects and also allowed childhood studies scholars to be aligned with the interests of children (Alanen 1994)—that has fed into a reading of children's rights after the United Nations Convention on the Rights of the Child, which understood those rights as manifestations of, or closely articulated with, an underlying everyday social and political interactivity (Freeman 1998; Hanson and Nieuwenhuys 2013). In this reading of the politics of children, even though empirical investigation into the areas in which children did politics provided fruitful insight and innovation, the question of how children do politics was often assumed. My intention in this chapter, then, is not to sleight the energy or direction of such thought within childhood studies, but simply to ask again the question of what is a politics *for children* and *of children*, in such a way that might interrogate often implicit and dominant assumptions. I want to ask this question not as separate questions (that separate at first base an "adult-centered" from a "child-centered" politics, "protection" from "rights," "best interests" from "liberation," and so on) but as conjoined inasmuch as they refer to two sides of the same question and inasmuch as they refer to a singular theoretical (albeit often very diverse empirically) problematic regarding *what kind of space is the space of children's politics*, a space which conjoins the fact of children doing politics with an external recognition of such doing. Let's be clear, a children's politics has never been afforded the luxury of a pure space from which children's interests could be defended, free from adult interests. Moreover, it is in this sense that a politics of childhood is also contingently, but intimately, a politics of gender.

This chapter argues that childhood studies has been defined not simply against an idea of "adulthood" but, perhaps more significantly, against "infancy." From its initial moments, it has sought to include children within a political space, but it has never systematically and theoretically engaged with the problematic of that space and, as such, has consistently thought of children in terms that attempt to scale-down or scale-up or "cut-and-paste" adult conceptions of the political. This chapter argues that, first, a more wholesale critique of the edifice of the political upon which children's (political) agency rests within childhood studies is needed and, second, a positive engagement with the question of infancy needs to be made. If adultist conceptualizations have rested on an idea of the primacy of speech, often within a gendered distribution between reproduction and necessity, on the one hand, and politics and freedom (or agency), on the other, then a politics thought with, not against, infancy suggests consideration of messier, more physical, and noisier forms of demonstration, alignment, and articulation. In such a demonstrative space, the sound of politics is different (see Oswell 2009; Rosen 2015). Moreover, in such a move to thinking of a *politics-with-infancy*, there is no simple position of the child and childhood with and from which researchers can align their knowledge production and critique; instead, a politics-with-infancy suggests a necessarily collective, negotiated, haptic, and diffracted "vision."

I start by briefly defining the contours of what I see as the existing problematic. I then consider two aspects of a rethought engagement with children's politics and infancy: first, in relation to a reframing of children's political space as a space of contestation and assembly, rather than of voice or even dialogue; and second, in relation to questions of infrastructure and the material resources and supports for a space of politics. My discussion leans on the work of Jacques Rancière and Judith Butler.

Defining the problematic

There are three defining features of the problematic: a mutually exclusive binary relation between, on the one hand, a politics imposed on children and, on the other, a politics internal to children's everyday lives; an acceptance that contemporary politics surpasses a domestic/public divide, yet, at the same time, the maintenance of an understanding (not overtly stated) of politics in terms of a classical conceptualization of the political actor as a form of "public man" and in the context of a *res publica*; and finally, a sense from some within childhood studies that mainstream political theory has ignored children, yet matched with a lack of motivation to engage systematically with mainstream political theory on the ground of a "children's politics."

Rightly childhood studies has been critical of the social structures through which children's lives have been, and are, governed and regulated, of the dominant ideologies and discourses of childhood, which are circulated and support reactionary perceptions and conceptualizations of children, but also of the multiple ways in which children have been, and are, ignored or erased in many affairs of public and social policy and political debate and consideration (Thomas 2013). Equally, childhood studies has made clear and evident how children, through their everyday interactions, shape and also make the worlds which they inhabit. These social interactions are seen as political; they are defined in the context of and often against adults and adult definitions of who children are and what they should be doing. For example, James and James foreground how children who are "out of place," with regard to normative adult ideas of childhood, are seen to cause both criminal and symbolic offense (James and James 2004). Or, for example, Danby and Baker talk about how the interactions of children in a pre-school classroom are political, with some children aligning the teacher against other children in such a way that the children "restore social order" differently to that of the adult teacher alone (Danby and Baker 1998).

There has been a schism in children's politics—between a politics *for children* and a politics *of children*—at the heart of sociologies of childhood for the last forty-five, if not more, years. In 1973, Norman Denzin stated that "children find themselves talked about, legislated over, tested and scrutinized" and that "the perspective of the caretaker is embodied in our definition of the child" (Denzin 1973: 2–3). In contrast to such a top-down, adultist conceptualization of children, Denzin argues that children, as for all human beings, should be understood "in active, interactionist terms." They are "symbol manipulating organisms ... capable of *mindful, self-conscious activity*" (Denzin 1973: 7). Denzin is critical of deficit models of children and, although hesitant to throw child development completely out of the window, wants to understand such development in interactionist terms, namely in the context of children's everyday experiences and active interactions (Denzin 1973: 9). A resolution to the schism is offered such that "children be accorded the rights to act like adults, be given the responsibility that comes with those rights, and be given access to the resources to organize and act out such rights" (Denzin 1973: 15). A solution to the deficit in a politics *for children* is found in an everyday politics *of children*. And yet understanding of such everyday politics is by virtue of constructing children "like adults": namely, a solution to the problem of the deficit is to model children *as adults*. In doing so, the solution to the deficit (one that is profoundly shaped in modern times by discourses of development and socialization) erases any reflection on *the infancy* of children's politics, namely reflection on the difference children make to *a conceptualization of the political*. Moreover, in the shift to a politics of children any close alignment of childhood and care, and the gendering of such relations, is erased in favor of an implicitly masculine conceptualization of the child as a political actor.

This difficult relation to gender has been central to a politics of childhood. Central to this has been a critique of understandings of children that locate them only inasmuch as they are products of families and reproduced through systems of care and welfare. This has meant that childhood studies scholars have been critical of "protectionist" ideas about childhood (see Archard 1993), but more extensively the project of giving children a voice and facilitating their rights has been dependent on the demand to "extricate children, conceptually, from parents, the family and professionals" (Mayall 2000: 243). The extrication of children from such ideas and practices of development, protection, and care (viz., a set of ideas and practices that place women and children in a normalized alignment) and the placing of children, conceptually, fully into the realm of the social and the sociological is also seen in terms of a movement of children from the a-political to the political: "The sociological project is to work initially on the task of extracting children theoretically from the family in order to study their social positioning as a social group" (Mayall 2000: 247). Yet for Mayall and others such a move does not simply mean an acceptance of a gendered division of labor and space that sees a public realm shaped by the supposedly masculine affairs of economics and politics and a feminized private realm of domesticity, mothers, children, and reproduction. On the contrary, the domestic is itself seen in terms of economics and politics (Mayall 2000: 248). The work of Carol Smart and colleagues (Smart et al. 2001) has, for example, been significant in conceptualizing family as a site of political contestation and negotiation, and her work has been very clearly aligned with Giddens's public policy work on "the democracy of the family" (Giddens 1998).

In mainstream political theory and political sociology, there is a tradition that sees a dissolution of the divide between private and public as constituting a broader societal shift which is typified by the decline of public man. For example, Hannah Arendt has argued that the modern age sees an increasing surpassing of the political by the exigencies of the private, of necessity, of reproduction, and of economics as *oikonomia* (i.e., as household management). This transition is aligned with the growth of modern issues of welfare and of the growth of the state (Arendt 1998). Or Richard Sennet, in his conclusion to *The Fall of Public Man*, presents two images of what he calls "intimate tyrannies": the first is "a life limited by children, mortgages on the house, quarrels with one's spouse" and the second "the police state in which all one's activities, friends, and beliefs pass through the net of governmental surveillance" (Sennett 1977: 337). Domestication (both petty homeliness and also state surveillance and control), in which the child becomes a dominant figure, is contrasted with an idea of the *res publica* and public man. Childhood studies may have issues with this reading of modernity, but in its critique of normative ideas about socialization or development, it has often failed to mark the infancy of children as a point of *difference in* and *against* a dominant model of political agency that is predicated on a free individual expressive subject within *res publica*. Often children's politics has been argued on the basis, not only of it freeing children, conceptually, from the household, but also from a realm of necessity seen in terms of reproduction and the biological. This is certainly the main thrust of the political ontology offered by James and Prout (1990) (see Oswell 2016). Much recent work on biopower, biopolitics, and hybrid humans/technologies/natures begins to shift the basis of this ontology (Prout 2005; Wells 2011; Lee 2014). And some feminist work in childhood studies raises significant questions about children's socially necessary labor and a gendered division of social reproductive labor (Rosen and Newberry, 2018). But any rethinking of children's politics must rethink also the conservative core republicanism at the heart of childhood studies. To think about the spaces of children's politics, or children's "spaces of appearance" in Arendt's terms (1998), implies a deconstruction not only of children's relation to family and welfare, but also their relation to politics itself, to the dominant models through which politics has been conceptualized. The original spirit of Mayall's articulation of a sociology for children with a politics of childhood needs to be pushed further in terms of the very givenness of the political itself, inasmuch as children can't simply be offered a ready-made mask of "political actor," but rather their presence in politics is itself a push for redrawing the terms, conditions, and positionalities of politics. In this sense, over and above the innovations of Alderson's research on the politics and rights of babies and infants, her work repeats this form of political actor (Alderson 2000). In order to think through this problematic I want to focus specifically on the work of Jacques Rancière and Judith Butler on speech and political space and to consider further, but also provisionally, the question of "what kind of space is the space of children's politics." In doing so, I will, first, consider questions about political contestation and assembly and, second, questions about the material support or infrastructuring of political space.

From voice to assembly

If politics, at its most radical moment, refers to the processes through which actors and resources bring about social change (viz., processes of disturbance and transition), then it refers to a different set of processes than "the social," which is the object of such disturbance and transition. It is important to understand the social practices, agencies, and dynamics that form a social system or social world. It is also important to understand how children are key social actors and agents in the social worlds they inhabit. To write "children into the script of social order" is an important aspect of a broader epistemological politics regarding the contribution of children to social order. Such sociological work has taken different perspectives (e.g., the Bourdieusian research of Alanen and Siisiäinen (2011) or the actor-network research of Prout [2005]). But in failing to differentiate "the political" from "the social," and in conflating "political actors" with "social actors," such work has offered empirical observation and theoretical analysis of the status quo, not of change as a political formation dependent on a transitional political moment. Such sociological work might consider the social dynamics within which people and resources are formed; it might also offer an account of the unequal distribution of resources between actors as constitutive of such dynamics; but the position and force of such actors in the overturning of one system or dynamic into another on the basis of such inequalities might be seen as political, and not only sociological. In this sense, to talk of a situation as political is to understand such a situation as something more than sociological. Martin Breaugh defines the social bond as collective existence, but the political bond as collective action (2013: 202–203), by which he means not simply collective agency, but concerted orchestrated agency that brings about a change in the structure of collective existence.

Jacques Rancière helps us think of this political formation and what might constitute such a political moment; moreover, he, perhaps unwittingly, allows us to think of such a moment in terms of the question of infancy. His engagement with the question of the political is framed in terms of its classical European "origins" (*arkhe*) in Aristotle. The patriarchal, Eurocentric, and slave-owning contexts for such thought clearly constitute limitations. For Rancière such an origin is a point of contestation and reinterpretation. Rather than repeat the idea that there is an anthropological divide between the human animal and other animals by virtue of speech, or reason through speech (*logos*), Rancière reads Aristotle's discussion about "man as a political animal" (*zōon politikon*), as a problem about recognition and dispute (1999: 21–42). It is not that Rancière is dismissive of the idea of a life committed to public affairs (*bios politicos*), but that he contests its foundationalist and essentialist assumptions (cf. Arendt 1998; Agamben 1998). He refuses an idea that who has and who doesn't have political speech might be based on the qualities, attributes, and capacities of the person (viz., refusing that there is an essentialist reason for not recognizing women or barbarians or slaves or children within the political community or *polis*). For us this means refusing essentialist ideas about adult reasonable and rational speech set against essentialist ideas about the babble, or lesser speech, of infants. On the one hand, Rancière sees the classification of people and things into different types of people and things in terms of what he refers to as *police*. He doesn't see this exactly in Foucauldian terms as a question of control or government (Rancière 2010: 94–96); rather, he sees this in terms of how the sensible (that which is and can be perceived and sensed) is distributed (e.g., in terms of those who might be seen to have some qualities and capacities rather than others). For example, small children are seen to embody, as a form of habitus, a lack of seriousness and a propensity for play. Groups of teenage black boys may be felt by some white adults as threatening and hyper-aggressive. These racist biases and prejudices are not simply cognitive constructions and classifications; they are felt and sensed as habitus, as a form of the distribution of the sensible. In contrast, and on the other hand, Rancière refers to *politics* as that which contests and overturns the distribution of the sensible that is policed. The contestation is predicated on a dispute or on the recognition of a *wrong*. He refers to dispute through the notions of *disagreement* or *dissensus* (Rancière 1999, 2010). Politics, in this sense, is a rare occurrence, inasmuch as it does not refer to a generality across all social existence. The wrong at the heart of politics is twofold; it refers both to the fact of domination (i.e., to forms of political subjectification and relations of dependency) and to the symbolic distribution of bodies into "those that one sees and those that one does not, those who have a logos … and those who have no logos, those who really speak and those whose voice merely mimics the articulate voice to express pleasure and pain" (Rancière 1999: 22). In contrast to Aristotle, to the presumption that politics is predicated on a primary distinction between those animals who speak (and who have capacity for justice, for thinking about what is useful and what is harmful) and those who only make noise (*phone*) (and who merely express sounds of pleasure and pain), Rancière argues that such a distinction (a distribution of bodies and the sensible) is dependent precisely on a prior articulation, namely on the account given by those who lay claim to having speech. He states: "Politics exists because the logos is never simply speech, because it is always indissolubly the *account* that is made of this speech" (1999: 22–23). Politics names the contestation of the distribution of the sensible on the basis of those who can speak and those who are deemed unable to speak, but also of the recognition of some sounds as speech and some as noise or babble. Although Rancière begins with the analogy of speech, it is clear that such an understanding of politics implies the recognition of more than speech. The sensible for Rancière refers to an idea of aesthetics "as the system of *a priori* [albeit defined in Foucauldian terms as a kind of historical *a priori*] forms determining what presents itself to sense experience" (2006: 13). The sensible is understood as *aesthesis*, as that which is perceptible, sensed, and experienced. The sensible is that which can be expressed and that which can be experienced as expression, such that expression is not necessarily vocal, but can imply an articulation across a range of media and mediums. In that sense then, we have an understanding of children's politics that is not reduced to children's voice and the recognition (or not) of that voice as speech (i.e., it is not simply about giving children a platform to speak or listening to what children say, although that is clearly important) nor is it reduced to children and adults in intergenerational dialogue, such that politics is defined as the sharing of experiences and positionalities through interactional talk. In that sense, the imperative "voice is not enough" would constitute a radical demand regarding our common sense of what constitutes the political, a demand more radical than found in Lundy's framing of the issue (2007). It is more than an invitation to participate. A children's politics would define that which ruptures the perceptions of those dominant in such a way that their perceptions are radically refigured and such that the participants of a new settlement includes those children and their sensibilities that were previously excluded.

Politics implies, for Rancière, the "demonstration of a gap in the sensible itself" (2010: 38). What was perceived and recognized as noise is placed next to the sound of speech as if they were equivalent, on the same stage. And the force that presents noise on the same stage is understood by Rancière as the righting of a wrong, as the demonstration of a dispute. The righting of such a wrong though is not on the basis of a more accurate and representative account; rather it is on the basis of those excluded, those seen only to emit noise, apparently simply placing themselves side-by-side on "a common stage" with those who, prior to such a moment, failed or refused to recognize their sounds as if it were speech. Rancière talks about this moment in terms of "the deployment of a specific scene of revelation" (1999: 25). This moment is quintessentially political: "Politics is primarily conflict over the existence of a common stage and over the existence and status of those present on it" (1999: 26–27). But those who contest the dominant order, who contest adultist authority and expertise, do so not because they have well-defined identities prior to the contestation and on the basis of which such contestation is made (i.e., in terms of interests and experiences). Rather, those who are not counted—those who are not taken into account and are seen as having no capacity to account for themselves—present themselves on the same stage, in common, with those who refuse their recognition, and in doing so they contest the prior terms of recognition and perception. They contest such terms on the basis of a wrong, namely the wrong of their prior exclusion. Central to such contestation is the contestation of the presumed prior identities. In that sense, any politics of children, we might assume, is also a contestation of the identities and established discourses of "child/adult," "children/adults," and "childhood/adulthood." Politics, in this sense, implies a radical re-thinking and a radical re-representation. In Rancière's terms politics implies the gauging of incommensurables: "The incommensurables of the equality of speaking beings and the distribution of social bodies are gauged in relation to each other, and this gauge has an effect on the distribution itself" (1999: 39–40).

The fact of the social and cultural diversities of children and adults, through gender, sexuality, race, ethnicity, class, and (dis)ability, is not questioned. Yet, the placing of children's perceptions and sensibilities (as more than those specified diversities) alongside those of the adults, who have presumed to know, to differentiate, and to do the work of writing social order, is political inasmuch as those now present on the stage do not simply repeat the words of adults, nor do they even speak as adults speak, but they upset the very terms and conditions of the relationship. And in this sense, this upsetting is not simply "dialogue." The psychoanalyst Thomas Ogden talks about the case of Robert, a blind schizophrenic teenager, who has a fear of spiders and who never washes for fear of being sucked down the plughole. Robert wore the same clothes day after day and his hair was matted with grease and dirt. In his account of the psychoanalytic sessions with Robert, Ogden talks about feeling "invaded by this patient." He says, "I felt as if he had managed to get inside of me—to get under my skin—by means of his odour that was saturating my furniture" (Ogden 1989: 57 quoted in Lafrance 2009: 17). Ogden understands his feelings about Robert in terms of Robert's determination to make his presence felt (which Ogden analyzes in terms of a sense of a "second skin") such that

> he attempted to ground himself in the sensation of his own distinct bodily odour, which was of particular importance to him in the absence of the capacity to form well-defined visual images ... His odour provided the rudiments of being someone (someone who had a particular odour), being somewhere (somewhere in which he could perceive his odour), and being something for another person (a person who could smell him, be infused by him, and remember him). (Ogden 1989: 58 quoted in Lafrance 2009: 17)

Although this example raises questions about sensibilities and the sensible, I am not suggesting that this is a form of politics because it is not clear that the register of the interaction has changed. The gauging of the two sets of sensibilities in a single measure on a single stage is political if, and only if, the measure itself is changed. If this meant that children spoke simply as we might expect and recognize them to speak, then it would mean we would continue to place them in the same position within any social order prior to such speaking. But if the process of being political is not based on prior political subjects becoming aware of their inequality or of the interests of their pre-defined community, then politics is radically precarious. This means two things: first, the political subjectivity of infants is such that any intentionality, any motivation to change the status quo does not take the appearance of the well-defined political subjects in relation to which we may be familiar. We can't map an infant politics onto those images of vanguardist demonstrators or articulate spokespersons in debating chambers. There will be a novelty that is genuinely surprising. Second, the language used to talk about the infancy of a children's politics is necessarily both partial and metaphoric. It is partial because it cannot claim to represent a constituency of one set of people against another. And it is metaphoric because it necessarily has a hesitancy to that which it represents, inasmuch as any "reality" is revealed *post hoc*, after the moment of politics. Moreover, the outcome of a children's politics is not that it cannot be seen and felt (inasmuch as the outcome constitutes a re-distribution of the sensible), but that its recognition by others is seen as caught up in the structure of the social that is at the core of the problem. All of this suggests both a novelty and a surprise, but also a sense of care, attentiveness, and support with regard to such fledgling moments. Whereas an adult vanguardist politics or the idea of political debate in an assembly might presume ready-made political actors, fully equipped to take on the task of social and political change, an infant politics, in contrast, is in need of support and infrastructure. Such infrastructure is needed as a basic and primary demand.

In such rethinking, children, inasmuch as they might be defined through their infancy, change the nature of political discourse, not simply in terms of what they say (i.e., the comprehendible content of their expressions) but by virtue of the range of form, substance, and force through which their presence articulates a politics. It would be incorrect to assume that a children's politics can simply and solely be conceptualized in terms of a (re)distribution of the sensible. Any children's politics as a basic command equally implies a (re)distribution of resources, bodies, materialities, and technologies. Any repositioning of children, vis-à-vis their equality, means thinking about the infrastructures through which voices can be heard, staged, and assembled and positions elevated. Infrastructure is not thought as simply technical (e.g., roads, pipes, cables, computer systems, etc.) nor is it thought to the exclusion of people, but rather in terms of the mix across the two (see Oswell 2013). In AbdouMaliq Simone's thinking, infrastructure is understood in terms of the "modes of provisioning and articulation" such that these are productive, reproductive, positioning, and distributive of people and things across places and territories over time. Infrastructures are defined through the overlapping and complex patterns of conjunctions that are not static or fixed, but "incessantly flexible, mobile, and provisional" (Simone 2004: 407–408). Judith Butler has a similar sense of infrastructure as an arrangement, both material and performative. But she emphasizes its supportive nature with regard to the vulnerability of bodies and people. Taft's research on participatory structures in children's and young people's workers movement in Peru considers the deep commitment to the creation of "collaborative intergenerational relationships," but also how "many adults have difficulty creating intergenerational dialogue without reverting to habituated and hegemonic adult/child relationships" (Taft 2015: 470). To talk about infrastructure is to talk also about the interdependency of lives: "There is no life without the conditions of life that variably sustain life, and those conditions are pervasively social, establishing not the discrete ontology of the person, but rather the interdependency of persons, involving reproducible and sustaining social relations, and relations to the environment and to non-human forms of life, broadly considered" (2009: 19). For Butler such support is increasingly recognized as a political demand, "a demand for a certain kind of inhabitable ground and its meaning and force derive precisely from that lack" (2015: 127). The demand is "not for all kinds of infrastructure, since some serve the decimation of livable life (e.g. military forms of detention, imprisonment, occupation, and surveillance, for instance), and some support livable life" (2015: 127). Butler talks about support for mobility in terms, for example, of the rights of women to walk on the streets at night, of Palestinians to walk through prohibited areas, or for black men in the United States to walk without being arrested or shot (2015: 128). For children, often infrastructures that facilitate political spaces are so lacking that their possibilities are only fleetingly glimpsed. A group of 14-year-old girls might demand a secure environment and transport between respective homes and a party across town at night: a demand for a right to the city, a demand for freedom of movement at all times of day, a demand that requires thinking through mobility, age, and gendered violence beyond the impasse of threat and protection.

Understanding children's, and others', vulnerabilities (as might be suggested in the work of Taft in her critique of neoliberal agency with regard to young women's activism (2011), Harris and Shields Dobson on suffering actors (2015), Mizen and Ofusu-Kusi on children's agency as vulnerability (2013), and Puar (2009) on debility and disability) allows us to have a more attenuated sense of agency. It also raises the questions about the relation between bodies, not only as lived experience, but as living bodies in need of support and infrastructure. Research suggests that all bodies, infantile and adult, are entangled through infrastructure and that (human) living requires such interdependency (Manning 2009), but some lives seem more fragile and more in need of support. Or perhaps it is simply that different bodies need to be at different times and spaces differently supported. To talk about children and vulnerability lets in the question of biology. Evelyn Thoman states that an "infant's behavior is the ultimate expression of its biological functioning" (Thoman 1980: 243 quoted in Gottlieb 2004: 57). But rather than write this off as a "social construction," it is important to unpack its biopolitics. Rather than dismiss the claims regarding infancy and biology, it is important to understand how those claims constitute a necessary heritage for the lives of some children, providing them with complex supportive infrastructures. To overturn or to out-live those infrastructures itself requires support and care and the alliances of others. Equally, it is important to consider that what constitutes "biology" (as physiology or as development, etc.) is too heavily laden with Western connotations and such connotations need to factored into any investigation and understanding (see Gottlieb 2004: 60–61).

To talk about children's politics in terms of both infancy and infrastructure through the writing of Butler lays bare the vulnerability of infant bodies in a way that doesn't isolate those bodies from other bodies and from infrastructure, but precisely allows us to think through their necessary correlation. Whose bodies and what infrastructures support children doing politics? Through what articulations are bodies and technologies assembled? If, for example, babies communicate not only through sound, but through poohing and peeing, crying and cuddling, what bodies and mechanisms fit together? What might it mean, as Alma Gottlieb says, to shift "the theoretical axis from the vocal cords to the urinary tract"? It would certainly "unsettle our language-based model of communication at the same time that it may violate our notions of bodily pollution" (Gottlieb 2004: 55). This is not to suggest an understanding of children's politics as carnivalesque (Bakhtin 1968), but simply to think about how different bodies assemble in relation to different media (pooh, urine, milk, salty water) and through different technologies (nappies, barrier cream, potties).

Conclusion

The paradox that infancy throws up for politics is that if politics is concerned with overturning current structures and institutions and the mobilization of resources and peoples with regard to such an overturning, then infancy is defined precisely as a condition without access to such means. Infancy is defined as without voice and without resources, but also as the body that inhabits such exclusion and negation. Childhood studies has been insistent on not letting a definition of children's politics fall back on such an idea of infancy, and it has insisted on a theoretical equivalence between children and adults as political actors and agents. And yet, in doing so, it has disavowed the difference that children make to politics. This chapter, then, has argued that childhood studies, but also mainstream political theory, needs to (re-) engage with the problematic of infancy in (children's) politics to think through that difference and to begin a reconceptualization of the political. The work of Rancière and Butler provide significant, but certainly not the only, points of departure. To think about infancy in politics means:

- we need to reconsider the media and mediums through which politics is demonstrated;
- we need to think about the infrastructures, the systems of support, the apparatuses and devices that facilitate the spaces through which politics appears and through which change occurs;

- and we need to consider vulnerability as a necessary facet of political alliances and mobilization, inasmuch as it signals a basic requirement of solidarity (that we cannot act alone, because on our own we are weak and helpless to bring about change) and, as such, taking care of others, with others, constitutes a central element to consider in thinking about counter-hegemonic political change.

To argue for these basic starting points is not to discredit the forms and practices of participation and decision-making that form the ground of much current formal and institutional children's politics. It is not an argument against children's councils or young people's parliaments. Nor is it necessarily against the practical impact of "ladders of participation" (Hart 1992) as a device for enabling and encouraging children's participation in formal organizational contexts. Rather to argue for these basic starting points, as I have done above, for a politics-with-infancy means to argue for a broader sense of politics than one constrained by ideas of intentionality and reasoned, well-argued debate and to open up our sensitivities to noises and stutterings within a broader hegemonic children's politics. Moreover, in this framing, post-adultification means building political infrastructures beyond an adult/child binary. It means foregoing a politics of childhood "in opposition" to adults, but embracing a politics of articulation across different constituencies of people and contexts. It is equally important to think about politics-with-infancy in relation to teenagers as to babies. To think about the infancy of children's politics does not mean posing a new ontological foundation for children's political agency. Infancy does not constitute a new model of political agency nor does it offer a new form of identity politics. Rather it simply presents a fissure in current conceptualizations of the political.

BIBLIOGRAPHY

Abate, M. A. (2010), *Raising Your Kids Right: Children's Literature and American Political Conservatism*, New Brunswick, NJ: Rutgers University Press.

Abate, M. A., and Kidd, K. B., eds (2011), *Over the Rainbow: Queer Children's and Young Adult Literature*, Ann Arbor, MI: University of Michigan Press.

Abebe, T., and Ofusu-Kusi, Y. (2016), "Beyond pluralizing African childhoods: Introduction," *Childhood: A Global Journal of Child Research*, 23 (3): 303–316.

Adam, B. (1995), *Timewatch: The Social Analysis of Time*, Cambridge, MA: Polity Press.

Adkins, L. (2017), "Speculative futures in the time of debt," *The Sociological Review*, 65 (3): 448–462.

Agamben, G. (1993), *Infancy and History: The Destruction of Experience*, trans. L. Heron, London: Verso.

Agamben, G. (1998), *Homo Sacer: Sovereign Power and Bare Life*, Stanford, CA: Stanford University Press.

Ahearn, L. M. (2001), "Language and agency," *Annual Review of Anthropology*, 30: 109–137.

Ahmed, S. (2004), *The Cultural Politics of Emotion*, Edinburgh: Edinburgh UP.

Ahmed, S. (2010), *The Promise of Happiness*, Durham, NC: Duke University Press.

Aitken, S. (2001), *The Geographies of Young People: The Morally Contested Spaces of Identity*, London: Routledge.

Alanen, L. (1994), "Gender and generation: Feminism and the 'child question,'" in J. Qvortrup, M. Bardy, G. Sgritta, and H. Wintersberger (eds), *Childhood Matters: Social Theory, Practice and Politics*, 27–42, Aldershot: Avebury.

Alanen, L. (2000), "Childhood as a generational condition: Towards a relational theory of childhood," in *Research in Childhood: Sociology, Culture and History*, Denmark: University of Southern Denmark.

Alanen, L. (2011), "Editorial: Critical childhood studies?" *Childhood*, 18 (2): 147–150.

Alanen, L. (2015), "Are we all constructivists now?" *Childhood*, 22 (2): 149–153.

Alanen, L. (2017), "Editorial: Childhood studies and the challenge of ontology," *Childhood*, 24 (2): 147–149.

Alanen, L., and Mayall, B., eds (2001), *Conceptualizing Adult-Child Relations*, London: Routledge.

Alanen, L., and Siisiäinen, M., eds (2011), *Fields and Capitals: Constructing Local Life*, Jyväskylä: University of Jyväskylä.

Alderson, P. (2000), *Young Children's Rights: Exploring Beliefs, Principles and Practice*, London: Jessica Kingsley.

Alderson, P. (2016), "The philosophy of critical realism and childhood studies," *Global Studies of Childhood*, 6 (2): 199–210.

Allen, J. (2011), ¡ *Venceremos?: The Erotics of Black Self-making in Cuba*, Durham, NC: Duke University Press.

Allen, J. (2013), "Race/Sex Theory 'Toward a new and more possible meeting,'" *Cultural Anthropology*, 28 (3): 552–555.

Alliance for Childhood (2017), "Playwork and Play", Available online: http://www.allianceforchildhood.org/playwork (accessed April 4, 2017).

Ansell, N. (2005), *Children, Youth and Development*, London: Routledge.

Ansell, N. (2009), "Childhood and the politics of scale: Descaling children's geographies?" *Progress in Human Geography*, 33: 190–209.

Ansell, N., Robson, E., Hajdu, F., and Van Blerk, L. (2012), "Learning from young people about their lives: Using participatory methods to research the impacts of AIDS in southern Africa," *Children's Geographies*, 10 (2): 169–186.

Appadurai, A. ed (1986), "Introduction: Commodities and the politics of value," in A. Appadurai (ed.), *The Social Life of Things: Commodities in Cultural Perspective*, 3–63, New York: Cambridge University Press.

Appadurai, A. (1996), *Modernity at Large: Cultural Dimensions of Globalization*, Minneapolis, MN: University of Minnesota Press.

Archard, D. (1993), *Children: Rights and Childhood*, London: Routledge.

Ardener, S. ed. (1975), *Perceiving Women*, London: Malaby Press.

Arendt, H. (1960), *Between Past and Future: Six Exercises in Political Thought*, London: Faber & Faber.

Arendt, H. (1998), *The Human Condition*, Chicago, IL: University of Chicago Press.

Asad, T. (2000), "Agency and pain: An exploration," *Culture and religion*, 1 (1): 29–60.

Austin, J. S. (1885), *Lectures on Jurisprudence or The Philosophy of Positive Law*, Robert Campbell (ed.), London: John Murray, Albemarle Street.

Bailey, M. (2016), "Black (gay) raw sex," in E. Johnson (ed.), *No Tea, No Shade: New Writings in Black Queer Studies*, Durham, NC: Duke University Press.

Bailey, M. (2013), *Butch Queens Up in Pumps*, Ann Arbor, MI: University of Michigan Press.

Bakhtin, M. (1968), *Rabelais and His World*, Cambridge, MA: MIT Press.

Balagopalan, S. (2002), "Constructing indigenous childhoods: Colonialism, vocational education and the working child," *Childhood: A Global Journal of Child Research*, 9 (1): 19–34.

Balagopalan, S. (2011), "Introduction: Children's lives and the Indian context," *Childhood*, 18 (3): 291–297.

Balagopalan, S. (2012), "The politics of failure: Street children and the circulation of rights in Calcutta, India," in O. Nieuwenhuys and K. Hanson (eds), *Reconceptualizing Rights in International Development: Living Rights, Social Justice, Translations*, Cambridge: Cambridge University Press.

Balagopalan, S. (2014), *Inhabiting "Childhood": Children, Labour and Schooling in Postcolonial India*, London: Palgrave.

Balagopalan, S. (2018), "Afterschool and during vacations': On labor and schooling in the postcolony," *Children's Geographies*, DOI: 10.1080/14733285.2018.1490008

Balibar, E. (1994), "Subjection and subjectivation," in J. Copjec (ed.), *Supposing the Subject*, 1–15, London: Verso.

Ball, S. J., Hull, R., Skelton, M., and Tudor, R. (1984), "The tyranny of the 'devil's mill': Time and task at school," in S. Delamont (ed.), *Readings on Interaction in the Classroom*, 41–57, London: Methuen.

Barad, K. (2003), "Posthumanist performativity: Toward an understanding of how matter comes to matter," *Signs: Journal of Women in Culture and Society*, 28 (3): 801–831.

Barad, K. (2007), *Meeting the Universe Halfway: Quantum Physics and the Entanglement of Matter and Meaning*, Durham, NC: Duke University Press.

Barnes, C. (2012), "Understanding the social model of disability: Past, present and future," in N. Watson, A. Roulestone, and C. Thomas (eds), *Routledge Handbook of Disability Studies*, 12–29, London: Routledge.

Barron, I. (2007), "An exploration of young children's ethnic identities as communities of practice," *British Journal of Sociology of Education*, 28 (6): 739–752.

Bateson, G. (1972), "A Theory of play and fantasy," in *Steps to an Ecology of Mind*, 177–193, New York: Ballantine.

Baxter, J. (2015), "The archaeological study of children," *Allegra Lab: Anthropology, Law, Art & World*. May 12. Available online: http://allegralaboratory.net/the-archaeological-study-of-children/

Beauvais, C. (2013), "Transmettre mai 68: construction et paradoxes de l'idéal révolutionnaire à travers l'album jeunesse contemporain," *Strenae*, 5 (n.p.).

Beauvais, C. (2015a), "Simone de Beauvoir and the ambiguity of childhood," *Paragraph*, 38 (3): 329–346.

Beauvais, C. (2015b), *The Mighty Child: Time and Power in Children's Literature*, Amsterdam: John Benjamins.

De Beauvoir, S. ([1948] 1967), *Ethics of Ambiguity*, trans. B. Frechtman. Secaucus, NJ: Citadel.

De Beauvoir, S. ([1952] 1975), *The Second Sex*, trans. H. M. Parshley, New York: Vintage.

Bekken, W. (2014), "'I want them to see that I feel normal': Three children's experiences from attending consultations in paediatric rehabilitation," *Disability & Society*, 29 (5): 778–791.

Bell, N. (2008), "Ethics in child research: Rights, reason and responsibilities," *Children's Geographies*, 6 (1): 7–20.

Benhabib, S. (1987), "The generalized and the concrete other: The Kohlberg-Gilligan controversy and feminist theory in Feminism as Critique," in S. Benhabib and D. Cornell (eds), *Feminism as Critique*, 77–95, Cambridge and Malden, MA: Polity Press.

Benhabib, S. (2013), "Reason-giving and rights-bearing: Constructing the subject of rights," *Constellations*, 20 (1): 38–50.

Bennett, J. (2010), *Vibrant Matter: A Political Ecology of Things*, Durham, NC: Duke University Press.

Beresin, A. (2010), *Recess Battles*, Jackson, MS: University Press of Mississippi.

Berlant, L. (2016), "The commons: Infrastructures for troubling times," *Environment and Planning D: Society and Space*, 34(3): 393–419.

Bernardini, S. (2016), "In the Shadow of the Shade, Thrown: Affect, Violence, and the (Dis)Orientations of Black Queer Youth," PhD diss., Department of Childhood Studies, Rutgers University, Camden, NJ, USA.

Bernstein, R. (2011), *Racial Innocence: Performing American Childhood from Slavery to Civil Rights*, New York: NYU Press.

Den Besten, O., Horton, J., and Kraftl, P. (2008), "Pupil involvement in school (re)design: Participation in policy and practice," *Co-Design*, 4 (4): 197–210.

Den Besten, O., Horton, J., Adey, P., and Kraftl, P. (2011), "Claiming events of school redesign: Materialising the promise of 'Building Schools for the Future,'" *Social and Cultural Geography*, 12: 9–26.

Bhaba, H. (1994), *The Location of Culture*, London: Routledge.

Bhaskar, R. (1993), *Dialectic: The Pulse of Freedom*, London and New York: Verso.

Bichler, S., and Nitzan, J. (2013), "Can Capitalists Afford Recovery? Economic Policy When Capital Is Power," *Working Papers on Capital as Power* No. 1, www.capitalaspower.com/2013/10/no-20131-bichler-and-nitzan-can-capitalists-afford-recovery/ (accessed March 16, 2017).

Biesta, G. (2006), *Beyond Learning. Democratic Education for a Human Future*, London: Paradigm.

Birla, R. (2009), *Stages of Capital: Law, Culture and Market Governance in Late Colonial India*, Durham, NC: Duke University Press.

Bissel, S. (2003), "The social construction of childhood: A perspective from Bangladesh," in N. Kabeer, G. B. Nambissan, and R. Subrahmanian (eds), *Child Labour and the Right to Education in South Asia: Needs versus Rights?* New Delhi: Sage.

Blackburn, M. (2002), "Disrupting the (hetero) normative: Exploring literacy performances and identity work with queer youth," *Journal of Adolescent & Adult Literacy*, 46 (4): 312–324.

Blackburn, M. V. (2007), "The experiencing, negotiation, breaking, and remaking of gender rules and regulations by queer youth," *Journal of Gay & Lesbian Issues in Education*, 4 (2): 33–54.

Blaise, M. (2013), "Charting new territories: Reassembling childhood sexuality in the early years classroom," *Gender and Education*, 27: 801–817.

Blazek, M. (2015), *Rematerialising Children's Agency: Practices in a Post-Socialist Estate*, Bristol: Policy Press.

Boggs, C. (2000), *The End of Politics: Corporate Power and the Decline of the Public Sphere*, New York: The Guilford Press.

Bonnett, M. (1999), "Education for sustainable development: A coherent philosophy for environmental education?" *Cambridge Journal of Education*, 29 (3): 313–324.

Bonnett, M. (2002), "Education for sustainability as a frame of mind," *Environmental Education Research*, 8 (1): 9–20.

Bordonaro, L. I. (2012), "Agency does not mean freedom. Cape Verdean street children and the politics of children's agency," *Children's Geographies*, 10 (4): 413–426.

Bordonaro, L. I., and Payne, R. (2012), "Ambiguous agency: Critical perspectives on social interventions with children and youth in Africa," *Children's Geographies*, 10 (4): 365–372.

Borgmann, C. (2009), "The meaning of 'life': Belief and reason in the abortion debate," *Columbia Journal of Gender and Law*, 18 (2): 551–608.

Bornstein, M., P. Rebello Britto, Y. Nonoyama-Tarumi, Y. Ota, O. Petrovic, and D. L. Putnick (2012), "Child development in developing countries," *Child Development*, 83 (1): 16–31.

Bourdillon, M., Levison, D., Myers, W., and White, B. (2010), *Rights and Wrongs of Children's Work*, New Brunswick, NJ: Rutgers University Press.

Boyden, J. (1997), "Childhood and policymakers: A comparative study on the globalization of childhood," in A. James and A. Prout (eds), *Constructing and Reconstructing Childhood*, London: Falmer.

Boyden, J. (2015), "Epistemological and Ideological Clashes in Research and Policy around Children and Childhood," *3rd International Conference of the International Childhood and Youth Research Network*. June 10. European University Cyprus, Nicosia, Cyprus.

Boyden, J., and Dercon, S. (2012), *Child Development and Economic Development: Lessons and Future Challenges*, Oxford: Young Lives, Department of International Development.

Boyle, J. (1991), "Is subjectivity possible? The post-modern subject in legal theory," *University of Colorado Law Review*, 62: 489–524.

Breaugh, M. (2013), *The Plebeian Experience: A Discontinuous History of Political Freedom*, New York: Columbia University Press.

Brewer, M. B. (1999), "The psychology of prejudice: Ingroup love or outgroup hate?," *Journal of Social Issues*, 55 (3): 429–444.

Brockenbrough, E. (2015), "Queer of color agency in educational contexts: Analytic frameworks from a queer of color critique," *Educational Studies*, 51 (1): 28–44.

Bronfenbrenner, U. (1979), *The Ecology of Human Development*, Cambridge, MA: Harvard University Press.

Brown, G. (1999), "Child's play," *Differences: A Journal of Feminist Cultural Studies*, 11(3): 79.

Brown, K. (2011), "Vulnerability: Handle with care," *Ethics and Social Welfare*, 5 (3): 313–321.

Brown, S. (2009), *Play*, New York: Avery.

Brown, W. (2005), *Edgework: Critical Essays on Knowledge and Politics*, Princeton, NJ: Princeton University Press.

Brown, W. (2015), *Undoing the Demos: Neoliberalism's Stealth Revolution*, New York: Zone Books.

Browne, K. (2006), "Challenging queer geographies," *Antipode*, 38 (5): 885–893.

Browne, K., Lim, J., and Brown, G., eds (2009), *Geographies of Sexualities: Theory, Practices and Politics*, Aldershot: Ashgate Publishing Ltd.

Bruhm, S., and Hurley, N., eds (2004), *Curiouser: On the Queerness of Children*, Minneapolis, MN: University of Minnesota Press.

"Building Vineland, New Jersey from a Vast Wilderness," *The History Girl*, http://www.thehistorygirl.com/2013/08/building-vineland-new-jersey-from-vast.htm (accessed December 14, 2016)

Burman, E. (1996), "Local, global or globalized? Child development and international child rights legislation," *Childhood: A Global Journal of Child Research*, 3(1): 45–66.

Burman, E. (2008), *Deconstructing Developmental Psychology*, London: Routledge.

Burman, E. (2017), *Deconstructing Developmental Psychology*, London: Routledge.

Burn, A., and Richards, C., eds (2014), *Children's Games in the New Media Age*, Surrey: Ashgate.

Burnside, B. S. (2015), "When the girls still wore headscarves: Integration and belonging in an after-school center in Berlin," *Diaspora, Indigenous and Minority Education*, 9 (2): 140–154.

Butler, J. (1997a), *Excitable Speech: A Politics of the Performative*, New York, London: Routledge.

Butler, J. (1997), "Merely cultural," *Social Text*, (52/53): 265–277.

Butler, J. (1997b), *Psychic Life of Power: Theories in Subjection*, Stanford, CA: Stanford University Press.

Butler, J. (1999), *Gender Trouble: Feminism and the Subversion of Identity*, 2nd edn, New York, London: Routledge.

Butler, J. (2009), *Frames of War: When Is Life Grievable?*, London: Verso.

Butler, J. (2015), *Notes toward a Performative Theory of Assembly*, Cambridge, MA: Harvard University Press.

Caillois, R. (1961), *Man, Play and Games*, New York: Schocken.

Callon, M. (2010), "Performativity, misfires and politics," *Journal of Cultural Economy*, 3 (2): 163–169.

Camastral, S. (2008), "No small change: Process-oriented play therapy for children of separating parents," *Australian and New Zealand Journal of Family Therapy*, 29 (2): 100–106.

Cameron, C. (2008), "Towards an affirmation model," in T. Campbell, F. Fontes, L. Hemingway, A. Soorenian, and C. Till (eds), *Studies: Emerging Insights and Perspectives*, 14–30, Leeds: The Disability Press.

Campbell, F. K. (2010), "Crippin' the Flâneur: Cosmopolitanism, and landscapes of tolerance," *Journal of Social Inclusion*, 1 (1): 75–89.

Canella, G., and Viruru, R. (2004), *Childhood and Postcolonization: Power, Education and Contemporary Practice*, London: Routledge.

Carlsson-Paige, N. (2008), *Taking Back Childhood*, New York: Penguin.

Carr, E. S., and Lempert, M. (2016), "Introduction: Pragmatics of scale," in E. S. Carr and M. Lempert (eds), *Scale: Discourse and Dimensions of Social Life*, 1–21, Oakland, CA: University of California Press.

Chakrabarti, D. (2000), *Provincializing Europe: Postcolonial Thought and Historical Difference*, Princeton, NJ: Princeton University Press.

Chapin, B. (2014), *Childhood in a Sri Lankan Village: Shaping Hierarchy and Desire*, New Brunswick, NJ: Rutgers University Press.

Charalambous, I. (2015), "Greek as an Additional Language (GAL) School Students in Cyprus in Late Modernity: An Ethnographic Study of Three Parallel Intensive Greek Language Classes in Two Greek-Cypriot State Primary Schools," PhD diss., King's College, London.

Chatterjee, P. (1993), *The Nation and Its Fragments: Colonial and Postcolonial Histories*, Princeton, NJ: Princeton University Press.

Chatterjee, P. (2004), *Politics of the Governed: Popular Politics in Most of the World*, New York: Columbia University Press.

Cheney, K. (2007), *Pillars of the Nation: Child Citizens and Ugandan National Development*, Chicago, IL: The University of Chicago Press.

Cheney, K. (2011), "Children as ethnographers: The importance of participatory research in assessing orphans' needs," *Childhood*, 18 (2): 166–179.

Cheney, K. (2014a), "Giving children a 'better life'? Reconsidering social reproduction and humanitarianism in intercountry adoption," *European Journal of Development Research*, 26 (2): 247–263.

Cheney, K. (2014b), "Conflicting protectionist and empowerment models of children's rights: Their consequences for Uganda's orphans and vulnerable children," in A. Twum-Danso Imoh and N. Ansell (eds), *Children's Lives in an Era of Children's Rights: The Progress of the Convention on the Rights of the Child in Africa*, 17–33, New York: Routledge.

Cheney, K., and Rotabi, K. (2017), "Addicted to orphans: How the global orphan industrial complex jeopardizes local child protection systems," in C. Harker and K. Hörschelmann (eds), *Conflict, Violence and Peace*, 89–107, Singapore: Springer.

Cheney, K., and Ucembe, S. (forthcoming), "The orphan industrial complex: The charitable commodification of children and its consequences for child protection," in K. Cheney and A. Sinervo (eds), *Disadvantaged Childhoods and Humanitarian Intervention: Processes of Affective Commodification*, London: Palgrave.

Christensen, P. (2004), "Children's participation in ethnographic research: Issues of power and representation," *Children and Society*, 18: 165–176.

Christensen, P., and Prout, A. ([2005] 2012), "Anthropological and sociological perspectives on the study of children," in S. Greene and M. Hill (eds), *Researching Children's Experiences*, 42–60, London: Sage Publications Ltd.

Christou, M., and Spyrou, S. (2016), "The hyphen in between: Children's intersectional understandings of national identities," *Children's Geographies*, 15 (1): 51–64.

Chudacoff, H. (2007), *Children at Play: An American History*, New York: NYU Press.

Clark, C. (2003), *In Sickness and in Play*, Chicago, IL: University of Chicago Press.

Clemenson, N. (2016), "Exploring ambiguous realms: Access, exposure and agency in the interactions of rural Zambian children," *Childhood: A Global Journal of Child Research*, 23 (3): 317–332.

Cockburn, T. (2012), *Rethinking Children's Citizenship: Theory, Rights and Interdependence*, Basingstoke: Palgrave.

Cohen, L. (2001), *Playful Parenting*, New York: Ballantine.

Cole, J., and Durham, D., eds (2008), *Figuring the Future: Globalization and the Temporalities of Children and Youth*, Santa Fe: School for Advanced Research.

Comarof, J., and Comarof, J. (1992), *Ethnography and the Historical Imagination*, Boulder, CO: Westview Press.

Connors, C., and Stalker, K. (2007), "Children's experiences of disability: Pointers to a social model of childhood disability," *Disability and Society*, 21 (1): 19–33.

Cook, D. T. (2002), "Interrogating symbolic childhood," in D. T. Cook (ed.), *Symbolic Childhood*, 1–14, New York: Peter Lang.

Cooper, F., and Stoler, A. (1989), "Introduction tensions of empire: Colonial control and visions of rule," *American Ethnologist*, 16 (4): 609–621.

Cordero Arce, M. (2012), "Towards an emancipatory discourse of children's rights," *International Journal of Children's Rights*, 20: 365–421.

Cordero Arce, M. (2015a), "Maturing children's rights theory," *International Journal of Children's Rights*, 23: 283–331.

Cordero Arce, M. (2015b), *Hacia un Discurso Emancipador de los Derechos de las Niñas y los Niños*, Lima: IFEJANT.

Corker, M., and Davis, J. M. (2000), "Disabled children – invisible under the law," in J. Cooper and S. Vernon (eds), *Disability and the Law*, 216–238, London: Jessica Kingsley.

Cornwall, A. (2016), "Towards a pedagogy for the powerful," *IDS Bulletin*, 47 (5): 75–87.

Corsaro, W. (1986), *The Sociology of Childhood*, London: Sage.

Cortés-Morales, S., and Christensen, P. (2014), "Unfolding the pushchair. Children's mobilities and everyday technologies," *REM–Research on Education and Media*, 6 (2): 9–18.

Crain, P. (2016), *Reading Children: Literacy, Property, and the Dilemmas of Childhood in Nineteenth-Century America*, Philadelphia, PA: University of Pennsylvania Press.

Credit Suisse Research Institute (2017), *Global Wealth Report*, http://publications. credit-suisse.com/tasks/render/file/index.cfm?fileid=12DFFD63-07D1-EC63-A3D5F67356880EF3 (accessed July 20, 2018).

Crosby, C., Duggan, L., Ferguson, R., Floyd, K., Joseph, M., Love, H., and Rosenberg, J. (2012), "Queer studies, materialism, and crisis: A roundtable discussion," *GLQ: A Journal of Lesbian and Gay Studies*, 18 (1): 127–147.

Crouch, B. (2012), "Finding a voice in the academy: The history of women's studies in higher education," *The Vermont Connection*, 33: 16–23.

Csikszentmihalyi, M. (2008), *Flow: The Psychology of Optimal Experience*, New York: Harper Collins.

Cunningham, H. (1995), *Children and Childhood in Western Society since 1500*, London: Longman.

Curran, T., and Runswick-Cole, K. (2014), "Disabled children's childhood studies: A distinct approach?" *Disability & Society*, 29 (10): 1617–1630.

Cussiánovich, A., and Méndez, D. (2008), *Movimientos Sociales de NATS en América Latina. Análisis histórico y balance político en los últimos treinta años*, Lima: IFEJANT.

Cvetkovich, A. (2012), *Depression: A Public Feeling*, Durham, NC: Duke University Press.

Danby, S., and Baker, C. (1998), "'What's the problem?' Restoring social order in the preschool classroom," in I. Hutchby and J. Moran-Ellis (eds), *Children and Social Competence: Arenas of Action*, London: Falmer Press.

Davis, H., and Sarlin, P. (2012), "On the risk of new relationality: An interview with Lauren Berlant and Michael Hardt," *Reviews in Cultural Theory*, Edmonton: Department of English and Film Studies, University of Alberta.

Davis, L. J. (1995), *Enforcing Normality: Disability, Deafness and the Body*, London: Verso.

"Death Notice: Vineland Pioneer Dead," *Philadelphia Inquirer*, Philadelphia, PA, July 31, 1909.

De Jong, S., Icaza, R., and Rutazibwa, O., eds (2019), *Decolonization and Feminisms in Global Teaching and Learning*, Abingdon: Routledge.

Denton, D. E. (1968), "Existentialism in American educational philosophy," *International Review of Education*, 14 (1): 97–102.

Denzin, N., ed. (1973), *Children and Their Caretakers*, New Brunswick, NJ: Transaction Books.

Dimock, W.-C. (2006), *Through Other Continents: American Literature across Deep Time*, Princeton, NJ: Princeton University Press, loc. 791 and 74.

Dirks, N. (2001), *Castes of Mind: Colonialism and the Making of Modern India*, Princeton, NJ: Princeton University Press.

Douzinas, C. (2000), *The End of Human Rights*, Oxford: Hart.

Duane, A. (2013), *The Children's Table: Childhood Studies and the Humanities*, Athens, GA: University of Georgia Press.

Dumenil, G., and Levy, D. (2005), "The neoliberal (counter-)revolution," in A. Saad-Filho and D. Johnston (eds), *Neoliberalism: A Critical Reader*, London: Pluto Press.

Duncheon, J. C., and Tierney, W. G. (2013), "Changing conceptions of time: Implications for educational research and practice," *Review of Educational Research*, 83 (2): 236–272.

Duschinsky, R. (2013), "Childhood innocence: Essence, education and performativity," *Textual Practice*, 27 (5): 763–781.

Dyson, A. (1997), *Writing Superheroes*, New York: Teacher's College.

Dyson, J. (2014), *Working Childhoods: Youth, Agency and the Environment in India*, Cambridge: Cambridge University Press.

Edelman, L. (2004), *No Future: Queer Theory and The Death Drive*, Durham, NC: Duke University Press.

Edwards, A., and D'Arcy, C. (2004), "Relational agency and disposition in sociocultural accounts of learning to teach," *Educational Review*, 56 (2): 148–155.

Edwards, R., Gillies, V., and Horsley, N. (2015), "Early intervention and evidence-based policy and practice: Framing and taming," *Social Policy and Society*, 15 (1): 1–10.

Elias, N. (1982), *Sociología Fundamental*, Barcelona: Gedisa.

Elkind, David. (2007), *The Power of Play*, Cambridge, MA: Perseus Press.

Elson, D. (1982), "The differentiation of children's labour in the capitalist labour market," *Development and Change*, 13 (4): 479–497.

Engle, P. L., Black, M. M., Behrman, J. R., Cabral De Mello, M., Gertler, P. J., Kapiriri, L., Martorell, R., and Young, M. E. (2007), "Strategies to avoid the loss of developmental potential in more than 200 million children in the developing world," *The Lancet*, 369: 229–242.

Ennew, J., and Milne, B. (1990), *The Next Generation: The Lives of Third World Children*, Philadelphia, PA: New Society Publishers.

Erikson, E. (1950), *Childhood and Society*, New York: Norton.

Escobal, J., and Flores, E. (2009), "Maternal migration and child well-being in Peru," *Young Lives Working Paper*, 56 (64): ISBN 978-1-904427-62-9

Esser, F. (2016), "Neither 'thick' nor 'thin': Reconceptualizing agency and childhood relationally," in F. Esser, M. S. Baader, T. Betz, and B. Hungerland (eds), *Reconceptualizing Agency and Childhood: New Perspectives in Childhood Studies*, 48–60, London and New York: Routledge.

Esser, F., Baader, M. S., Betz, T., and Hungerland, B., eds (2016), *Reconceptualizing Agency and Childhood: New Perspectives in Childhood Studies*, London: Routledge.

Evans, R. (2011), "'We are managing our own lives … ': Life transitions and care in sibling-headed households affected by AIDS in Tanzania and Uganda," *Area*, 43: 384–396.

Fabian, J. (1983), *Time and the Other: How Anthropology Makes Its Object*, New York: Columbia University Press.

Farmer, P. (2005), *Pathologies of Power: Health, Human Rights, and the New War on the Poor*, Berkeley, CA: University of California Press.

Fass, P. (2005), "Children in global migrations," *Journal of Social History*, 38 (4): 937–953.

Federici, S. (2014), "From commoning to debt: Financialization, microcredit, and the changing architecture of capital accumulation," *South Atlantic Quarterly*, 113 (2): 231–244.

Feinberg, J. (1974), "The rights of animals and unborn generations," in W. Blackstone (ed.), *Philosophy and Environmental Crisis*, Athens, GA: The University of Georgia Press.

Feinstein, A. (2012), *The Shadow World: Inside the Global Arms Trade*, London: Penguin.

Feinstein, A. (2013), *The Shadow World: Inside the Global Arms Trade*, New York: Farrar, Straus and Giroux

Feldman, M. A., Battin, S. M., Shaw, O. A., and Luckasson, R. (2013), "Inclusion of children with disabilities in mainstream child development research," *Disability & Society*, 28 (7): 997–1011.

Ferguson, R. A. (2004), *Aberrations in Black: Toward a Queer of Color Critique*, Minneapolis, MN: University of Minnesota Press.

Filmer, D. (2008), "Disability, poverty, and schooling in developing countries: Results from 14 household surveys," *The World Bank Economic Review*, 22: 141–163.

Fisher, R. (2010), "Young writers' construction of agency," *Journal of Early Childhood Literacy*, 10 (4): 410–429.

Forst, R. (2010), "The justification of human rights and the basic right to justification: A reflexive approach," *Ethics*, 120 (4): 711–740.

Foucault, M. ([1975] 1995), *Discipline and Punish*, trans. A. Sheridan, New York: Random House.

Foucault, M. (1977), *Discipline and Punish: The Birth of the Prison*, New York: Vintage Books.

Foucault, M. (1980), *Power/Knowledge. Selected Interviews and Other Writings 1972–1977*, C. Gordon (ed.), New York: Pantheon Books.

Foucault, M. (1982), "The subject and power," *Critical Inquiry*, 8 (4): 777–795.

Foucault, M. (1995), *Discipline and Punish: The Birth of the Prison*, 2nd edn, New York: Vintage.

Fox, N. J., and Alldred, P. (2017), *Sociology and the New Materialism: Theory, Research, Action*, Los Angeles, CA: Sage.

Franklin, A., and Sloper, P. (2009), "Supporting the participation of disabled children and young people in decision-making," *Children and Society*, 23 (1): 3–15.

Fraser, N. (1997), *Justice Interruptus: Critical Reflections on the "Postsocialist" Condition*, London: Routledge.

Fraser, N. (2009), "Feminism, capitalism and the cunning of history," *New Left Review*, 56 (Mar–Apr): 97–117.

Fraser, N., and Honneth, A. (2003), *Redistribution or Recognition*, London: Verso.

Fraser, N. (2016), "Expropriation and exploitation in racialized capitalism: A reply to Michael Dawson," *Critical Historical Studies*, Spring: 163–178.

Freeman, M. (1992), "Taking children's rights more seriously," *International Journal of Law and the Family*, 6: 52–71.

Freeman, M. (1998), "The sociology of childhood and children's rights," *International Journal of Children's Rights*, 6: 433–444.

Freeman, M. (2007), "Why it remains important to take children's rights seriously," *International Journal of Children's Rights*, 15: 5–23.

Freeman, M. (2011), "Children's rights as human rights: Reading the UNCRC," in J. Qvortrup, W. A. Corsaro, and M.-S. Honig (eds), *The Palgrave Handbook of Childhood Studies*, Basingstoke: Palgrave Macmillan.

Freud, S. ([1905] 1960), *Jokes and Their Relation to the Unconscious*, trans. James Stachey, New York: Norton.

Fricker, M. (2009), *Epistemic Injustice: Power and the Ethics of Knowing*, Oxford: Oxford University Press.

Friedl, E. (2002), "Why are children missing from textbooks?" *Anthropology News*, 43 (5): 9.

Froerer, P. (2011), "Children's moral reasoning about illness in Chattisgarh, Central India," *Childhood: Journal of Global Child Research*, 18 (3): 367–383.

Fuller, L. L. (1969), *The Morality of Law*, New Haven, CT and London: Yale University Press.

Gabrielson, C. (2013), *Tinkering: Kids Learn by Making Stuff*, Sebastopol, CA: Maker Media.

Gagen, E. (2004), "Making America flesh: Physicality and nationhood in early twentieth-century physical education reform," *Cultural Geographies*, 11: 417–442.

Gagen, E. (2015), "Governing emotions: Citizenship, neuroscience, and the education of youth," *Transactions of the Institute of British Geographers*, 40: 140–152.

Gallacher, L., and Gallagher, M. (2008), "Methodological immaturity in childhood research?" *Childhood*, 15 (4): 499–516.

Genishi, C., and Haas Dyson, A. (2014), "Play as precursor for literacy development," in L. Brooker, M. Blaise, and S. Edwards (eds), *The Sage Handbook of Play and Learning in Early Childhood*, 228–239, London: Sage.

Ghai, A. (2001), "Marginalization and disability: Experiences from the third world," in M. Priestley (ed.), *Disability and the Life Course: Global Perspectives*, 26–37, Cambridge: Cambridge University Press.

Giddens, A. (1998), *The Third Way: The Renewal of Social Democracy*, Cambridge: Polity Press.

Gilligan, C. (1982), *In a Different Voice*, Cambridge, MA: Harvard University Press.

González, C. (2010), "Visibilizando el Co-Protagonismo Infantil: el Caso del Proyecto 'Banco de los Niños', una Experiencia de Participación y Solidaridad," *Revista Internacional NATS*, 20: 39–46.

Gonzalez, C., and Bell, H. (2016), "Child-centered play therapy for Hispanic children with traumatic grief: Implications for treatment outcomes," *International Journal of Play Therapy*, 25 (3): 146–153.

Goodley, D., and Runswick-Cole, K. (2010), "Emancipating play: Dis/abled children, development and deconstruction," *Disability & Society*, 25 (4): 499–512.

Gordon, B. (2006), "The paper doll house," in *The Saturated World: Aesthetic Meaning, Intimate Objects, Women's Lives, 1890–1940*, Knoxville, TN: University of Tennessee.

Gottlieb, A. (2004), *The Afterlife Is Where We Come from*, Chicago, IL: Chicago University Press.

Graeber, D. (2011), *Debt: The First 5000 Years*, Brooklyn, NY and London: Melville House Publishing.

Grier, B. (2006), *Invisible Hands: Child Labor and the State in Colonial Zimbabwe*, Portsmouth, NH: Heinemann.

Grimes, N., and Collier, B. (2012), *Barack Obama: Son of Promise, Child of Hope*, New York: Simon and Schuster.

Grindheim, L., and Ødegaard, E. (2013), "What is the state of play?" *International Journal of Play*, 2 (1): 4–6.

Guha, R. (1998), *Dominance without Hegemony: History and Power in Colonial India*, Cambridge, MA: Harvard University Press.

Guldberg, H. (2009), *Reclaiming Childhood: Freedom and Play in an Age of Fear*, London: Routledge.

Habermas, J. (2010), "The concept of human dignity and the realistic Utopia of human rights," *Metaphilosophy*, 41 (4): 464–480.

Hackett, A., Procter, L., and Seymour, J. (2015), *Children's Spatialities: Embodiment, Emotion and Agency*, Basingstoke: Palgrave Macmillan.

Hacking, I. (1999), *The Social Construction of What?*, Harvard, MA and Cambridge: Harvard University Press.

Haiven, M. (2014), *Cultures of Financialization: Fictitious Capital in Popular Culture and Everyday Life*, London: Palgrave Macmillan.

Hague Conference on Private International Law (1993), *The 1993 Hague Convention on Protection of Children and Co-operation in Respect of Intercountry Adoption*, The Hague, Netherlands: Hague Conference on Private International Law.

Hajisoteriou, C. (2010), "Europeanising intercultural education: Politics and policy making in Cyprus," *European Educational Research Journal*, 9 (4): 471–483.

Halberstam, J. (2005), *In a Queer Time and Place: Transgender Bodies, Subcultural Lives*, New York: NYU Press.

Halberstam, J. J. (2011), *The Queer Art of Failure*, Durham, NC: Duke University Press.

Halberstam, J. J. (2012), *Gaga Feminism: Sex, Gender, and the End of Normal*, Beacon Press.

Hall, G. S. (1907), "A study of dolls," in Theodate L. Smith (ed.), *Aspects of Child Life and Education*, New York: Ginn, loc. 3211.

Hall, S. (1992), "Cultural studies and its theoretical legacies," in L. Grossberg and C. Nelson (eds), *Cultural Studies*, New York: Routledge.

Hall, S. M. (2015), "Everyday family experiences of the financial crisis: Getting by in the recent economic recession," *Journal of Economic Geography*, 16 (2): 305–330.

Hallward, P. (2010), "Communism of the intellect, communism of the will," in C. Douzinas and S. Zizek (eds), *The Idea of Communism*, 111–130, London: Verso.

Hanson, K., and Neiuwenhuys, O. (2013), "Living rights, social justice, translations," in K. Hanson and O. Nieuwenhuys (eds), *Reconceptualizing Children's Rights in International Development: Living Rights, Social Justice, Translations*, 3–26, Cambridge: Cambridge University Press.

Haraway, D. (1992), "The promises of monsters: A regenerative politics for inappropriate/d others," in L. Grossberg, C. Nelson, and P. Triechler (eds), *Cultural Studies*, 295–337, New York: Routledge.

Hardison, O. B., and Golden, L. (1995), *Horace for Students of Literature: The "Ars Poetica" and Its Tradition*, Gainesville: University Press of Florida.

Hardman, C. (1973), "Can there be an anthropology of children?" *Journal of the Anthropology Society of Oxford*, 4 (1): 85–99.

Harker, C. (2005), "Playing and affective time-spaces," *Children's Geographies*, 3 (1): 47–62.

Harris, A., and Shields Dobson, A. (2015), "Theorizing agency in post-girlpower times," *Continuum: Journal of Media & Cultural Studies*, 29 (2): 145–156.

Hart, D., Aitkins, R., and Ford, D. (1998), "Urban America as the context for the development of moral identity in adolescence," *Journal of Social Issues*, 54 (3): 513–530.

Hart, J., Galappatti, A., Boyden, J., and Armstrong, M. (2007), "Participatory tools for evaluating psychosocial work with children in areas of armed conflict: A pilot in eastern Sri Lanka," *Intervention*, 5 (1): 41–60.

Hart, R. (1992), *Children's Participation: From Tokenism to Citizenship*, Florence: UNICEF.

Hart, R. (2002), "Containing children: Some lessons on planning for play from New York City," *Environment and Urbanization*, 14 (2): 135–148.

Harvey, D. (2007), *A Brief History of Neoliberalism*, Oxford: Oxford University Press.

Hashemi, G., Kuper, H., and Wickenden, M. (2017), "SDGs, Inclusive health and the path to universal health coverage," *Disability and The Global South*, Special issue on the SDGs, 4 (1): 1088–1111.

Hecht, T. (1998), *At Home in the Street: Street Children of Northeast Brazil*, Cambridge: Cambridge University Press.

Heidbrink, L. (2014), "Collisions of Debt and Interests: Youth Negotiations of (In)debt(ed) Migration," 10th Joint Area Centers Symposium "Children and Globalization: Issues, Policies and Initiatives," University of Illinois at Urbana-Champaign, April 10–12, 2014.

Heidegger, M. (1927/1962), *Being and Time*, trans. J. Macquarrie and E. Robinson, New York: Harper.

Hekman, S. (2008), "Constructing the ballast: An ontology for feminism," in S. Alaimo and S. Hekman (eds), *Material Feminisms*, 85–119, Bloomington and Indianapolis, IN: Indiana University Press.

Helgesen, E. (2015), "Miku's mask: Fictional encounters in children's costume play," *Childhood*, 22 (4): 535–550.

Hendrick, H. (1997), *Children, Childhood and English Society 1880–1990*, New York: Cambridge University Press.

Hirschfeld, L. (2002), "Why don't anthropologists like children?" *American Anthropologist*, 104 (2): 611–627.

Holbraad, M., and Pedersen, M. A. (2017), *The Ontological Turn: An Anthropological Exposition*, Cambridge: Cambridge University Press.

Hollos, M. (2002), "The cultural construction of childhood: Changing conceptions among the Pare of northern Tanzania," *Childhood: A Global Journal of Child Research*, 9 (2): 167–189.

Holloway, S. (2014), "Changing children's geographies," *Children's Geographies*, 3: 47–62.

Holloway, S., and Valentine, G. (2000), "Spatiality and the new social studies of childhood," *Sociology*, 34: 763–783.

Holt, L. (2004), "The 'voices' of children: De-centring empowering research relations," *Children's Geographies*, 2 (1): 13–27.

Holt, L. (2010), "Young children's embodied social capital and performing disability," *Children's Geographies*, 8 (1): 25–37.

Honey, M., and Kanter, D. (2013), *Design Make Play*, New York: Routledge.

Honig, M.-S. (2009), "How is the child constituted in childhood studies?" in J. Qvortrup, W. A. Corsaro, and M.-S. Honig (eds), *The Palgrave Handbook of Childhood Studies*, 62–77, Basingstoke: Palgrave Macmillan.

Honneth, A. (1995), "Decentered autonomy: The subject after the fall," in C. W. Wright (ed.), *The Fragmented World of the Social: Essays in Social and Political Philosophy*, 261–271, Albany, NY: State University of New York Press.

Honwana A. (2012), *The Time of Youth: Work, Social Change and Politics in Africa*, Sterling, VA: Kumarian Press.

Hopkins, P. (2010), *Young People, Place and Identity*, London: Routledge.

Hopkins, P., and Pain, R. (2007), "Geographies of age: Thinking relationally," *Area*, 39: 287–94.

Hopkins, T. K., and Wallerstein, I. (1986), "Commodity chains in the world-economy prior to 1800," *Review (Fernand Braudel Center)*, 10 (1): 157–170.

Horton, J. (2008), "A 'sense of Failure'? Everydayness and research ethics," *Children's Geographies*, 6 (4): 363–383.

Horton, J. (2010), "How children's popular culture matters," *Social and Cultural Geography*, 11: 377–398.

Horton, J. (2015a), "Young people and debt: Getting on with austerities," *Area*, 49 (3): 280–287. DOI: 10.1111/area.12224

Horton, J. (2015b), "For geographies of children, young people and popular culture," *Geography Compass*, 8: 1–13.

Horton, J. (2016), "Anticipating service withdrawal: Young people in spaces of neoliberalisation, austerity and economic crisis," *Transactions of the Institute of British Geographers*, 41: 349–362.

Horton, J., and Kraftl, P. (2006a), "What else? Some more ways of thinking about and doing children's geographies," *Children's Geographies*, 4: 69–95.

Horton, J., and Kraftl, P. (2006b), "Not just growing up, but *going on*: Children's geographies as becomings, materials, spacings, bodies, situations," *Children's Geographies*, 4: 259–276.

Horton, J., and Kraftl, P. (2018), "Rats, assorted shit and 'racist groundwater': Towards extra-sectional understandings of childhoods and social-material processes," *Environment and Planning D: Society and Space*, online early.

Howard, N. (2012), "Protecting children from trafficking in Benin: In need of politics and participation," *Development in Practice*, 22 (4): 460–472.

Huijsmans, R., George, S., and Gigengack, R. (2014), "Theorising age and generation in development: A relational approach," *European Journal of Development Research*, 26 (2): 163–174.

Huizinga, J. (1950), *Homo Ludens*, Boston, MA: Beacon Press.

Hultman, K., and Lenz Taguchi, H. (2010), "Challenging anthropocentric analysis of visual data: A relational materialist methodological approach to educational research," *International Journal of Qualitative Studies in Education*, 23 (5): 525–542.

Hunleth, J. (2011), "Beyond on or with: Questioning power dynamics and knowledge production in 'child-oriented' research methodology," *Childhood*, 18: 81.

Hurtig, J. (2008), *Coming of Age in Times of Crisis: Youth, Schooling, and Patriarchy in a Venezuelan Town*, New York: Palgrave Macmillan.

Icaza, R. (2017), "Decolonial feminism and global politics: Border thinking and vulnerability as a knowing otherwise," in M. Woons and S. Weier (eds), *Critical Epistemologies of Global Politics*, 26–45, Bristol: E-International Relations. Available online: http://www.e-ir.info/wp-content/uploads/2017/06/Critical-Epistemologies-of-Global-Politics-E-IR.pdf.

IDA (2016), *High level political forum. Ensuring that no one is left behind*. Position paper by Persons with Disabilities, New York: International Disability Alliance. Available online: http://www.internationaldisabilityalliance.org/blog/day-one-high-level-political-forum-2016.

Importance of Play Group (2017), "Taking Play Seriously—About," *The Importance of Play*, n.d. Available online: http://www.importanceofplay.eu/about/ (accessed April 4, 2017).

Irvine, J. T. (2016), "Going upscale: Scales and scale-climbing as ideological projects," in E. S. Carr and M. Lempert (eds), *Scale: Discourse and Dimensions of Social Life*, 213–231, Oakland, CA: University of California Press.

Isenberg, J. P., and Quisenberry, N. (2002), "A position paper of the Association for Childhood Education International PLAY: Essential for all children," *Childhood Education*, 79 (1): 33–39.

Jaarsma, A. S., Kinaschuk, K., and Xing, L. (2016), 'Kierkegaard, despair and the possibility of education: Teaching existentialism existentially," *Studies in Philosophy and Education*, 35 (5): 445–461.

Jackson, M. (1998), *Minima Ethnographica: Intersubjectivity and the Anthropological Project*, Chicago, IL: University of Chicago Press.

Jacobs, J. (2006), "A geography of big things," *Cultural Geographies*, 13: 1–27.

Jagose, A. (1996), *Queer Theory: An Introduction*, New York: NYU Press.

James, A. (2007), "Giving voice to children's voices: Practices and problems, pitfalls and potentials," *American Anthropologist*, 109 (2): 261–272.

James, A. L. (2010), "Competition or integration: The next step in childhood studies," *Childhood: A Global Journal of Child Research*, 17 (4): 485–499.

James, A., and James, A. L. (2001), "Childhood: Toward a theory of continuity and change," *Annals of the American Academy of Political and Social Science*, 575: 25–37.

James, A., and James, A. L. (2004), *Constructing Childhood*, New York: Palgrave Macmillan.

James, A., and James, A. L. (2008), *Key Concepts in Childhood Studies*, Los Angeles, CA: Sage Publications Ltd.

James, A., and James, A. L. (2012), *Key Concepts in Childhood Studies*, London: Sage Publications Ltd.

James, A., Jenks, C., and Prout, A. (1998), *Theorizing Childhood*, Cambridge: Polity.

James, A., and Prout, A., eds (1990), *Constructing and Reconstructing Childhood: Contemporary Issues in the Sociological Study of Childhood*, London: Falmer Press.

James, A., and Prout, A. (1990), *Constructing and Reconstructing Childhood: New Directions in the Sociological Study of Childhood* (2nd edn [1997] Published by Routledge ed.), Oxford: Routledge.

James, A., and Prout, A. (1997), *Constructing and Reconstructing Childhood: Contemporary Issues in the Sociological Study of Childhood*, Washington, DC: Falmer Press.

Janssen, D. (2008), "Re-queering queer youth development: A post-developmental approach to childhood and pedagogy," *Journal of LGBT Youth*, 5 (3): 74–95.

Jaschik, S. (2009), "The evolution of American women's studies," *Inside Higher Education*. March 27. Available online: https://www.insidehighered.com/news/2009/03/27/women.

Jeffrey, C. (2012), "Geographies of children and youth II," *Progress in Human Geography*, 36: 245–253.

Jenks, C. (1982), "Introduction: Constituting the child," in C. Jenks (ed.), *The Sociology of Childhood: Essential Readings*, 9–24, London: Batsford.

Johansson, B. (2011), "Doing adulthood in childhood research," *Childhood*, 19 (1): 101–114.

Johnson, E. P. (2011), *Sweet Tea: Black Gay Men of the South*, Chapel Hill, NC: University of North Carolina Press.

Jones, E., and Reynolds, G. (2011), *The Play's the Thing: Teachers' Roles in Children's Play*, New York: Teachers' College Press.

Jones, L., Bellis, M. A., Wood, S., Hughes, K., McCoy, E., Eckley, L., Bates, G., Mikton, C., Shakespeare, T., and Officer, A. (2012), "Prevalence and risk of violence against children with disabilities: A systematic review and meta-analysis of observational studies," *Lancet*, 380 (9845): 899–907.

Joosen, V. (2017), "Age studies and children's literature," in C. Beauvais and M. Nikolajeva (eds), *The Edinburgh Companion to Children's Literature*, 79–89, Edinburgh: Edinburgh University Press.

Joosen, V., ed. (2018), *Connecting Childhood and Old Age in Popular Media*, Jackson, MS: University of Mississippi Press.

Kakkori, L., and Huttunen, R. (2012), "The Sartre-Heidegger controversy on humanism and the concept of man in education," *Educational Philosophy and Theory*, 44 (2): 351–365.

Kallio, K., and Häkli, J. (2013), "Children and young people's politics in everyday life," *Space and Polity*, 17: 1–16.

Katz, C. (2004), *Growing Up Global: Economic Restructuring and Children's Everyday Lives*, Minneapolis, MN: University of Minnesota Press.

Katz, C. (2008), "Cultural geographies lecture: Childhood as spectacle: Relays of anxiety and the reconfiguration of the child," *Cultural Geographies*, 15(1): 5–17.

Kelen, K., and Sundmark, B., eds (2012), *The Nation in Children's Literature: Nations of Childhood*, New York: Routledge.

Kelly, P., and Kamp, A. (2015), *A Critical Youth Studies for the 21st Century*, Leiden: Brill.

Kelz, R. (2016), *The Non-Sovereign Self, Responsibility and Otherness: Hannah Arendt, Judith Butler and Stanley Cavell on Moral Philosophy and Political Agency*, Basingstoke: Palgrave.

Kent, G. (1995), *Children in the International Political Economy*, Basingstoke: Houndmills.

Kesby, M. (2007), "Methodological insights on and from children's geographies'," *Children's Geographies*, 5 (3): 193–205.

Kidd, K. (2011), "The child, the scholar, and the children's literature archive," *The Lion and the Unicorn*, 35 (1): 2–3.

Kincaid, J. R. (1992), *Child-Loving: The Erotic Child and Victorian Culture*, New York: Routledge.

Kirby, P., Lanyon, C., Cronin, K., and Sinclair, R. (2003), *Building a Culture of Participation: Involving Children and Young People in Policy, Service Planning, Delivery and Evaluation*, London: Department for Education and Skills.

Klocker, N. (2007), "An example of thin agency: Child domestic workers in Tanzania," in R. Panelli, S. Punch, and E. Robson (eds), *Global Perspectives on Rural Childhood and Youth: Young Rural Lives*, 81–148, London: Routledge.

Komulainen, S. (2007), "The ambiguity of children's 'voice' in social research," *Childhood*, 14 (1): 11–28.

Kraftl, P. (2006), "Building an idea: The material construction of an ideal childhood," *Transactions of the Institute of British Geographers*, 31: 488–504.

Kraftl, P. (2012), "Utopian promise or burdensome responsibility? A critical analysis of the UK government's building schools for the future policy," *Antipode*, 44: 847–870.

Kraftl, P. (2013a), "Beyond 'voice', beyond 'agency', beyond 'politics'? Hybrid childhoods and some critical reflections on children's emotional geographies," *Emotion, Space and Society*, 9: 13–23.

Kraftl, P. (2013b), *Geographies of Alternative Education*, Bristol: Policy Press.

Kraftl, P. (2014), "Liveability and urban architectures: Mol(ecul)ar biopower and the becoming-lively of Sustainable Communities," *Environment and Planning D: Society and Space*, 13: 274–292.

Kraftl, P., Christensen, P., Horton, J., and Hadfield-Hill, S. (2013), "Living on a building site: Young people's experiences of emerging 'Sustainable Communities' in England," *Geoforum*, 50: 190–199.

Kraftl, P., Horton, J., and Tucker, F. (2014), "Children's geographies," *Oxford Bibliographies in Childhood Studies*, published online; DOI: 10.1093/OBO/9780199791231-0080

Kuper, H., Monteath-Van Dok, A., Wing, K., Danquah, L., Evans, J., Zuurmond, J., and Gallinetti, J. (2014), "The impact of disability on the lives of children; cross-sectional data including 8,900 children with disabilities and 898,834 children without disabilities across 30 countries," *PLoS One*, 9 (9): e107300.

Kyriakou, N. (2015), "Investigating Teachers' and Language Learners' Use of Language in Public Primary Schools in Cyprus," PhD diss., University of Exeter, Exeter.

Lafrance, M. (2009), "Skin and the self: Cultural theory and Anglo-American psychoanalysis," *Body and Society*, 15 (3): 3–24.

Lanclos, D. (2003), *At Play in Belfast*, New Brunswick: Rutgers University Press.

Landis, C. K. (1875), "The settlement of vineland in New Jersey," *Fraser's Magazine*, 11 (January 1875): 121–122.

Landreth, G. (2001), "Facilitative dimensions of play in the play therapy process," in G. Landreth (ed.), *Innovations in Play Therapy*, 3–22, London: Routledge.

Langa, P. (2008), Ruling, in *MEC for Education: Kwazulu-Natal and Others v Pillay* (CCT 51/06) [2007] ZACC 21; 2008 (1) SA 474 (CC); 2008 (2) BCLR 99 (CC), through the *Southern African Legal Information Institute*, Available online: http://www.saflii.org/za/cases/ZACC/2007/21.pdf (accessed November 28, 2016).

Lansdown, G. (2012), *Using the Human Rights Framework to Promote the Rights of Children with Disabilities*, New York: UNICEF.

Lareau, A. (2003), *Unequal Childhoods: Race, Class and Family Life*, Berkeley, CA: University of California Press.

Lather, P. (2013), "Methodology-21: What do we do in the afterward?" *International Journal of Qualitative Studies in Education*, 26 (6): 634–645.

Latour, B. (2005), *Reassembling the Social: An Introduction to Actor-Network-Theory*, Oxford and New York: Oxford University Press.

Law, J. (2004), *After Method: Mess in Social Science Research*, London and New York: Routledge.

Lazos, S. (2012), "Are student teaching evaluations holding back women and minorities? The perils of 'doing' gender and race in the classroom," in G. Muhs, Y. Niemann, C. González, and A. Harris (eds), *Presumed Incompetent: The Intersections of Race and Class for Women in Academia*, 164–185, Boulder, CO: University Press of Colorado.

Lazzarato, M. (2011), *The Making of the Indebted Man*, Cambridge, MA: MIT Press.

Lee, N. (1998), "Towards an immature sociology," *The Sociological Review*, 46: 458–481.

Lee, N. (2000), "Faith in the body? Childhood, subjecthood and sociological enquiry," in A. Prout (ed.), *The Body, Childhood and Society*, 149–171, Basingstoke: Palgrave Macmillan.

Lee, N. (2001), *Childhood and Society: Growing Up in an Age of Uncertainty*, London: McGraw-Hill Education.

Lee, N. (2013), *Childhood and Biopolitics: Climate Change, Life Processes and Human Futures*, New York: Palgrave Macmillan.

Lee, N. (2014), *Childhood and Biopolitics*, Basingstoke: Palgrave.

Lee, N., and Motzkau, J. (2011), "Navigating the biopolitics of childhood," *Childhood*, 18: 7–19.

Lefort, C. (1986), *The Political Forms of Modern Society: Bureaucracy, Democracy, Totalitarianism*, J. Thompson (ed.), Cambridge, MA: MIT Press.

Leibel, M. (2004), *A Will of Their Own: Cross-Cultural Perspectives on Working Children*, London: Zed Books.

Liebel, M. (2015), "Protecting the rights of working children instead of banning child labour," *International Journal of Children's Rights*, 23: 529–547.

Lieberman, C. (1985), "The existentialist 'school' of thought: Existentialism and education," *The Clearing House*, 58 (7): 322–326.

Lesko, N., and Talburt, S. (2012), "Enchantment," in S. Talburt and N. Lesko (eds), *Keywords in Youth Studies: Tracing Affects, Movements, Knowledges*, 279–289, New York and London: Routledge.

Lester, S., and Russell, W. (2014), "Turning the world upside down: Playing as the deliberate creation of uncertainty," *Children*, 1: 241–260.

Levi-Strauss, C. (1966), "The science of the concrete," in *The Savage Mind*, Chicago, IL: University of Chicago Press.

Levine, D. (1988), *The Flight from Ambiguity: Essays in Social and Cultural Theory*, Chicago, IL: University of Chicago Press.

Levine, S. (1999), "Bittersweet harvest: Children, work and the global march against child labour in the postapartheid state," *Critique of Anthropology*, 19 (2): 139–155.

Lieberman, C. (1985), "The existentialist 'school' of thought: Existentialism and education," *The Clearing House*, 58 (7): 322–326.

Lindroos-Hovinheimo, S. (2015), "Excavating foundations of legal personhood: Fichte on autonomy and self-consciousness," *International Journal for the Semiotics of Law*, 28: 687–702.

Lindsey, R. A. (1972), "Existentialism: Is it bankrupt as an educational philosophy?" *The Clearing House*, 47 (4): 195–197.

Linn, S. (2006), *The Case for Make Believe*, New York: New Press.

Lobo, M. (2016), "Co-inhabiting public spaces: Diversity and playful encounters in Darwin, Australia," *Geographical Review*, 106 (2): 163–173.

Lorimer, H. (2005), "Cultural geography: The busyness of being 'more-than-representational,'" *Progress in Human Geography*, 29: 83–94.

Louv, R. (2005), *Last Child in the Woods*, Chapel Hill, NC: Algonquin Books.

Love, H. (2009), *Feeling Backward*, Cambridge, MA: Harvard University Press.

Lundy, L. (2007), "'Voice' is not enough: Conceptualizing article 12 of the United Nations Convention on the Rights of the Child," *British Educational Research Journal*, 33 (6): 927–942.

Maccormick, N. (1997), "Law as institutional normative order," *Rechtstheorie*, 28: 219–234.

Mackinnon, C. (1991), "Difference and dominance: On sex discrimination," in K. T. Bartlett and R. Kennedy (eds), *Feminist Legal Theory*, 81–94, San Francisco, CA: Westview Press.

MacNell, L., Driscoll, A., and Hunt, A. (2015), "What's in a name: Exposing gender bias in student ratings of teaching," *Journal of Collective Bargaining in the Academy*, 0 (52). Available online: http://thekeep.eiu.edu/jcba/vol0/iss10/52.

Mahmood, S. (2011), *Politics of Piety: The Islamic Revival and the Feminist Subject*, Princeton, NJ: Princeton University Press.

Manalansan IV, M. F. (2003), *Global Divas: Filipino Gay Men in the Diaspora*, Durham, NC: Duke University Press.

Manning, E. (2009), "What if it didn't all begin and end with containment? Toward a leaky sense of self," *Body and Society*, 15 (3): 33–45.

Marsh, J., and Bishop, J., eds (2014), *Changing Play: Play, Media and Commercial Culture from the 1950s to the Present Day*, Berkshire: Open University Press.

Marston, S. A., Woodward, K., and Jones III, J. P. (2007), "Flattening ontologies of globalization: The Nollywood case," *Globalizations*, 4 (1): 45–63.

Martin, Randy (2002), *Financialization of Daily Life*, Philadelphia, PA: Temple University Press.

Marx, K. (2003), *The Class Struggles in France: From the February Revolution to the Paris Commune*, Chippendale, NSW, Australia: Resistance Books.

Marx, K. ([1844] 2009), "Sobre la Cuestión Judía," in B. Bauer (ed.), *La Cuestión Judía*, Barcelona: Anthropos.

Mason, M. (1990), "Internalised oppression," in R. Reiser and M. Mason (eds), *Disability Equality in Education*, London: ILEA. http://pf7d7vi404s1dxh27mla5569.wpengine.netdna-cdn.com/files/library/Mason-Michelene-mason.pdf

Mason, M. (2013), "In the ivory tower, men only: For men, having children is a career advantage. For women, it's a career killer," *Slate.com*. June 17. Available online: http://www.slate.com/articles/double_x/doublex/2013/06/female_academics_pay_a_heavy_baby_penalty.html

Mayall, B., ed. (1994), *Children's Childhoods Observed and Experienced*, London: Falmer.

Mayall, B. (2000), "The sociology of childhood in relation to children's rights," *International Journal of Children's Rights*, 8: 243–259.

Mayall, B. (2002), *Towards a Sociology for Childhood: Thinking from Children's Lives*, Milton Keynes: Open University Press.

Mazzei, L. A. (2013), "A voice without organs: Interviewing in posthumanist research," *International Journal of Qualitative Studies in Education*, 26 (6): 732–740.

Mbembe, A. (1992), "Provisional notes on the postcolony," *Africa: Journal of the International African Institute*, 62 (1): 3–37.

Mbembe, A. (2003), "Necropolitics," *Public Culture*, 15 (1): 11–40.

Mendus, S. (2015), "Care and human rights: A reply to Virginia Held," in R. Cruft, S. M. Liao, and M. Renzo (eds), *Philosophical Foundations of Human Rights*, 642–652, Oxford: Oxford University Press.

Mengel, F., Sauermann, J., and Zolitz, U. (2016), "Gender Bias in Performance Evaluations: Evidence from Random Student-Teacher Assignment," *American Economic Association Annual Meeting*, January 5. San Francisco.

Mergen, B. (1992), "Children's play in American autobiographies: 1870–1914," in Kathryn Grover (ed.), *Hard at Play: Leisure in America, 1840–1940*, Amherst, MA: University of Massachusetts Press.

Mickenberg, J. (2006), *Learning from the Left: Children's Literature, the Cold War, and Radical Politics in the United States*, New York: Oxford University Press.

Mickenberg, J., and Nel, P., eds (2008), *Tales for Little Rebels: A Collection of Radical Children's Literature*, New York: New York University Press.

Mill, J. S. (2015), "Considerations on representative government," in M. Philp and F. Rosen (eds), *On Liberty, Utilitarianism and Other Essays*, 179–405, Oxford: Oxford University Press.

Milteer, R. M., and Ginsburg, K. R. (2012), "The importance of play in promoting healthy child development and maintaining strong parent-child bond: Focus on children in poverty," *Pediatrics*, 129 (1): 204–213.

Mimiaga, M. J., Reisner, S. L., Bland, S., Cranston, K., Isenberg, D., Driscoll, M. A., VanDerwarker, R., and Mayer, K. H. (2010), "'It's a quick way to get what you want': A formative exploration of HIV risk among urban Massachusetts men who have sex with men who attend sex parties," *AIDS Patient Care and STDs* 24 (10): 659–674.

Mimiaga, M. J., Reisner, S. L., Bland, S. E., Driscoll, M. A., Cranston, K., Isenberg, D., VanDerwarker, R., and Mayer, K. H. (2011), "Sex parties among urban MSM: An emerging culture and HIV risk environment," *AIDS and Behavior*, 15 (2): 305–318.

Ministry of Education and Culture (2017), "Annual Report 2016" [in Greek]. Available online: http://moec.gov.cy/etisia-ekthesi/index.html

Minge-Kalman, W. (1978), "The Industrial Revolution and the European family: The institutionalization of 'childhood' as a market for family labor," *Comparative Studies in Society and History*, 20 (3): 454–468.

Mintz, S. (2012), "Why the history of childhood matters," *Journal of the History of Childhood and Youth*, 5 (1): 17.

Mitchell, K., and Elwood, S. (2012), "Mapping children's politics: The promise of articulation and the limits of nonrepresentational theory," *Environment and Planning D*, 30: 788–804.

Mizen, P. (2002), "Putting the politics back into youth studies: Keynesianism, Monetarism and the changing state of youth," *Journal of Youth Studies*, 5: 15–20.

Mizen, P., and Ofusu-Kusi, Y. (2013), "Agency as vulnerability: Accounting for children's movement to the streets of Accra," *Sociological Review*, 61 (2): 363–382.

Mohr, R. (2007), "Identity crisis: Judgment and the hollow legal subject," *Law Text Culture*, 11: 106–128.

Mol, A. (2002), *The Body Multiple: Ontology in Medical Practice*, Durham, NC: Duke University Press.

Mol, A. (1999), "Ontological politics: A word and some questions," in J. Law and J. Hassard (eds), *Actor Network Theory and After, 74–89*, Oxford: Blackwell.

Morris, V. C. (1966), *Existentialism in Education*, New York: Harper & Row.

Morrow, V., and Crivello, G. (2015), "What is the value of qualitative longitudinal research with children and young people for international development?" *International Journal of Social Research Methodology*, 18 (3): 267–280.

Moser, S. (2015), 'Educating the nation: Shaping student-citizens in Indonesian schools," *Children's Geographies*, 14 (3): 247–262.

Muñoz, J. E. (1999), *Disidentifications: Queers of Color and the Performance of Politics*, Minneapolis, MN: University of Minnesota Press.

Mutua, K., and Swadener, B., eds (2004), *Decolonizing Research in Cross-Cultural Contexts: Critical Personal Narratives*, Albany, NY: State University of New York Press.

Naffine, N. (2003), "Who are law's persons? From Cheshire cats to responsible subjects," *The Modern Law Review*, 66: 346–367.

Nandy, A. (1992), "Reconstructing childhood: A critique of the ideology of adulthood," in *Traditions, Tyranny and Utopias: Essays in the Politics of Awareness*, New Delhi: Oxford University Press.

Narotzky, S., and Besnier, N. (2014), "Crisis, value, and hope: Rethinking the economy," *Current Anthropology*, 55 (S9): S4–S16.

Nash, C. J., and Brown, K. eds (2012), *Queer Methods and Methodologies: Intersecting Queer Theories and Social Science Research*, London: Routledge.

Neuiwenhuys, O. (1998), "Global childhoods and the politics of contempt," *Alternatives*, 23 (3): 267–289.

Neuiwenhuys, O. (2001), "By the sweat of their brow? Street children, NGOs and children's rights in Addis Ababa," *Africa*, 71 (4): 539–557.

Neuiwenhuys, O. (2013), "Theorizing childhood: Why we need postcolonial perspectives," *Childhood*, 20 (1): 3–8.

"New Jersey, Births and Christenings Index, 1660–1931. FHL Film no. 494183." http://www.ancestry.com

Newberry, J. (2017), "Interiority and the government of the child," *Focaal–Journal of Global and Historical Anthropology*, 77: 76–89.

Newbery, J. (1770), *A Little Pretty Pocket-Book : Intended for the Instruction and Amusement of Little Master Tommy, and Pretty Miss Polly*, London: Printed for Newbery and Carnan.

Ngutuku, E., and Okwany, A. (2017), "Youth as researchers: Navigating generational power issues in adolescent sexuality and reproductive health research," *Childhood in Africa*, 4 (1): 70–82.

Niblett, W. R. (1954), "On existentialism and education," *British Journal of Educational Studies*, 2 (2): 101–111.

Nino, C. S. (1989), *The Ethics of Human Rights*, Oxford: Clarendon Press.

Nodelman, P. (2008), *The Hidden Adult: Defining Children's Literature*, Baltimore, MD: Johns Hopkins.

Norrie, A. (2004), "Dialectics, deconstruction and the legal subject," in J. Joseph and J. M. Roberts (eds), *Realism Discourse and Deconstruction*, 217–245, London and New York: Routledge.

Oakley, A. (1994), "Women and children first and last: Parallels and differences between children's and women's studies," in B. Mayall (ed.), *Children's Childhoods: Observed and Experienced*, 13–23, Washington, DC: Falmer Press.

Ochs, E., and Izquierdo, C. (2009), "Responsibility in childhood: Three developmental trajectories," *Ethos: Journal of the Society for Psychological Anthropology*, 37 (4): 391–413.

Ogden, T. (1989), *The Primitive Edge of Experience*, New Brunswick, NJ: Jason Aronson.

Oldman, D. (1994), "Adult-child relations as class relations," in J. Qvortup, M. Bardy, G. Sgritta, and H. Wintersberger (eds), *Childhood Matters: Social Theory, Practice and Politics*, Aldershot: Avebury.

Oliver, M. (2009), *Understanding Disability. From Theory to Practice*, 2nd edn, Basingstoke: Palgrave Macmillan.

O'Neill, W. F. (1964), "Existentialism and education for moral choice," *The Phi Delta Kappan*, 46 (2): 48–53.

"Open letter: A better approach to child work," (2016), *Open Democracy: Beyond Trafficking and Slavery*. January 27. Available online: https://www.opendemocracy.net/open-letter-better-approach-to-child-work.

Opie, I., and Opie, P. (1959), *Lore and Language of Schoolchildren*, Oxford: Clarendon Press.

Oswell, D. (2009), "Yet to come? Globality and the sound of an infant politics," *Radical Politics Today*, 1 (1): 1–18.

Oswell, D. (2013), *The Agency of Children: From Family to Global Human Rights*, Cambridge: Cambridge University Press.

Oswell, D. (2016), "Re-aligning children's agency and re-socialising children in childhood studies," in F. Esser, M. Baader, T. Betz, and B. Hungerland (eds), *Reconceptualising Agency and Childhood: New Perspectives in Childhood Studies*, London: Routledge.

Pacini-Ketchabaw, V., and Clark, V. (2016), "Following watery relations in early childhood pedagogies," *Journal of Early Childhood Research*, 14: 98–111.

Panikkar, R. (1982), "Is the notion of human rights a Western concept?" *Diogenes*, 30: 75–102.

Parcero, J. A. C. (2007), *El Lenguaje de los Derechos*, Madrid: Trotta.

Parnell, R., and Patsarika, M. (2016), *Designing with Children: A Guide for Architects and Educators*, London: Routledge.

Pells, K. (2012), "Rights are everything we don't have: Clashing conceptions of vulnerability and agency in the daily lives of Rwandan children and youth," *Children's Geographies*, 10 (4): 427–440.

Penn, H. (2010), "Shaping the future: How human capital arguments about investment in early childhood are being (mis)used in poor countries," in N. Yelland (ed.), *Contemporary Perspectives on Early Childhood Development*, Maidenhead: Open University Press.

Penn, H. (2011), "Travelling policies and global buzzwords: How international non-governmental organizations and charities spread the word about early childhood in the global South," *Childhood*, 18 (1): 94–113.

Philippou, S. (2009), "Greek-Cypriot pupils' representations of national others: A study of the impact of 'Europe' in a primary school curricular intervention," *Mediterranean Journal of Educational Studies*, 14 (2): 117–160.

Philo, C. (2003), "'To go back up the side hill': Memories, imaginations and reveries of childhood," *Children's Geographies*, 1: 7–23.

Philo, C. (2016), "Childhood is measured out by sounds and sights and smells, before the dark hour of reason grows' Children's Geographies at 12," *Children's Geographies*, 14: 623–640.

Phiri, D., and Abebe, T. (2016), "Suffering and thriving: Children's perspectives and interpretations of poverty and well-being in rural Zambia," *Childhood: A Global Journal of Child Research*, 23 (3): 378–393.

Pimlott-Wilson, H. (2015), "Individualising the future: The emotional geographies of neoliberal governance in young peoples' aspirations," *Area*, online early.

PLAN International (2013), *Outside the Circle: A research initiative by PLAN International into the rights of children with disabilities to education and protection in West Africa.* Woking, Plan International.

"Playwork and playworkers" (2017), *Play and Playground Encyclopedia*, n.d. Available online: https://pgpedia.com/p/playwork-and-playworkers (accessed April 4, 2017).

Pomfret, D. (2009), "Raising Eurasia: Race, Class and Age in French and British Colonies," *Comparative Studies in Society and History*, 51 (2): 314–343.

Povinelli, E. (1999), "Settler modernity and the quest for an indigenous tradition," *Public Culture*, 11 (1): 19–48.

Prout, A. (2000), *The Body, Childhood and Society*, Basingstoke: Palgrave Macmillan.

Prout, A. (2005), *The Future of Childhood*, London: Routledge Falmer.

Prout, A., and James, A. (1997), "A new paradigm for the sociology of childhood? Provenance, promise and problems," in A. James and A. Prout (eds), *Constructing and Reconstructing Childhood*, 7–33, NY: Routledge Falmer.

Puar, J. (2009), "Prognosis time: Towards a geopolitics of affect, debility and capacity," *Women and Performance: A Journal of Feminist Theory*, 19 (2): 161–172.

Pugh, T. (2010), *Innocence, Heterosexuality, and the Queerness of Children's Literature*, Abingdon, Oxon: Routledge.

Punch, S. (2015), "Possibilities for learning between childhoods and youth in the minority and majority worlds: Youth transitions as an example of cross-world dialogue," in J. Wyn and H. Cahill (eds), *Handbook of Children and Youth Studies*, New York: Springer.

Punch, S. (2016), "Exploring Children's Agency across Majority and Minority World Contexts," in S. Punch and K. Tisdall (eds), *Reconceptualising Agency and Childhood: New Perspectives in Childhood Studies*, 183–196, London: Routledge.

Punch, S., and Tisdall, K., eds (2016), *Children and Young People's Relationships: Learning across Majority and Minority Worlds*, Routledge.

Pupavac, V. (2001), "Misanthropy without borders: The international children's rights regime," *Disasters*, 25 (2): 95–112.

Pykett, J. (2015), *Brain Culture: Shaping Policy through Neuroscience*, Bristol: Policy Press.

Qvotrup, J. (1985), "Placing children in the division of labour," in P. Chase and R. Collins (eds), *Family and Economy in Modern Society*, 129–145, London: Palgrave.

Qvortrup, J. (2004), "Editorial: The waiting child," *Childhood*, 11 (3): 267–273.

Qvortrup, J., Bardy, M., Sgritta, G., and Wintersberger, H. (eds) (1994), *Childhood Matters*, Aldershot: Avebury Press.

Raad voor Strafrechtstoepassing en Jeungdbescherming [Council for Criminal Justice and Protection of Juveniles] (2016), *Bezinning op Interlandelijke Adoptie (Reflection on Intercountry Adoption)*, The Hague: Raad voor Strafrechtstoepassing en Jeungdbescherming.

Raby, R., and Pomerantz, S. (2015), "Playing it down/playing it up: Girls' strategic negotiations of academic success," *British Journal of Sociology of Education*, 36 (4): 507–525.

Raithelhuber, E. (2016), "Extending agency: The merit of relational approaches for childhood studies," in F. Esser, M. S. Baader, T. Betz, and B. Hungerland (eds), *Reconceptualizing Agency and Childhood: New Perspectives in Childhood Studies*, 89–101, London and New York: Routledge.

Rancière, J. (1999), *Disagreement: Politics and Philosophy*, Minneapolis, MN: University of Minnesota Press.

Ranciere, J. (2004), "Who is the subject of the rights of man?" *The South Atlantic Quarterly*, 103 (2/3): 297–310.

Rancière, J. (2006), *The Politics of Aesthetics*, London: Continuum.

Rancière, J. (2010), *Dissensus: On Politics and Aesthetics*, London: Continuum.

Rautio, P. (2013), "Children who carry stones in their pockets: On autotelic material practices in everyday life," *Children's Geographies*, 11: 394–408.

Rautio, P. (2014), "Mingling and imitating in producing spaces for knowing and being: Insights from a Finnish study of child–matter intra-action," *Childhood*, 21 (4): 461–474.

Renold, E., and Mellor, D. (2013), "Deleuze and Guattari in the nursery: Towards an ethnographic multi-sensory mapping of gendered bodies and becomings," in R. Coleman and J. Ringrose (eds), *Deleuze and Research Methodologies*, 23–41, Edinburgh: Edinburgh University Press.

Reynolds, K. (2007), *Radical Children's Literature: Future Visions and Aesthetic Transformations in Juvenile Fiction*, London: Palgrave Macmillan.

Ricoeur, P. (2000), *The Just*, Chicago and London: The University of Chicago Press.

Rikowski, Glenn (2003), "Alien life: Marx and the future of the human," *Historical Materialism*, 11 (2): 121–164.

Ringwalt, J. E. (1880), "Fun for the fireside: The paper-doll's house," *Godey's Lady's Book and Magazine*, 101: 160–162.

Robinson, K. H., and Davies, C. (2008), "She's kicking ass, that's what she's doing," *Australian Feminist Studies*, 23 (57): 343–358.

Robson, E., Bell, S., and Klocker, N. (2007), "Conceptualizing agency in the lives and actions of rural young people," in R. Panelli, S. Punch, and E. Robson (eds), *Global Perspectives on Rural Childhood and Youth: Young Rural Lives*, 135–148, London: Routledge.

Rogoff, B. (2003), *The Cultural Nature of Human Development*, Oxford: Oxford University Press.

Rose, J. (1984), *The Case of Peter Pan, or The Impossibility of Children's Fiction*, London: Macmillan.

Rose, N. (2007), *The Politics of Life Itself: Biomedicine, Power, and Subjectivity in the Twenty-First Century*, Princeton, NJ: Princeton University Press.

Rosen, D. (2007), "Child soldiers, international humanitarian law, and the globalization of childhood," *American Anthropologist*, 109 (2): 296–306.

Rosen, R. (2015), "'The scream': Meanings and excesses in early childhood settings," *Childhood*, 22 (1): 39–52.

Rosen, R. (2017), "Time, temporality, and woman–child relations," *Children's Geographies*, 15(3): 374–380.

Rosen, R., and Newberry, J. (2018), "Love, labour and temporality: Reconceptualising social reproduction with women AND children in the frame," in R. Rosen and K. Twamley (eds), *Feminism and the Politics of Childhood: Friends or Foes?*, London: University College London Press.

Roth, R. (1998), "Scrapbook houses: A late nineteenth-century children's view of the American home," in E. Thompson (ed.), *The American Home: Material Culture, Domestic Space, and Family Life*, 301–323, Winterthur, DE: Winterthur Museum.

Rottenberg, C. (2017) "Neoliberal feminism and the future of human capital," *Signs*, 42 (2): 329–348.

Ruddick, Sue (2003), "The politics of aging: Globalization and the restructuring of youth and childhood," *Antipode*, 334–362.

Ruppert, E., Law, J., and Savage, M. (2013), 'Reassembling social science methods: The challenge of digital devices," *Theory, Culture and Society*, 30 (4): 22–46.

Ryan, K. (2012), "The new wave of childhood studies: Breaking the grip of bio-social dualism?" *Childhood*, 19: 439–452.

Ryan, K. (2014), "Childhood, biosocial power and the 'anthropological machine': Life as a governable process?" *Critical Horizons*, 15: 266–283.

Sæverot, H. (2011), "Kierkegaard, seduction, and existential education," *Studies in Philosophy and Education*, 30 (6): 557–572.

Sabatello, M. (2013), "Children with disabilities: A critical appraisal," *International Journal of Children's Rights*, 21: 464–487.

Said, E. (1978), *Orientalism*, London: Routledge.

St. Croix, T. (2012), "If someone is not a success in life it's their own fault': What Coalition youth policy says about young people and youth workers," UK: In Defence of Youth Work. Available online: https://indefenceofyouthwork.com/2012/08/15/if-someone-is-not-a-success-in-life-its-their-own-fault-coalitionyouth-policy-revisited/ (accessed May 9, 2017).

St. Pierre, E. (2013), "The posts continue: Becoming," *International Journal of Qualitative Studies in Education*, 26 (6): 646–657.

Sallie, A., Marston, S. A., Jones III, J. P., and Woodward, K. (2005), "Human geography without scale," *Transactions of the Institute of British Geography*, NS 30: 416–432.

Sandel, M. (1984), "The procedural republic and the unencumbered self," *Political Theory*, 12 (1): 81–96.

Sandiland, R. (2017), "A clash of conventions? Participation, power and the rights of disabled children," *Social Inclusion*, 5 (3): 93–103.

Sartre, J.-P. ([1943] 1958), *Being and Nothingness*, trans. H. E. Barnes, London: Routledge.

Sartre, J.-P. (1950), *What is Literature ?* trans. B. Frechtman, New York: Philosophical Papers.

Sartre, J.-P. (1988), *What Is Literature? and Other Essays*, Cambridge, MA: Harvard University Press.

Sayer, A. (2001), "For a critical cultural political economy," *Antipode*, 33 (4): 687–708.

Sayer, A. (2011), *Why Things Matter to People: Social Science, Values and Ethical Life*, Cambridge: Cambridge University Press.

Scheer, J., and Groce, N. (1988), "Impairment as a human constant: Cross-cultural and historical perspectives on variation," *Journal of Social Issues*, 44 (1), 23–37.

Scheper-Hughes, N. (2008), "A talent for life: Reflections on human vulnerability and resilience," *Ethnos: Journal of Anthropology*, 73 (1): 25–56.

Scheurich, J. J. (1995), "A postmodernist critique of research interviewing," *Qualitative Studies in Education*, 8 (3): 239–252.

Scholz, S. J. (2010), "That all children should be free: Beauvoir, Rousseau, and childhood," *Hypatia*, 25 (2): 394–411.

Schulten, S. (2012), *Mapping the Nation: History and Cartography in Nineteenth-Century America*, Chicago, IL: University of Chicago Press.

Schwartzman, H. B. (1978), *Transformations: The Anthropology of Children's Play*, New York: Plenum Press.

Sedgwick, E. K. (1991), "How to bring your kids up gay," *Social Text*, 29 (1): 18–27.

Sen, S. (2005), *Colonial Childhoods: The Juvenile Periphery of India*, London: Anthem Press.

Sennett, R. (1977), *The Fall of Public Man*, New York: Alfred A Knopf Inc.

Serres, A., and Bonnani, S. (2009), *Quand nous aurons mangé la planète (Once We Have Eaten Up The Planet)*, Paris: Rue du Monde.

Seven, J., and Christy, J. (2013), *A Rule Is to Break: A Child's Guide to Anarchy*, San Francisco, CA: Manic D Press.

Shain, F. (2013), "'The girl effect': Exploring narratives of gendered impacts and opportunities in neoliberal development," *Sociological Research Online*, 18 (2).

Shakespeare, T. (1997), "Cultural representation of disabled people: Dustbins for disavowal," in L. Barton and M. Oliver (eds), *Disability Studies: Past Present and Future*, 217–233, Leeds: The Disability Press.

Shakespeare, T. (2013), *Disability Rights and Wrongs Revisited*, Basingstoke: Palgrave.

Shakespeare, T., and Watson, N. (2010), "Beyond models: Understanding the complexity of disabled people's lives," in S. Scambler and G. Scambler (eds), *New Directions in the Sociology of Chronic and Disabling Conditions: Assaults on the Lifeworlds*, 55–77, Basingstoke: Palgrave Macmillan.

Shoveller, Jean A., and Johnson, Joy L. (2006), "Risky groups, risky behaviour, and risky persons: Dominating discourses on youth sexual health," *Critical Public Health*, 16 (1): 47–60.

Sicart, M. (2014), *Play Matters*, Cambridge, MA: MIT Press.

Simone, A. (2004), "People as infrastructure: Intersecting fragments in Johannesburg," *Public Culture*, 16 (3): 407–429.

Singal, N., and Muthukrishna, N. (2014), "Introduction: Education, childhood and disability in countries of the South–Re-positioning the debates," *Childhood*, 21 (3): 293–307.

Singh, V., and Ghai, A. (2009), "Notions of self: Lived realities of children with disabilities," *Disability& Society*, 24 (2): 129–145.

Skeggs, B. (2008), "The dirty history of feminism and sociology: Or the war of conceptual attrition," *Sociological Review*, 56 (4): 670–690.

Skelton, T. (2008), "Research with children and young people: Exploring the tensions between ethics, competence and participation," *Children's Geographies*, 6 (1): 21–36.

Skelton, T. (2013), Children, young people and politics: Transformative possibilities for a discipline?" *Geoforum*, 49: 4–6.

Skelton, T., and Gough, K. V. (2013), "Introduction: Young people's im/mobile urban geographies," *Urban Studies*, 50 (3): 455–466.

Slodovnick, A., and Gauthier, M. (2008), *La carie*, Montréal: Les 400 Coups.

Sloth-Nielsen, J., and Mezmur, B. D. (2008), "A dutiful child: The implications of Article 31 of the African Children's Charter," *Journal of African Law*, 52 (2): 159–189.

Smart, C., Neale, B., and Wade, A. (2001), *The Changing Experience of Childhood: Families and Divorce*, Cambridge: Polity Press

Solberg, A. (1996), "'The challenge in child research: From 'being' to 'doing,'" in J. Brannen and M. O'Brien (eds), *Children in Families: Research and Policy*, London: Falmer Press.

Solomon, T. M., Halkitis, P. N., Moeller, R. M., Siconolfi, D. E., Kiang, M. V., and Barton, S. C. (2011), "Sex parties among young gay, bisexual, and other men who have sex with men in New York City: Attendance and behavior," *Journal of Urban Health*, 88 (6): 1063–1075.

Spivak, G. (1992), *Thinking Academic Freedom in Gendered Post-coloniality*, T. B. Davie Memorial Lecture (ed.), Cape Town: University of Cape Town.

Spivak, G. (2004), "Righting wrongs," *South Atlantic Quarterly*, 103: 523–581.

Spyrou, S. (2011), "The limits of children's voices: From authenticity to critical, reflexive representation," *Childhood*, 18 (2): 151–165.

Spyrou, S. (2013), "Children and the sexualized construction of otherness: The imaginary perceptions of Russian and Romanian immigrant women in Cyprus," *Journal of International Migration and Integration*, 14 (2): 327–343.

Spyrou, S. (2016), "Researching children's silences: Exploring the fullness of voice in childhood research," *Childhood: A Global Journal in Child Research*, 23 (1): 7–21.

Spyrou, S. (2017), "Editorial: Time to decenter childhood?" *Childhood*, 24 (4): 433–437.

Spyrou, S. (2018), *Disclosing Childhoods: Research and Knowledge Production for a Critical Childhood Studies*, London: Palgrave Macmillan.

Stephens, S. (1995), "Children and the politics of culture in 'late captialism'," in S. Stephens (ed.), *Children and the Politics of Culture*, 3–50, Princeton, NJ: Princeton University Press.

Stephens S. (1996), "Children and the politics of culture in late capitalism," in Sharon Stephens (ed.), *Children and the Politics of Culture*, Princeton, NJ: Princeton University Press.

Stephens, S. (1997), "Nationalism, nuclear policy and children in Cold War America," *Childhood*, 4 (1): 103–123.

Stockton, K. B. (2009), *The Queer Child, or Growing Sideways in the Twentieth Century*, Durham, NC: Duke University Press.

Stone, E., and Priestley, M. (1996), "Parasites, pawns and partners: Disability research and the role of non-disabled researchers," *The British Journal of Sociology*, 47 (4): 699–716.

Strathern, M. (2004), *Partial Connections*, Updated edn, Walnut Creek: Altamira Press.

Sutton-Smith, B. (1997), *The Ambiguity of Play*, Cambridge, MA: Harvard University Press.

Swain, J., and French, S. (2000), "Towards an affirmative model of disability," *Disability and Society*, 15: 569–582.

Swanson, K. (2010), *Begging as a Path to Progress: Indigenous Women and Children and the Struggle for Ecuador's Urban Spaces*, Athens, GA: University of Georgia Press.

Swinton, W. (1875), *Elementary Course in Geography: Designed for Primary and Intermediate Grades, and as a Complete Shorter Course*, New York: Ivison, Blakeman, Taylor, and Company.

Symes, C. (2012), "No time on their hands: Children and the narrative architecture of school diaries," *Time & Society*, 21 (2): 156–174.

Taft, J. (2011), *Rebel Girls: Youth Activism and Social Change across the Americas*, New York: New York University Press.

Taft, J. (2015), "'Adults talk too much': Intergenerational dialogue and power in the Peruvian movement of working children," *Childhood*, 22 (4): 460–473.

Talburt. S., and Lesko, N. (2012), "An Introduction to Seven Technologies of Youth Studies," in S. Talburt and N. Lesko (eds), *Keywords in Youth Studies: Tracing Affects, Movements, Knowledges*, 1–10, New York and London: Routledge.

Tam, P. (2012), "Children's bricolage under the gaze of teachers in sociodramatic play," *Childhood*, 20 (2): 244–259.

Taylor, A. (2013), *Reconfiguring the Natures of Childhood*, London: Routledge.

Taylor, A., Blaise, M., and Giugn, M. (2013), "Haraway's 'bag lady story-telling': Relocating childhood and learning within a 'post-human landscape'," *Discourse*, 34: 8–62.

Taylor, A., and Pacini-Ketchabaw, V. (2015), "Learning with children, ants, and worms in the Anthropocene: Towards a common world pedagogy of multispecies vulnerability," *Pedagogy, Culture & Society*, 23 (4): 507–529.

Taylor, A., Pacini-Ketchabaw, V., and Blaise, M. (2012), "Children's relations with the more-than-human world," *Contemporary Issues in Early Childhood*, 13: 81–85.

Terzi, L. (2004), "The social model of disability: A philosophical critique," *Journal of Applied Philosophy*, 21 (2): 141–157

Theodorou, E. (2008), "Authoring spaces: Identity negotiation among immigrant students at a Cypriot public primary school," PhD diss., University of Virginia, Charlottesville.

Theodorou, E. (2014a), Χαρτογραφώντας τη διαπολιτισμική εκπαιδευτική πολιτική στην Κύπρο: Θεωρία, παραδοχές και πράξη [Mapping intercultural education policy in Cyprus: Theory, assumptions, and practice], Συγκριτική και Διεθνής Εκπαιδευτική Επιθεώρηση, 22: 101–128.

Theodorou, E. (2014b), "Constructing the 'other': Politics and policies of intercultural education in Cyprus," in L. Vega (ed.), *Empires, Post-Coloniality and Interculturality, Comparative and Education Society in Europe Series*, 251–272, Rotterdam: Sense Publishers.

Thoman, E. (1980), "Infant development viewed in the mother-infant relationship," in Quilligan, E. J. (ed.), *Fetal and Maternal Medicine*, 243–265, New York: John Wiley and Sons.

Thomas, A. (2014), *Making Makers: Kids, Tools and the Future of Invention*, Sebastopol, CA: Maker Media.

Thomas, C. (2007), *Sociologies of Disability and Illness: Contested Ideas in Disability Studies and Medical Sociology*, 37–56, Basingstoke: Palgrave Macmillan.

Thomas, C. (2010), "Medical sociology and disability theory," in G. Scambler and S. Scambler (eds), *New Directions in the Sociology of Chronic and Disabling Conditions: Assaults on the Lifeworld*, 37–56, Basingstoke: Palgrave Macmillan, Chap 3.

Thomas, N. (2007), "Towards a theory of children's participation," *International Journal of Children's Rights*, 15 (2): 199–218.

Thomas, N. (2013), "Children and politics," in Montgomery, H. (ed.), *Oxford Bibliographies in Childhood Studies*, New York: Oxford University Press, http://www.oxfordbibliographies.com/view/document/obo-9780199791231/obo-9780199791231-0067.xml

Thomas, N., and O'Kane, C. (1998), "The ethics of participatory research with children," *Children & Society*, 12: 336–348.

Thomson, J., and Philo, C. (2004), "Playful spaces? A social geography of children's play in Livingston, Scotland," *Children's Geographies*, 2 (1): 111–130.

Thorne, B. (2007), "Editorial: Crafting the interdisciplinary field of childhood studies," *Childhood*, 14: 147–152.

Thornham, H., and Myers, C. (2012), "Architectures of youth: Visibility, agency and the technological imaginings of young people," *Social & Cultural Geography*, 13: 783–800.

Thrift, N. (2000), "Afterwords," *Environment and planning D*, 18: 213–255.

Tisdall, K. M. (2012), "The challenge and challenging of childhood studies? Learning from disability studies and research with disabled children," *Children & Society*, 26 (3): 181–191.

Tisdall E., and Punch, S. (2012), "Not so 'new'? Looking critically at childhood studies," *Children's Geographies*, 10: 249–264.

Trouillot, M. (1995), *Silencing the Past: Power and the Production of History*, Boston, MA: Beacon Press.

Tsing, A. L. (2009), "Supply chains and the human condition," *Rethinking Marxism*, 21 (2): 148–176.

Tsing, A. L. (2005), *Friction: An Ethnography of Global Connection*, Princeton, NJ and Oxford: Princeton University Press.

Tuhiwai Smith, L. (1999), *Decolonizing Methodologies: Research and Indigenous Peoples*, London: Zed Books.

Tulve, N., Stefaniak, A. B., Vance, M. E., Rogers, K., Mwilu, S., LeBouf, R. F., Schwegler-Berry, D., Willis, R., Thomas, T. A., and Marr, L. C. (2015), "Characterization of silver nanoparticles in selected consumer products and its relevance for predicting children's potential exposures," *Int J Hyg Environ Health*, 218: 345–357.

Twamley, K., Rosen, R., and Mayall, B. (2017), "The (im)possibilities of dialogue across feminism and childhood scholarship and activism," *Children's Geographies*, 15 (2): 249–255.

Twum-Danso, A. (2016), "From the singular to the plural: Exploring diversities in contemporary childhoods in sub-Saharan Africa," *Childhood*, 23 (3): 455–468.

Twum-Danso Imoh, A. (2012), "The Convention on the Rights of the Child: A product and facilitator of a global childhood," in A. Twum-Danso Imoh and R. Ame (eds), *Childhoods at the Intersection of the Local and Global*, 17–33, New York: Palgrave Macmillan.

Uprichard, E. (2008), "Children as 'beings and becomings': Children, childhood and temporality," *Children & Society*, 22: 303–313.

UNICEF (2011), *Calls for Children with Disabilities to Be Included in All, Development (3 December)*, New York: UNICEF, http://www.unicef.org/media/media_60790.html

UNICEF (2013), *State of the World's Children: Children with Disabilities*, New York: UNICEF, http://www.unicef.org/sowc2013/

UN (1989), *Convention on the Rights of the Child*, New York: United Nations, https://downloads.unicef.org.uk/wpcontent/uploads/2010/05/UNCRC_united_nations_convention_on_the_rights_of_the_child.pdf

UN (2007), *UN Convention on the Rights of Persons with Disabilities*, New York: United Nations, http://www.un.org/disabilities/convention/conventionfull.shtml

UN (2013), "General Comment No. 17 on the Right of the Child to Rest, Leisure, Play, Recreational Activities, Cultural Life and the Arts (art. 31)," April 17. Committee on the Rights of the Child.

UN (2015), *Sustainable Development Goals*, New York: United Nations, http://www.un.org/sustainabledevelopment

United Nations General Assembly (1989), "Convention on the Rights of the Child, adopted by the General Assembly of the United Nations on 20 November 1989 (art. 31)," *United Nations, Treaty Series*, 1577: 54. Available online: https://treaties.un.org/Pages/showDetails.aspx?objid=08000002800007fe&clang=_en (accessed April 4, 2017).

Valentin, K., and Meinert, L. (2009), "The adult North and the young South: Reflections on the civilizing mission of children's rights," *Anthropology Today*, 25 (3): 23–28.

Vallargada, K. (2011), "Adam's escape: Children and the discordant nature of colonial conversions," *Childhood: A Global Journal of Child Research*, 18 (3): 298–314.

Van Blerk, L., and Ansel, N. (2006), "Children's experiences of migration: Moving in the wake of AIDS in Southern Africa," *Environment and Planning D: Society and Space*, 24: 449–471.

Vygotsky, L. (1978), *Mind in Society*, Cambridge, MA: Harvard University Press.

Wagner, N., Rieger, M., and Voorvelt, K. (2016), "Gender, ethnicity and teaching evaluations: Evidence from mixed teaching teams," *ISS Working Paper Series*, 32, The Hague, Netherlands: International Institute of Social Studies.

Wall, B. (1991), *The Narrator's Voice: The Dilemma of Children's Fiction*, London: Macmillan.

Wallace, J.-A. (2008), "Technologies of 'the child': Towards a theory of the child-subject," *Textual Practice*, 9 (2): 285–302.

Warner, M. (1993), *Fear of a Queer Planet: Queer Politics and Social Theory*, Minneapolis, MN: University of Minnesota Press.

Wells, K. (2009), *Childhood in a Global Perspective*, Cambridge: Polity Press.

Watson, A. (2009), *The Child in International Political Economy*, London: Routledge.

Watson, N. (2002), "Well I know this is going to sound very strange to you but I don't see myself as a disabled person: Identity and disability," *Disability and Society*, 17 (5): 509–527.

Watson, N. (2012), "Theorising the lives of disabled children: How can disability theory help?" *Children & Society*, 26 (3): 192–202.

Wells, K. (2011), "The politics of life governing childhood," *Global Studies of Childhood*, 1 (1): 15–25.

WHO and World Bank (2011), *World Report on Disability*, New York: United Nations. http://www.who.int/disabilities/world_report/2011/report.pdf

Wicke, J. (1991), "Postmodern identity and the legal subject," *University of Colorado Law Review*, 62: 455–473.

Wickenden, M. (2011), "Whose voice is that?: Issues of identity, voice and representation arising in an ethnographic study of the lives of disabled teenagers who use Augmentative and Alternative Communication (AAC)," *Disability Studies Quarterly*, 31 (4).

Wickenden, M., and Elphick, J. (2016), "Don't forget us, we are here too! Listening to the perspectives and priorities of disabled children and their families living in contexts of poverty," in S. Grech and K. Soldatic (eds), *Disability in the Global South: A Critical Handbook*, New York: Springer.

Wickenden, M., and Kembhavi, G. (2014), "Ask us too! Doing participatory research with disabled children in the Global South," *Childhood*, 21 (3): 400–417.

Wilkinson, R., and Pickett, K. (2009), *The Spirit Level. Why Equality is Better for Everyone*, London: Penguin Books.

Willett, R. (2016), "Makerspaces as the future of public libraries: A discourse analysis of library journal articles about makerspaces," *Library Quarterly: Information, Community, Policy*, 86 (3): 1–17.

Willett, R., Richards, C., Marhs, J., Burn, A., and Bishop, J. (2013), *Children, Media and Playground Cultures: Ethnographic Studies of School Playtimes*, Basingstoke: Palgrave.

Williams, T. (2016a), "Oriented towards action: The political economy of primary education in Rwanda," *ESID Working Paper* No. 64, Manchester: Effective States and Inclusive Development.

Williams, T. (2016b), "Theorizing children's subjectivity: Ethnographic investigations in rural Rwanda," *Childhood: A Global Journal of Child Research*, 23 (3): 333–347.

Wilson, K. (2015), "Towards a radical re-appropriation: Gender, development and neoliberal feminism," *Development and Change*, 46 (4): 803–832.

Witchger Hansen, M., Siame, M., and Van Der Veen, J. (2014), "A qualitative study: Barriers and support for participation for children with disabilities," *African Journal of Disability*, 3 (1): 112.

Wohlwend, Karen E. (2011), *Playing Their Way into Literacies: Reading, Writing, and Belonging in the Early Childhood Classroom*, New York: Teachers College Press.

Woodyer, T. (2012), "Ludic geographies: Not merely child's play," *Geography Compass*, 6: 313–326.

Woodyer, T., Martin, D., and Carter, S. (2017), "Ludic geographies," in B. Evans, J. Horton, and T. Skelton (eds), *Geographies of Childhood and Youth, Volume 9: Play, Recreation, Health and Wellbeing*, Singapore: Springer.

World Bank (2006), *World Bank Development Report 2007: Development and the Next Generation*, Washington, DC: World Bank.

Worth, N. (2009), "Understanding youth transition as 'becoming': Identity, time and futurity," *Geoforum*, 40: 1050–1060.

Wyness, M. (2015), *Childhood*, Cambridge: Polity Press.

Youdell, D. (2003), "Identity traps or how black [1] students fail: The interactions between biographical, sub-cultural and learner identities," *British Journal of Sociology of Education*, 24 (1): 3–20.

Youdell, D. (2006), *Impossible Bodies, Impossible Selves: Exclusions and Student Subjectivities*, Dordrecht, NL: Springer.

Youdell, D. (2012), "Fascinating 'Pacific Islander': Pedagogies of expropriation, return and resistance and other lessons from a 'multicultural day'," *Race, Ethnicity and Education*, 15 (2): 141–155.

Youdell, D. (2016), "New biological sciences, sociology and education," *British Journal of Sociology of Education*, 37: 788–800.

Youdell, D., and Armstrong, F. (2011), "A politics beyond subjects: The affective choreographies and smooth spaces of schooling," *Emotion, Space and Society*, 4: 144–150.

Young-Breuhl, E. (2012), *Childism: Confronting Prejudice against Children*, New Haven, CT: Yale University Press.

Zelizer, V. (1985), *Pricing the Priceless Child*, Princeton, NJ: Princeton University Press.

Zembylas, M. (2010), "Critical discourse analysis of multiculturalism and intercultural education policies in the Republic of Cyprus," *The Cyprus Review*, 22 (1): 39–59.

Zembylas, M., and Lesta, S. (2011), "Greek-Cypriot students' stances and repertoires towards migrants and migrant students in the Republic of Cyprus," *Journal of International Migration and Integration*, 12 (4): 475–494.

INDEX